**Urban
Land Policy
for the
1980s**

Books from
The Lincoln Institute of Land Policy

The Lincoln Institute of Land Policy is a school that offers intensive courses of instruction in the field of land economics and property taxation. The Institute provides a stimulating learning environment for students, policymakers, and administrators with challenging opportunities for research and publication. The goal of the Institute is to improve theory and practice in those fundamental areas of land policy that have significant impact on the lives and livelihood of all people.

Constitutions, Taxation, and Land Policy   Michael M. Bernard

Constitutions, Taxation, and Land Policy—Volume II
   Michael M. Bernard

Federal Tax Aspects of Open-Space Preservation   Kingsbury Browne

Taxation of Nonrenewable Resources   Albert M. Church

Conflicts over Resource Ownership   Albert M. Church

Taxation of Mineral Resources   Robert F. Conrad and R. Bryce Hool

World Congress on Land Policy, 1980   Edited by Matthew Cullen and
   Sharon Woolery

Land Readjustment   William A. Doebele

The Rate of Return   Edited by Daniel M. Holland

Incentive Zoning   Jerold S. Kayden

Building for Women   Edited by Suzanne Keller

Urban Land Policy for the 1980s   Edited by George Lefcoe

Fiscal Federalism and the Taxation of Natural Resources   Edited by
   Charles E. McLure, Jr., and Peter Mieszkowski

State Land-Use Planning and Regulation   Thomas G. Pelham

The Role of the State in Property Taxation   Edited by H. Clyde Reeves

Land-Office Business   Gary Sands

The Art of Valuation   Edited by Arlo Woolery

Urban Land Policy for the 1980s

The Message for State and Local Government

Edited by
George Lefcoe
University of Southern California
Law Center

LexingtonBooks
D.C. Heath and Company
Lexington, Massachusetts
Toronto

Library of Congress Cataloging in Publication Data

Main entry under title:
   Urban land policy for the 1980s.

   1. Urban policy—United States—Congresses. 2. Land use, Urban—
United States—Congresses. 3. Municipal finance—United States—Congresses.
4. Housing policy—United States—Congresses. I. Lefcoe, George.
HT123.U7457   1982   333.77'0973   82-48492
ISBN 0-669-06157-3

Copyright © 1983 by D.C. Heath and Company

Published simultaneously in Canada

Printed in the United States of America

International Standard Book Number: 0-669-06157-3

Library of Congress Catalog Card Number: 82-48492

Contents

Contents

Figures and Tables

Acknowledgments

I would like to acknowledge the help of those whose efforts made the work possible in addition to our authors and the conference participants whose names appear in the final pages. Kadi Kurgpold served as conference administrator and prepared the manuscript for publication. Sharon Woolery was our reporter; much of the material for the book was taken from her transcript. Lowdon Wingo, my conference co-chairman, helped considerably in shaping the program. Arlo Woolery, the director of The Lincoln Institute of Land Policy, is responsible for maintaining the environment in which this kind of effort can be undertaken. To all of them, a heartfelt thanks.

Preface

This volume began as a conference: The Urban Land Policy in the Reagan Years: The Message for State and Local Governments. Convened in February 1982 at the University of Southern California Law Center under the auspices of The Lincoln Institute of Land Policy, it was attended by more than one hundred people, all involved in land-use policy, state and local government and land development, representing varied professions and political persuasions. Our central question was: What do the Reagan years hold in store for urban land policy?

The Reagan years refer to both a time frame and a set of identifiable policies. The relevant policies include both the implicit impacts of the Reagan budget and the explicit norms of the new Federalism. Applicable policies encompass notions about the proper role of the central government in urban land-use planning and specific existing federal programs in energy, environmental protection, public-facilities funding, education, housing and housing finance. Each of these topics is addressed in one of the chapters of this book, as it was in the various sessions of our conference.

To help the busy reader I offer a synopsis of each chapter, emphasizing particularly the conclusions reached on the central theme. Our starting point, appropriately enough, is an analysis of the impacts of the Reagan budget on state and local governments. Professors Kimbell and Shulman offer their forecasts on national economic growth, corporate and individual income trends, and federal deficits. The authors report a number of items of special interest to local and state officials.

1. Unlike the 1973-1975 recession, local government spending will not be counter-cyclical. In those years the increase in federal grants-in-aid helped cover declining local tax revenues.
2. Business growth, spurred by tax relief, requires local investments in bridges, roads, schools, and the like. It may be frustrated by the inability of local governments to finance new capital improvements from either current revenues or borrowing.
3. Kimbell and Shulman conclude, "This obviously will slow the growth of the faster growing regions of California and stay the incipient boom that is now developing in the Central Valley. However, it could inure to the benefit of the older cities of Los Angeles, San Francisco, and Oakland, where in some cases there is surplus infrastructure capacity."

Part II of this book moves the urban-land-policy debate to a national and historic plane, as Professor Hicks argues against explicit government policies to channel urbanization into declining areas or away from growing ones. Hicks disputes the traditional distinction between urban and rural land, contending that even agriculture is in the process of freeing itself from its dependency on the soil, while in most rural resort towns, vacationers can buy the *National Enquirer* and a six-pack of Perrier water. America, he explains, spent the nineteenth century coming to its industrial cities, which were beautiful for what they made possible but not for themselves, and has spent the twentieth century, at first unnoticed, moving away from them. The trend parallels that of the move from a manufacturing to a service-based economy, the same move that has given many of the older industrial centers a new life as office cores. Trying to stop these historic trends with tax dollars is more than futile; in its wastefulness it misdirects public effort which should be directed toward easing the transition for people left jobless during this period of painful adjustment.

In part III, Professor Hall describes and Professor Denman faults British land-planning policy, a thirty-five-year effort to moderate if not to contravene market forces. Hall explains that in some important ways British policy currently is reversing itself as the present government moves to halt high-spending local-government authorities, to accelerate the sale of public housing to tenants, and to nurture the development efforts of private builders. At the same time, we in the United States are showing keen interest in British efforts to revive declining industrial areas through such strategies as the enterprise zone and the use of public redevelopment corporations. He observes that any nation "deeply struck by recession is likely to grasp at any kind of growth that is happening. . . ."

Professor Denman cautions that public intervention in a free society should always be preceded by a modest but definite sense of mission. British land planning, he contends, went awry because the government never decided which of many conflicting land policies it was planning for. This led inevitably into rules and regulations that changed precipitously, were often ambiguous, and never left the citizen knowing with confidence where he stood under the law. Sharing the Reagan administration's enthusiasm for private-sector initiatives, Denman sees micro as stronger than macro; hence, until private incentives coincide with public goals, public land planning is bound to fail.

The energy and environmental aspects of the Reagan program form the substance of part IV. Dale Keyes divides his presentation accordingly, the first half dealing with energy issues, the second with environmental ones (clean air, water pollution, and hazardous-waste management). On the energy side, he suggests that in the short run energy costs ought to rise with gas decontrol. This raises no direct problem for local governments as less than 5 percent of their budgets depends on fuel costs. Indirectly, local governments may be petitioned to underwrite fuel price increases, especially for the poor. While some local-policy advocates have thought rising energy costs might slow the march to suburbia as firms and households seek to reduce commuting costs, Keyes suggests that people are more likely to stand firm on their location preferences but insulate their dwellings better or substitute smaller houses and fuel-efficient cars to meet rising energy costs. He concludes that "a major reshaping of urban America is simply not in order."

The message concerning the administration's environmental efforts is mixed. The federal government's demurrer to the states to set air and water quality standards could bring with it some difficult state-level contests in which the benefits of near-term economic gains derived from allowing polluting industries to expand in already-threatened air basins must be balanced against the possibility of longer term withdrawals by amenity-conscious employers. Washington will soon cease subsidizing sewage-treatment plants to handle anticipated growth in suburbia; federal taxpayers will no longer pay to cleanse the effluent of the affluent. But, Mr. Keyes warns, a reduction in ambient water-quality standards "could produce state 'bidding wars' for polluting industries."

Governor Lamm, in commenting on Dale Keyes's chapter, expresses concern over a public-lands-management program that seems set on using private-marketplace criteria. Lamm cautions against selling the national heritage to cover budget deficits and regards some administration leasing efforts as unnecessary.

In the next three chapters (part V) we examine the problems of financing public facilities and services in times of financial constraint. George Peterson calls our attention to the budget effect of the fact that "bridges don't vote" but that government employees and the beneficiaries of public services do. "The *only* aggregate budget item actually reduced in dollar terms by California localities after Proposition 13 was the capital item," he observes. Capital spending on infrastructure (roads, bridges, sewers, and so forth) accounted for little more than half the share of state and local budgets in 1980 than it had in 1960.

That these budget items should decline along with others is to be expected. Measuring the seriousness of the shortfall is far from simple.

Great reliance has been placed on federal standards for highways, wastewater-treatment plants, and bridges. Yet the standards bore no necessary relationship to acceptable minimum-service levels. For instance, one-half of the claimed federal deficiency in bridges was due to "deck geometry"—bridges narrower than the approaching highways. While some bridge widenings would certainly help traffic flow, others might offer only slight improvement at great cost. Peterson sees the problems as targeted. Interstate highways (the older routes especially) and mass transit in older cities (New York and Philadelphia most notably) are in terrible shape. But some of the older sewer and water systems are outperforming more recent additions.

Addressing the question of how best to secure our public facilities needs, Peterson reports that independent authorities charge more than city-operated ones and are better run. Cities with professional managers take better care of their infrastructure than those where elected professional officials exercise managerial authority. Taxes earmarked for capital improvements reach their intended destinations while general funds are increasingly diverted from capital spending. If the experience in Cleveland proves typical, voters are willing to endorse tax hikes earmarked for debt repayment and badly needed capital-facilities investments.

Does Peterson suggest that the best way to protect our public infrastructure is, therefore, to remove it from the general political arena into special-purpose enclaves where revenues cannot be invaded by elected officials nor maintenance dictated by other than sound business practices? The answer is no, because that achieves efficiency at the expense of an open public debate on spending priorities and budget trade-offs, a debate Peterson views as essential to democracy. His recommendation is for public enlightenment, followed by responsible public choice.

Gary Hoachlander's chapter is on school finance. In California, Proposition 13 cutbacks since 1977-1978 have reduced school budgets 15 percent (12 percent adjusting for declines in average daily attendance). Although the impacts of proposed federal cuts will be limited (federal aid accounts for only 2-3 percent of the total school budget), many of the same urban districts most affected by Proposition 13 (San Francisco, Oakland, Los Angeles) will experience losses in the 4-5-percent range.

A determined optimist, Hoachlander sees the financial pinch as a time for reform. He surveys three types of proposed changes: tuition tax credits, vouchers, and school-district reorganization and financial restructuring. Acknowledging the increased opportunity for individual choice that tax credits and vouchers promise, he reviews the formidable technical difficulties in their implementation. To set up a tax credit, as the administration has recently proposed, several considerations demand attention: (1) What types of schools would be eligible? (for example, may church schools be included constitutionally?) (2) What counts as tuition for tax-credit purposes? (For example, transportation? a summer in France for the wealthy preppy? voluntary busing for the inner-city resident seeking to attend a suburban school?) If detailed regulations are necessary to resolve these and other questions, much of the gain in consumer choice may be offset by bureaucratic constraints on private schools, which is why so many private-school supporters want neither tax credits nor vouchers, fearing a loss of freedom that is not worth the revenues. (3) May parents whose income-tax liability does not equal the amount of the credit be eligible to receive a cash refund for the tuition they pay? If so, the costs will be overwhelming. If not, the poor will be disadvantaged.

Professor Hoachlander urges bringing education policy closer to parental desires. He perceives the greatest barrier to a locally supported school system in the earlier school-consolidation movement which left 40 percent of the state's pupils in 4 percent of its districts. If these big-city districts could be reduced in size to something approaching 20,000 pupils per district, people might begin to feel some affinity for their school organization. Redrawing district lines is facilitated by Proposition 13, since school finance is no longer tied to the local-property-tax base; state financing has freed it. Dividing the big-city districts into smaller ones might make them more responsive to their constituents which, in turn, could lead to the enactment of local income or special taxes to supplement state aid. School attendance across district boundaries could be permitted since state support is based largely on average daily attendance. Parents could be allowed the option of placing their children in schools near their work places (children could ride to school with their parents and be within easy reach in the event of an emergency). As Hoachlander views it, although we have experienced the budget cutbacks necessitated by Proposition 13, we have yet to realize the opportunities made possible by freeing school finance from the property tax.

The third chapter in this section describes the ways local governments have found to raise revenues after Proposition 13. Along with his chapter, Patrick Coughlan supplies two tables of the various taxes cities have used, demonstrating how inventive local officials can be. Seeking to match service levels to effective demand, communities are asking voters to approve special taxes and to pay user charges for police, fire, recreation, and other services previously supported by general funds. Hoping to provide public services more efficiently, communities are increasingly contracting with private firms for their performance and are entering joint-powers agreements with neighboring governments to realize economies of scale. Cities are also looking to developers to finance the capital improvements needed to serve their projects and to provide means of maintaining these facilities upon completion, such as through home-owner-association fees. Increasingly, planning-department filing fees are calibrated to meet the actual costs of processing development applications. Some cities have even made clear to developers that unless needed amenities are donated, development permission will be withheld.

Part VI presents two rather different approaches to housing, each with its own directive for public policy. Wallace Smith contends that the time has come to stop subsidizing the savings industry, and instead to create a government lender dedicated to financing the American dream, restoring to the one-income, child-raising family the opportunity for home ownership. He decries the attempted administration bail-out of the savings and loans. Even military appropriations have been cut, and yet the All Savers Bill became law eight weeks after being presented, despite claims, now proven, that far more could be lost in taxes than would be gained in new savings. The trend toward indexing savings and mortgage debt to inflation so that lenders may be assured the benefits of a comfortable spread makes no sense to Smith. For borrowers the new mortgage devices are precisely the ones that led to massive foreclosures in the Great Depression. For the economy as a whole, Smith sees them as inflationary. Smith also advocates a compulsory-savings program crossed with social security to make mortgage loans.

The second housing chapter, by Ira S. (Jack) Lowry, is in its own way just as startling. His careful research in the rental housing market has led him to conclude that most of the media and a good many elected officials, along with any number of leading home builders, have misunderstood the present rental housing picture if they believe there is a shortage of rental housing. We are feeling the impact of a surplus, not a shortage, if those terms are measured in terms of returns to investors. Landlords have been going broke. Operating expenses have risen in the past decade 1.6 times faster than revenue, considerably in excess of the consumer price index (CPI), while rents have declined in real terms. The only rental properties trading at high values are those that can be converted to condominiums or other uses. Vacancy rates are low because landlords would prefer a full house at losing prices to a high vacancy rate with the occupied units yielding higher rents.

If the federal government were to continue subsidizing new rental construction it would make matters worse by encouraging those who are subsidized to leave market-rate apartments, creating vacancies and, in some cases, abandonments. Similarly, rent controls are bound to be counterproductive. Lowry recommends subsidizing the operation of existing rental dwellings by helping truly needy renters with an income or rent supplement.

Like a dutiful teacher, I endeavored to identify the issues and organize the inquiry. I was not expecting to find a unifying message, but when I reviewed the essays one emerged. The trends described in this volume will push state and local officials into a more entrepreneurial position in land policy.

Local officials, faced with spending cuts in their subventions from higher levels of government, and barred to voter resistance and high borrowing costs from bonding to finance capital improvements, will need to conceive of the land within their jurisdictions not just as a property-tax base but as the only factor of production which they can reach directly. As they attempt to improve local economies, they will doubtless learn the lesson of thirty-five years of British land policy, that swimming against the economic tides is enervating and futile. The best they can do is to take an accurate measure of the current and swim with it, only faster.

A few years ago some local officials might have hoped that rising fuel prices would have dictated a trend towards more compact development patterns, and that federal air- and water-quality standards coupled with massive funding of infrastructure to mitigate pollution would remove from their calendars the most intractible debates about land-use priorities, the environment versus development imbroglio. That expectation is no longer realistic. They will be left to their own devices in resolving these disputes, and in funding whatever infrastructure their decisions require.

On the cheerful side, local officials may find a public more receptive to the need for public-facilities improvements as a necessary condition for economic development. They will probably find, as well, that their constituents have no ideological commitments except that public works be done efficiently, whether that means increasing the number of public front-line service providers or contracting with private firms.

Increasingly, private developers are being asked to finance public facilities. In return, some firms can be expected to demand the lifting of uneconomic public regulations and the sharing of public powers on their behalf (including eminent domain and the right to form special assessment districts). As federal subsidies to housing construction are withdrawn and the workhorse of home-mortgage finance, the savings association, is lamed by unpredictable interest-rate fluctuations, political demands for housing will only be realized with the help of inventive and vigorous entrepreneurs with whom local officials will be compelled to negotiate to secure both acceptable levels of suburban growth and urban renewal.

Part I
The Reagan Budget

1

Reaganomics: Implications for California Governments

Larry J. Kimbell
and *David Shulman*

On March 10, 1981, President Reagan sent to the Congress of the United States a set of revisions to the Carter administration's budget, prefaced with the following objectives:

First, we must cut the growth of government spending.

Second, we must cut tax rates so that once again work will be rewarded and savings encouraged.

Third, we must carefully remove the tentacles of excessive government regulation which are strangling our economy.

Fourth, while recognizing the independence of the institution, we must work with the Federal Reserve Board to develop a monetary policy that will rationally control the money supply.

Fifth, we must move, surely and predictably, toward a balanced budget.

Progress on Three Objectives: Failure on One, Doubts on the Others

Government spending will increase for defense and decrease for non-defense, in constant dollars. Tax rates have been cut significantly and special savings incentives have been introduced. Regulation is taking a decisively new course: toward less regulation and more faith in the free-market system.

However, not all objectives are still supported. Less than one year later, the Reagan administration has abandoned the hope of a balanced budget for fiscal year 1984. Its support of the Federal Reserve Board was strong at the beginning, when things looked good, but weakened noticeably as the economy fell into sharp recession.

A Perspective on Reaganomics

Reaganomics is a curious mixture of traditional conservative economic thinking and maverick, gadfly notions. The traditional remedies include:

3

1. Gradually lower money growth until inflation is under control (that is, less than 2 percent per year).
2. Lower taxes and *lower government spending* (that is, aim for a balanced budget or a federal surplus).
3. Rely on the free market as the chief regulator of producers' behavior and protector of consumers' interests.

Reagan's notion, which cannot be found in the traditional conservative economic literature, is the prediction that large tax cuts pay for themselves within one or two fiscal years so there is no urgent need to cut spending when taxes are cut. This notion, relying on the so-called Laffer curve, underlies the Kemp-Roth proposals that were championed by Reagan during the election campaign. They were largely adopted by Congress in the Economic Recovery Tax Act of 1981, which features a 23-percent reduction in personal-income-tax rates, phased in over three years.

Herbert Stein, formerly chairman of the Council of Economic Advisers under President Nixon, suggested in the *Wall Street Journal* (July 18, 1978) that the odds that Kemp-Roth would raise revenues were about the same as finding human life on Mars.

Milton Friedman, writing in *Newsweek*, critized Kemp-Roth for exaggerated promises, reminding readers that there is no such thing as a free lunch. The Laffer curve, on the other hand, suggested taxpayers could have lower tax rates without loss of government services, a veritable free lunch.

The Kemp-Roth recommendation, to cut tax rates and keep spending, was largely indistinguishable from the Keynesian remedies for a recession although the argument was shifted to alleged supply-side effects. This argument was attacked in the *1979 Annual Report* of the Federal Reserve Bank of Minneapolis under the title "The Tax-Cut Illusion" as follows:

> A shift from explicit taxes to deficits does not lower the real tax burden, whatever else it may do. Increasing federal debts is a way to conceal taxes, not a way to reduce them.

These three rejections of the Laffer curve were amplified manyfold, since many other economists—conservative and liberal alike—rejected the idea that a large tax rate reduction pays for itself almost immediately with higher revenues.

The Reagan administration has paid a very high price for not rejecting the Laffer curve. Bond-market investors remain very worried about the deficit and show no sign of changing their views. Interest rates remain at unprecedented levels, given inflation and the recession. Recovery will be slow or may stall entirely if rates do not drop. Housing is in the worst depression since the 1930s. Savings and loan associations and mutual banks are under such severe cost pressures that many will require federal assistance if rates do not drop dramatically. Unemployment will rise above 9 percent and may remain there over a year if interest rates do not fall relative to inflation. Investment fell sharply in the fourth quarter of 1981, certainly not a supply-side victory.

Reaganomics is working to reduce inflation and change the composition of federal spending. Given time, less inflation will help set the stage for stronger investment and higher productivity. But Reaganomics is not working to balance the budget in the next few fiscal years. The traditional conservative prediction—that slowing money growth will lower inflation—is roughly on target, but the supply-side predictions so far are dead wrong.

In January 1982, many of Reagan's economic advisers as well as several prominent Republican senators urged the president to cut the projected budget deficits. Recommendations included raising excise taxes and slowing defense expansion. The president eventually rejected this advice and stayed with the supply-side arguments.

Recession Brings an Education to the White House

Table 1-1 compares the Reagan projections made in March 1981 with the UCLA forecast made in December 1981. The federal budget for fiscal 1983, which is now being prepared, will differ from our assumptions, but table 1-1 illustrates the magnitude of the gap that budget analysts now face.

The UCLA base forecast now calls for growth in GNP in current dollars in 1982 of 5.3 percent, 7.5 percent less than the administration forecast in March 1981. In contrast with our forecast of March 1981, we now expect personal income to be $107 billion lower and corporate profits $80 billion lower in 1982 than Reagan's March estimates. Ironically much of this reduction results from the fact that the current rate of inflation is less than the administration was forecasting in March 1981. The UCLA forecast now anticipates that the GNP deflator in 1982 will increase 7.1 percent in 1982, 1.1 percent below the Reagan projections.

Federal revenues are expected to be lower and expenditures higher than Reagan assumed last March. We now project a deficit in 1984 of more than $100 billion. Revenues are predicted to be $51 billion lower and outlays $61 billion higher than contained in Reagan's first budget, which included massive unspecified budget cuts. However, the easy cuts have been made. Most of the defense budget and social security are off limits; interest payments cannot be controlled. The rest of the budget is not large enough; hence the deficit will be large.

**State and Local Government Expenditures
Are No Longer Counter-Cyclic**

In the most intense phase of the recession of 1973-1975, real state and local government purchases of goods and services grew at the annual rate of 2.9

Table 1-1
Why the Balanced Budget Disappeared: Projections

| | Billions of Dollars | | |
	1982	1983	1984
Receipts			
Reagan	651	710	772
UCLA	620	668	721
Difference	30	42	51
Outlays			
Reagan	696	733	772
UCLA	728	778	832
Difference	− 33	− 45	− 61
Deficit			
Reagan	− 45	− 23	1
UCLA	− 108	− 110	− 111
Difference	63	87	112
	Percent Change		
	1982	1983	1984
GNP			
Reagan	12.8	12.4	10.8
UCLA	5.3	11.1	9.5
Difference	7.5	1.3	1.3
Real GNP			
Reagan	4.2	5.0	4.5
UCLA	− 1.7	4.2	3.8
Difference	5.9	0.8	0.7
Price deflator			
Reagan	8.2	7.0	6.0
UCLA	7.1	6.6	5.5
Difference	1.1	0.4	0.5

Note: Reagan projections are from March 1981, and UCLA base forecast projections are from December 1981.

percent and employment expanded at the rate of 5.1 percent (see table 1-2). Tax revenues adjusted for inflation were falling, but federal grants-in-aid increased rapidly enough to completely offset lower tax receipts, leaving total real revenues constant. Corporate-profit tax collections adjusted for inflation, fell at the annual rate of 37 percent, but real grants grew at a 21-percent rate. During the current recession, on the other hand, real grants-in-aid are expected to drop at the annual rate of 14 percent from third quarter 1981 to first quarter 1982. With total real receipts falling at a 7.6 percent rate, real state and local expenditures will drop at a 2.6-percent rate. Moreover, further budget cuts must be made later because many of the operating surpluses prevalent in 1981 will turn to deficits in 1982. The outlook calls for real purchases of state and local governments to decline until 1983, when the real spending level will be the same as in the first quarter of 1976, eight years earlier.

Table 1-2
Payroll Jobs over Two Business-Cycle Episodes
(average annual percent change)

	Stagflation 1973:4-74:3	*Free Fall 1974:3-75:1*	*Expansion 1975:1-79:1*	*Stagflation 1979:1-81:3*	*Free Fall 1981:3-82:1*	*Expansion 1982:1-84:4*
Payroll jobs (nonagricultural)						
California	2.6	−2.7	5.3	2.4	−2.0	3.0
United States	1.3	−4.4	3.8	1.3	−2.8	1.9
Private sector						
California	2.0	−4.8	6.3	2.7	−2.2	3.5
United States	0.9	−6.4	4.1	1.5	−3.1	2.3
Government sector						
California	4.9	5.7	1.2	0.9	−1.5	0.6
United States	3.1	5.1	2.0	0.3	−1.0	0.1

As shown in table 1-2, private-sector job losses during the current free-fall period are expected to be about half as rapid as in the 1974-1975 recession. However, since government jobs will be declining instead of growing rapidly, total payroll jobs will drop almost as rapidly as before.

Capital spending by state and local governments has already been sharply curtailed and is predicted to drop more, as discussed further in the following section.

**Incidence of Monetary Policy
on State and Local Growth**

Although much has been said about the impact of fiscal policy on the state and local sector, the impact of monetary policy is perhaps of equal importance. The current monetary policy of the Federal Reserve Board, slowing the growth of the monetary aggregates in the face of a huge federal deficit, has substantially increased real interest rates. For our purposes, we will define the real interest rate as the yield on long-term government bonds minus the percentage change in the GNP deflator over the previous year. Table 1-3 presents the historical nominal and real interest rates from 1976 to 1981 and the forecast rates for 1982-1984.

An increase in the real interest rate is analogous to imposing an excise tax on borrowers and redistributing the proceeds proportionally among lenders. Thus net borrowers in the economy face what is in effect a tax *increase* and net lenders receive a tax decrease. This means that despite tax-rate reductions in the individual and corporate sectors of the economy, many net borrowers may be actually facing a de facto tax *increase*.

This effect is first felt with a decline in the demand for capital goods and consumer durables. As a result, the industrial Midwest was the first and hardest hit casualty of the slow-money-growth policy. However, as time elapses, the effects of high real interest rates are more subtle. Economic growth and migration become casualties as well.

If this view of the world is correct, then the impact of the current monetary policy is antisupply side because growing sectors and regions of the economy also bear the burdens of high real interest rates. The effects described are probably more short run in nature in that ultimately the accumulation of capital in the lending sectors of the economy will increase the supply of capital and lower the real interest rate. However, in the meantime, the increase in real interest rates will work their antisupply-side effects. This is especially important for growing areas that require huge infusions of capital to finance infrastructure.

Another aspect of the problem is that unusually high new-mortgage interest rates relative to the average of existing mortgage rates works to defer

Table 1-3
Historical and Forecasted Interest Rates

	1977	1978	1979	1980	1981	1982 Forecast	1983 Forecast	1984 Forecast
Long-term government-bond yield	7.7	8.5	9.3	11.4	13.6	11.9	11.4	10.2
Percent change GNP deflator	5.8	7.3	8.5	9.0	9.2	7.1	6.6	5.5
Real interest rate	1.9	1.2	0.8	2.4	4.4	4.8	4.8	4.7

interregional migration. That is, people are reluctant to move when a move would automatically penalize them through an automatic set-up in housing costs caused by an increase in mortgage interest rates. This makes it difficult for fast-growing industries to attract people from other regions, thus slowing their growth. We might call this effect an immigration tax.

The Infrastructure Problem

Public capital can be viewed as complementary to private capital. Much private investment would not take place without public investment in bridges, roads, sewers, transit systems, and education, for example. As a result of President Reagan's program we expect state and local investment, as measured in 1972 dollars, to decline 31 percent to $20.5 billion in 1980 to $14.1 billion in 1984. *Business Week* (October 26, 1981) called the situation a crisis.

This decline will obviously make it more difficult for private industry to undertake the major investment boom that was predicated upon the new accelerated cost-recovery system (ACRS) of depreciation allowances. If industry is forced to bear the public infrastructure costs, then many of the advantages of ACRS would be dissipated.

This obviously will slow the growth of the faster-growing regions of California and stay the incipient boom that is now developing in the Central Valley. However, it could inure to the benefit of the older cities of Los Angeles, San Francisco, and Oakland, where in some cases there is surplus infrastructure capacity. These older areas will thus become more attractive for growth and development. Should this happen, some of the reductions in the income-redistribution programs, which are greatly affecting the older urban areas, would be offset by direct employment in the private sector.

The inability of state and local governments to finance infrastructure is predicated on three factors. The first is the drastic cut in grants-in-aid to state and local governments that was discussed earlier. The second is the incidence of monetary policy that raises real interest rates on borrowings. Third, changes in the tax code have made tax-exempt state- and local-government bonds less attractive to investors.

The sweeping changes in the tax code have taken away much of the relative advantages of low-risk tax-exempt bonds. Individuals and commercial banks, the primary buyers of tax-exempt securities, now have many more tax-exempt alternatives. For example, there are the new all-savers certificates and individual retirement accounts (IRAs), and the new liberalized leasing rules will allow banks to shelter income through the normal commercial lending process. The reduction of the maximum tax on unearned income from 70 percent to 50 percent is also important. This decrease alone has to cause an increase in the tax-exempt bond yields. Lastly, the reduction in grant-in-aid has increased the risk of default so the risk premiums on state and local bonds will increase.

The increase in the cost of debt to state and local governments will make the bond alternative less attractive for financing public infrastructure. Thus most of what is left to finance infrastructure would be an increase in local taxation. Whether such increases are politically possible in the post-Propositions 13 and 2½ era remains to be seen. However, the across-the-board reduction in individual-income-tax rates raises the effective cost of local taxes to individuals by reducing the related federal tax benefits.

UCLA Forecast for California

The recession in the U.S. economy in late 1981 was felt in California, though prospects call for a less severe impact in California. Table 1-4 presents a summary of the December 1981 UCLA Forecast for California. These are the highlights of the California outlook:

1. The sharp recession has led to a substantial downward revision of our estimate for personal-income growth in 1982, from 10 percent in September to 7.8 percent in December.
2. Government employment was strongly counter-cyclic in the 1973-1975 recession, when it grew over 5 percent in both California and the United States. This time there will be no quick fix or increase in government jobs to fight unemployment; government employment will decline in 1982. Stopping inflation remains the dominant priority in Washington, D.C.
3. Employment in the aircraft and aircraft parts industry has weakened in the past year. Commercial airliner production will drop in 1982 and the L-1011 program will be shut down permanently.
4. Electronic-component producers are caught in a severe price war. Job losses in this cyclic industry have already occurred and will get worse.
5. Nonresidential construction has helped offset the severe depression in housing for the past two years. Although housing is expected to begin a slow recovery, weakness in government capital spending (in a state of collapse) and business fixed investment do not augur well for this sector.
6. Unemployment in California is expected to rise to about 9 percent, less than in the recession of 1973-1975, and slightly better than in the United States in general. Employment gains in the following recovery are expected to be slower, however, than they were in 1976-1978 when the money supply grew far too fast to hold down inflation.

Table 1-4
Summary of the UCLA Forecast for California

	1974	1975	1976	1977	1978	1979	1980	1981	1982	1983	1984
Personal Income and Gross State Product (billions of dollars)											
Personal income	128.2	141.3	157.4	175.6	198.8	228.5	259.6	290.1	312.7	346.5	384.0
Gross state product	154.1	170.8	192.1	217.7	248.7	283.2	315.5	352.2	374.0	420.2	469.4
(1972 Dollars)	135.8	136.2	145.0	154.3	163.8	172.5	173.2	177.4	176.1	185.6	197.0
California compared with the United States											
Personal Income *(percent change)*											
California	11.8	10.3	11.4	11.6	13.2	14.9	13.6	11.8	7.8	10.8	10.8
United States	9.7	8.2	10.0	10.5	11.9	12.9	11.1	11.1	7.0	9.6	8.6
California income as a percent of United States	11.0	11.2	11.3	11.4	11.5	11.8	12.0	12.1	12.2	12.3	12.6
Wages and salaries per non-agricultural payroll employee *(percent change)*											
California	6.9	7.4	6.4	6.5	6.6	8.4	9.6	8.1	7.0	6.7	6.6
United States	6.9	7.1	7.0	6.4	6.9	7.9	7.9	9.0	6.2	6.2	5.8
Nonagricultural payroll employment *(percent change)*											
California	2.8	0.2	3.9	5.5	6.9	5.1	2.3	1.8	-0.5	2.7	3.9
United States	2.0	-1.7	3.2	3.9	5.1	3.6	0.8	1.1	-0.7	2.4	1.8
Unemployment Rate											
California	7.3	9.8	9.1	8.2	7.1	6.2	6.8	7.4	8.8	8.5	7.3
United States	5.6	8.5	7.7	7.0	6.0	5.8	7.1	7.6	8.9	8.4	7.9
Consumer prices *(percent change)*											
California	10.2	10.4	6.1	7.1	8.0	10.9	15.6	10.3	5.7	6.4	5.5
United States	11.0	9.1	5.7	6.5	7.7	11.3	13.5	10.4	5.9	6.4	5.8
California Building Activity											
Residential building-permit activity *(thousands of units)*	125.9	131.4	222.0	269.9	239.2	208.2	146.5	109.8	133.0	183.2	200.0
Total valuation *(million $)*	6,904	7,653	11,519	15,201	16,315	17,953	16,655	16,760	17,552	22,810	26,993

7. Housing activity will slowly revive in 1982 but it will be 1983 before permits for the year average 180,000 or more, still well below the 270,000-unit rate of 1977.
8. Home prices in California are expected to increase less than in the United States generally for an extended period of time—a healthy development.

As a result of the recession and the budget-cutting efforts of the Reagan administration, state and local governments all over the United States are struggling to adjust to new budget realities. These new policies are intended primarily to cut back the secular growth of government spending, and this is being accomplished. Another incidental effect,however, is that, at least for this recession, state- and local-government spending is likely to move with the general business cycle instead of being strongly counter-cyclic as it was in the 1973-1975 period.

California has special problems due to adjustments (still under way) to the effects of Proposition 13, and income-tax indexation, which was passed immediately after Proposition 13. As shown in figure 1-1, public-sector employment by state and local governments in California dropped sharply after Proposition 13 passed in June 1978. No similar precipitous drop is anticipated. Nevertheless, the impact of the recession implies substantially less revenue since personal income is now much lower. For example, in September 1981, before the outline of the recession was clearly visible, we had projected that personal income would grow $29 billion, or 10.0 percent, in 1982. We now project growth of $22.6 billion, or 7.8 percent. Although we do not project state revenues, a rough rule of thumb—that state revenues move slightly more than 1 percent for each 1-percent change in personal income in California—implies between $0.5 and $1.0 billion less revenue than was indicated in September. The recession means that efforts to prepare a balanced state budget for fiscal year 1982-1983 are more challenging than they were several months ago.

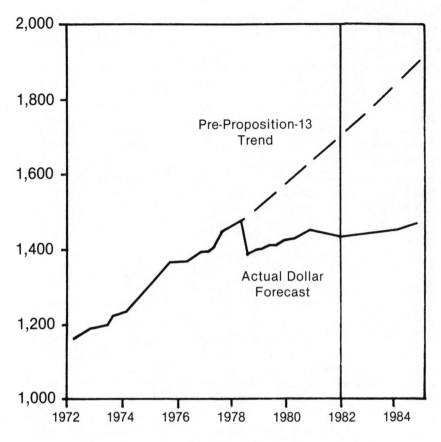

Figure 1-1. Public-Sector Employment (Thousands)

Comments

David Doerr

Three points deserve attention: (1) the impact of the 1982 federal budget on California; (2) the fiscal and legal implications of the new-federalism proposal; and (3) my suggestions for the new federalism.

First, the initial round of 1982 federal budget cuts affected California by $1.5 billion: $300 million was lost through CETA job eliminations; $180 million was slashed through the Aid for Dependent Children (AFDC) cut which eliminated 122,000 persons and reduced benefits for another 330,000; food stamps were cut; unemployment-insurance benefits were cut for people leaving the military. There were a number of other cuts as well.

Second, it might be helpful to examine the so-called new-federalism proposal announced in the president's recent State of the Union speech; we will look at the fiscal ramification only and not any policy aspects. Briefly, the proposal is to shift $20 billion in the aggregate with the federal government taking over the states' share of Medicaid, and the states would take over the federal share of AFDC costs and the food-stamp program. In addition, the federal government will set up a trust fund of about $28 billion to pay for the transfer of other grant programs to the states. Beginning late in 1987 through 1991, that fund will be phased out.

What might we expect? Will the revenues balance the added costs? That appears to be the intent. Our state controller has said that in the first four years the shift will cost us $6 billion over a four-year span. Even if there is presently a deficit, the program could be fine-tuned to balance in the initial years.

In 1987, the states would begin to fund what had been funded by the federal trust fund. Sixty percent of the revenue in the federal trust fund would be derived from the federal oil-windfall-profits tax. When the federal trust fund phases out, is a state windfall-profits tax viable as a replacement? The tax folks generally feel that it would be very difficult, if not impossible, to administer that kind of a tax on a state level. Since California has oil, it could probably use another kind of oil-based tax such as a severance tax. States that do not have oil as a natural resource would have more difficulty than would California.

Legislators do not like to impose taxes, especially to fill a tax cut by some other level of government. One of the taxes in this trust fund is a federal excise tax on telephone service; this excise tax has been declining, but California is trying to levy the difference as the federal tax declines. Since the trust-fund tax base will be phased out at 25 percent a year, taxes at the state level would have to be raised four years in a row, which might be even more politically unpopular than to do it just once.

California has a two-thirds vote requirement on any increase in state taxes as a result of Proposition 13, so a bipartisan agreement is required in the legislature to raise taxes. Suppose a two-thirds vote were achieved and the government somehow manages to raise taxes every year for four years to fill the deficit. This raises a final question, perhaps the most interesting of all. Can the state of California constitutionally spend the money for these purposes under Article XIIIB, the Gann Initiative?

The 1979 initiative limited the growth in state and local government spending to the lesser of consumer price index (CPI) or per-capita income growth. Presently, we are probably $1.5 billion below our limit. Projections indicate that the cushion will gradually decrease to $500-700 million in 1987. Our share of the transferred programs will be about $2.8 to $3 billion. So we in California would be trying to fit a $3-billion expenditure into a spending frame of perhaps $500 million.

There are possibly two relevant exceptions to the spending limit. First, funds can be spent in excess of the limit for federally mandated programs. But one of the purposes of the shift is to remove federal control in order to give the states options. So the programs would not be federally mandated. The second possibility is some involved language in the constitution that the state can raise its spending limit for programs transferred by another level of government, but only if both agencies mutually agree on the amount of the shift and the increase in the transferee's budget produces a corresponding reduction in the transferor's budget.

We must conclude that there may well be constitutional problems if the state has to spend additional local tax dollars for these transferred federal programs.

Third, another approach merits consideration for the new federalism that the federal government pay the costs of any program it mandates upon state and local governments. In California there is a comparable provision for the costs of state-mandated programs imposed on local governments. It was the cornerstone of President Reagan's major tax-reform proposal in California when he was governor. It is consistent with accountability and responsibility in government; he who calls the tune should pay the piper. This might be a more realistic proposal for the state of California than the one being suggested.

Discussion

Gideon Kanner: Professor Shulman, do you think California is particularly vulnerable to high interest rates because of the boom in residential housing here in the 1970s and resulting prices higher than in other states?

David Shulman: Yes.

Donald Denman: As a visitor from Cambridge, England, I am interested in the statement that house prices have become so high that no one can buy homes. Then who indeed is buying them? Somebody must be.

Larry Kimbell: Homeowners already in the game can finance new home prices from their equities. It's a pyramid game. In the mid 1970s we underbuilt and had lots of new jobs and migration. That combination seems to have pushed up home prices. Now some people in California, such as those on our faculty, are discovering that a modest West Los Angeles dwelling would finance a mansion, a forty-acre farm, and a cow and a pig in many other places. A net loss of population among potential home-buying ranks finally brought us to a crisis.

Cary Lowe: David Shulman, I read your article in the *Los Angeles Times* about the need for a federal bailout of savings and loans, a medium- to long-term capitalization of their existing debt that could be redeemed at a future time. This should be of great concern to local and state governments since under Proposition 13, without new homes being built, the base is not going to grow. How might such a bailout actually be accomplished?

David Shulman: Congress would appropriate more money into the Federal Savings and Loan Insurance Corporation. Federal Home Loan Bank advances would be made through direct appropriation. That would put the industry in quasi-receivership, which means it would not make loans. Last year, of all new mortgages created in the United States, 40 percent came from federal and state housing finance agencies, and 60 percent came from the private sector. This year, the public-sector percentage will be greater unless Stockman shuts down the federal credit agencies. For all practical purposes, the savings and loans are leaving the market. They are in a holding pattern. The effects are already apparent in the housing market. November 1981 was the lowest month for new housing starts in California since permit numbers have been kept.

Fred Kahane: Over time, if interest rates remain high and housing starts continue to decline, wouldn't that induce more people to save and others to borrow for housing if the demand is there and has not been met?

David Shulman: We are in transition now from a period of high to low inflation—a very painful adjustment. One of the results is high real-interest rates which in the long run should attract more capital into savings, causing the real rate to drop at some time in the future.

Jack Spahn: Do you think in the foreseeable future we are going to see take-out interest rates below 12 percent or 13 percent?

David Shulman: November or December 1981, I would have said that we would. Now I am not sure. We thought that rates would be in the 13-15 percent range by spring-summer of 1982. We no longer think that.

Jack Spahn: Do you think there is any hope for that within the next two years?

Larry Kimbell: Our model, our theory, our predictions all said "down" and history has said the opposite. So we find the current rates inexplicable, puzzling, and damaging. We haven't decided what went wrong in the last prediction, but it flies in the face of the recession, the declining rate of inflation, even the current deficit. But we are taking another look.

Jack Spahn: Do you see us coming back to a fixed interest rate on long-term mortgages?

David Shulman: In the immediate future, no. In the longer term, 1990 and beyond, if the inflation rate is down and we have stable 2-to-3-percent inflation, I think we will see lenders making fixed-rate loans. In the intermediate term, even if rates drop, lenders will maintain variable or balloon loans. But after three or four years with a stable inflation rate and competitive lending market, we should experience a return to long-term, fixed-rate mortgages.

Leroy Graymer: Many transactions involve sellers of homes carrying their own paper for at least a short time. Do you have figures on the percentage of home sellers carrying their own paper?

David Shulman: Something like 60 percent of all the transactions involve sellers carrying their own paper. Frank Mittelbach has studied this.

Frank Mittelbach: This is a significant proportion.

David Shulman: If money every eases, there will be a backlog of previously sold houses to finance, creating a double burden on institutions to lend both for new sales as well as refinancing of old sales.

Leroy Graymer: Isnt't there another element? Home sellers will then be paid off; they will have cash. What will they do with it?

Larry Kimbell: Sellers may not be paid in full. Some of these loans will have been discounted as much as 50 cents on the dollar if they fall due before rates decline and while house prices are soft. The below-market seller-made loans are the equivalent of a price cut. If house prices have declined, there may not be so much to refinance.

Part II
National Urban Land Policy

2 National Urban Land Policy: Facing the Inevitability of City and Regional Evolution

Donald A. Hicks

A traditional consideration of national urban land policy invariably invites a treatment of land as the focus of intergovernmental and intersectoral squabbles and the subject of endless tension between efficiency and equity, profit and preservation, community sovereignty and national goals. Yet it is tempting to suggest that there is more to consider under the rubric of national urban land policy. There may be a new and useful way of looking at things which, as we proceed from issue to traditional issue, from small to large scale, from city to countryside, suggests that conventional assumptions about land and the uses to which it is put are crumbling. New ways of looking at old problems often have as their first effect—if not the doing away with the problems—a shift of the terrain of the debate.

The matter of a national policy regarding land and its uses has become much more complex, largely without our being aware of it and for reasons few have yet to appreciate fully. Traditional perspectives on land use emphasize its intergovernmental, economic, fiscal, energy, and environmental aspects along with the ever-present efficiency-equity trade-offs. While often complex, these discussions are familiar even though their outcomes may be predictable. Today each of these traditional perspectives is receiving a long-overdue reexamination. As usual, changing realities have paced these reexaminations by a full stride. Any consideration of a national urban land policy must take into account the greater synchronization between what land is, how it is used, and how both concepts are being defined. In the end, it may be the very national (federal) policy apparatus that broadcasts the need for new, better, more coherent policies able to handle small-scale and broad-scale problems all in a sweep of brilliance that obscures our view of where we are and where we are going. Perhaps our land-related problems are no longer what they seem to be. Perhaps the problems lie more with the political and policy apparatuses that periodically evidence concern over land and its uses than with land and its uses in themselves.

Urban Land-Rural Land: The Vanishing
Natural Distinction

Early in our history land was a medium for influence, a basis for economic power, and an insulator via space from unwanted social influences. To go to the country meant getting out of town—keeping city ways and influences at arm's length. Soon mail-order catalogs, automobiles, radio and newspapers, and other technological developments eroded the barriers between urban and rural life. Rural communities were the producers, urban communities were net consumers. Rural communities first lost their youth to jobs in the growing cities and later their unique qualities disappeared in lifestyles built on new ways of organizing rural-agricultural resources that surged back into the countryside. Cities had reshaped the hinterland, if not in their own image, then at least to serve their own purposes.

Today the rural-to-urban population-migration stream has all but dried up. No longer does the cityward shift of rural folk compensate in part for the larger shift of city residents out of large central and even suburban cities. Increasingly, one-time rural areas and small towns are the destinations of people who wish to leave metropolitan areas altogether. As these relocations of jobs and people, capital, innovation, and income wash away the distinction between urban and rural, the extended spatial dimensions of the new urban America are revealed. Nearly all of the United States is now urban—defined less by where we work and sleep and more by the conditions that define both our own lives and our accessibility to the lives of others.

Likewise, land as a production factor demands redefinition. The passage from an agrarian to an industrial era a century and more ago altered radically the intrinsic meaning and significance of land. Increasingly there arose alternative bases for wealth and power. Land ownership was joined by industrial entrepreneurship, advanced education, and official position as the wellsprings of wealth and power. Today, in the late industrial era, the essential physical capital that is required by the high-technology industries of the Silicon Valley in California or the Silicon Prairie in Texas can quickly be transported to a new location. So fragile are the anchors of an increasing portion of our economy to specific places that location or place is rapidly receding in significance.

The traditional land-based extractive industries of the primary sector of the economy—mineral mining and food and fiber production—have undergone revolutionary transformations. The role that land plays in these activities has not escaped unaltered. The primary sector of the economy traditionally has viewed land as a vault or storehouse; locked within this treasure chest was either a substance of value itself (for example, coal) or properties that were necessary to the production of things of value (for example, the chemical composition of rich soil). Yet the important point is that the historical circumstances of a nation, its location on a technological time line and a wide variety of other social, political, and economic factors have always determined what precisely about land was of value.

Nothing locked in the land was inherent value; social circumstances and technological capacities create value. A conspiracy of price, alternative sources, recovery technologies, and industrial demands has caused the value of coal to rise and fall over the past two centuries. High and low sulphur content and assorted other distinctions have been called into existence and assigned meaning as the value of coal is set and reset by dozens of forces. Likewise, there was a time in the not too distant past when oil itself was considered a nuisance. The rising interest in oil shale and natural gas for meeting our energy needs as well as the mushrooming demand for countless ores and minerals in expanding and revolutionizing industrial-production processes have literally assured that the role of land in the extractive primary sector of the economy has been subject to virtually incessant redefinition since the Industrial Revolution.

Similarly, agriculture itself, with historically the most direct dependence on the essential features of land (for example, soil composition, exposure to climate, susceptibility to erosion, and so on), is freeing itself from land as we have known it (that is, in terms of its physical, chemical, and locational endowments). It is highly probable that food and fiber production will increasingly be amenable to a variety of nontraditional arrangements. Carbon-dioxide fertilization, biological-nitrogen fixation, photosynthetic enhancement, drip irrigation, breeding for growth in salt water, multiple and extensive cropping, no-tillage agriculture, organic-waste recycling, and many other technological advancements and organizational strategies constitute just a few of the battles that have begun the liberation of agriculture from the soil. The extended implication is that prime land in the agricultural sector is no longer considered to be the gift of nature but rather the resultant of myriad forces increasingly being brought under the control of organized collective life.

**Plastic Land: The Coming Revolution in Land
and Its Uses**

Traditionally land, like so many other resources, has been perceived as two-dimensional, with width and breadth and measured in acres.

> The total land area is viewed as a two-dimensional space to be allocated among competing uses, primarily on the basis of economic and social utility, modified by political tradeoffs. (The Council of State Governments, 1975:8)[1]

As a matter of fixed wealth, generally the prime concern was for the distribution of its largesse. This makes eminently good sense in agrarian economies where the tie to the land was the lifeline to the larger economy. To be landless was to be shut off from the wealth generated by the larger economy.

Today land is viewed as multidimensional. We are learning that wealth is not fixed, awaiting only compassionate redistribution; instead, it can be created through the productive chemistry of technology, population, and other natural resources and how we organize them. While the land speculator's sales line, "One thing about land is that they're not making any more of it," emphasizes the view of land as a static commodity, what land represents in our society has always been in a state of flux. Though the controversies implicating land in itself during our industrial era have evolved into controversies over location for the most part, there is ever less that happens in the economic life in an advanced nation that seems to depend on a specific kind or characteristic of land itself or even now of its location. No longer do steel mills or automobile plants have to locate inside or nearby the Great Lakes or the deposits of iron ore so as to be able to build automobiles economically enough to be able to produce for a mass market. No longer even does agriculture have to be located where the soil is naturally black and deep, rich and fertile, well watered and amply warmed by the sun.

The intrinsic values of land understood as either location or composition have been reduced as a result of technological developments that change how we produce, the requirements for production, and what we produce. As petroleum-derived plastics and glues and other substances replace sheet steel, screws, and nuts and bolts in the automobile and other manufacturing industries, and dozens of technological and organizational strategies have come to be used in farming, even agricultural production is on the verge of being taken off the farm in much the same way factories have been able to leave town. The significance of land itself and the uses to which it is put have increasingly been brought under our control. Fish are farmed in special man-made ponds, forests are started in trays on shelves under corrugated metal roofs, cattle are created in test tubes, poultry are manufactured in high-rise structures, the diurnal cycle is wrung out of the growing process as round-the-clock daylight is simulated for entire fields of crops by banks of electric lights, and new hybrid grains are grown without soil and even in salt water. All these developments challenge more traditional conceptions of land and its properties, locations, and uses. It is this brave new world that the following thoughts on a national land use policy intend to explore. The intellectual backswing necessary to justify this unconventional approach to urban land that now encompasses nearly all of the United States and the national policies governing its uses requires that we first delineate a series of relevant urban and economic changes.

Transformation of the Urban-Industrial
United States

Despite the U.S.'s relative youth as a nation-state, it has inhabited the industrial era as long as any nation. A century-long period of political and economic consolidation in the United States followed nearly two centuries as a colony to a succession of one or another European superstates. In time the extractive industries of mining, fishing, and farming which characterized an essentially agrarian economy were joined in the early nineteenth century by fledgling enterprises involved in the fashioning of raw materials into finished products. The arrival of the industrial era had preceded relatively slowly in its Western European seedbeds principally because of the resistance it encountered in displacing a land-based economy and a medieval social order insinuated with it.

In the United States by the late eighteenth century, however, novel ideas were imported as easily as population. With no deeply entrenched agrarian arrangements to hinder its progress, the industrial era caught on and developed rapidly. Accompanying rampant industrialization was a rapid urbanization process. The nineteenth century was an era of great city building for the United States just as it was for Western Europe.[2] The array of Northeastern and North Central industrial cities from Boston to Chicago, Detroit to Baltimore, as well as those cities of secondary status from South Bend to Dayton and on east to Hartford stand today defining a network of settlements overlaid on an industrial hierarchy of places that so ably and predictably generated wealth for the new nation. Each of these settlements had come into existence to fulfill the evolving needs of the emerging industrial order.[3] Their growth was often rapid, as evidenced by the quality and arrangement of the physical capital stock.

These early industrial centers may be more aptly seen as the aftermath of a series of implosions of factory jobs and factory workers stacked in massive piles of bricks and mortar near unevenly distributed natural-resource endowments (coal, iron ore, rivers) that offered the raw materials and transportation options for the strengthening industrial economy. Although these industrial centers were designed to be beautiful cities, they were not. The economic miracle (which became a social one gradually leading to improved jobs, homes, education, health and quality of life for millions of Americans over a half dozen generations) was the beauty these industrial cities offered. That the system of industrial cities, the spatial arrangements within and between them, and the physical forms of factories, public buildings, and residential areas that were erected to serve the functions assigned to these early industrial cities succeeded is largely explained by the fact that growth and development could proceed de novo without first having to clear out the rubbish of medieval cities and without having to accommodate a medieval past.

The urban United States, then, is a curious amalgam. It combines a relatively long industrial tradition with a relatively short urban one. Other nations produced large cities before the United States had, but no nation had erected such large cities so rapidly in the service of the industrial process. Our oldest cities reflect these early origins and functions; in a very real sense they often remind us of accoutrements of the early mills and factories they were meant to serve rather than vice versa.

During the nineteenth century, immigrants from abroad and migrants of the United States from rural areas contributed to the rapid growth of industrial era settlements of the Northeast and Midwest. Yet by late in the nineteenth century, the city as an economic and technological entity was already beginning to lose its grip on manufacturing jobs—the mainstay of the new industrial economy—and the population base it had captured. Since 1900, the central cities' share of metropolitan manufacturing employment has been declining.[4] No one seemed to notice, however. At best it appeared that the spatial arrangements of the industrial era were simply spreading out to embrace ever more land and resources. It did not seem to matter if urban settlements were using space more than ever before to sift and sort people and activities across land and if the political boundaries were unable to embrace the expanding scale of local economic and social organization. Even though the move away from central cities in 1900 that would rapidly expand through the next century had begun in the 1880s, these deconcentrations were so compensated for by growth through immigration of population and industrial births and secondary expansions of businesses in place that the net consequence was steady and predictable growth and expansion.

Today, looking back over figures that in aggregate tell no lies, we can see that the United States has spent the bulk of the twentieth century moving away from those very cities that it never was quite able to abide intellectually or culturally in the first place but still had kept populating during the nineteenth century. But it was not until the process was already several decades old that the net consequence of the building deconcentration would be obvious to all. By 1920 the majority of the population could be defined as urban, and by mid-century growth rates in suburbs would surpass those in central cities.

By this time, the cumulative effect of the city's loosening hold on people and jobs began to be felt acutely. With three-quarters of the nation residing in metropolitan areas, the nation's dominant cities began to show the telltale signs of decades of flows of jobs, people, and seedbed qualities for industrial entrepreneurship leading away from cities. City after city, particularly the oldest and largest, began to be characterized first by retarded growth rates relative to the suburban jurisdictions surrounding them, then later by absolute population declines as well.[5] During the decade of the

1970s, compared to the decade that preceded it, the number of U.S. cities that lost jobs declined while the number of cities losing population increased.[6] Some, like St. Louis, in the three decades since mid-century have lost nearly half the population they had at their peak; New York City lost half its manufacturing base during the same period.[7]

By the end of the 1970s, the suburbanization process which was just less than a century old was joined by a nonmetropolitan growth process that saw the nation's nonmetropolitan area growth rate eclipse the growth rate of metropolitan areas for the first time since the nation had begun moving to its cities. Urban United States was spreading out with such relentless predictability that during the 1970s nearly one in six of the nation's metropolitan areas (especially the oldest and largest) actually lost population rather than simply failed to grow.

Behind this industrial era process is unquestionably the transformation of the nation's economy from being manufacturing-dominated to being increasingly service-dominated. While the manufacturing sector continues to grow, it does so at a rate that no longer enables it to dictate what the settlements that serve the nation will do (function) or will look like (form). Technological revolutions in the linking technologies of transportation and communication greased the skids and allowed the significance of physical distance to lose its sting; the friction of physical accessibility was lessened even though the distances between home and factory and factory workers and office workers were able to increase. (After 1876, when the telephone and telegraph allowed the message to be transmitted without the messenger, the barriers to the deconcentration of the life we know as urban began to topple.)

In short, the twin transformations of the industrial era economy and the cities whose forms and functions reflected that era had proceeded to the point that the industrial economy's hegemony was to be only something less than a century and a half long. This dual transformation of the nation's economy and its cities requires that the assumptions underlying a wide variety of understandings and expectations be reconsidered. Included in this reexamination are issues involving land and the uses to which it is put. This time, as had been the case in Western Europe at the waning of the agrarian era, the United States has a past, an industrial past, with which to contend. Political arrangements and social assumptions are increasingly a drag on adapting to economic and technological change.

Inevitable Evolution: Public Policy and the Passing of the Industrial Era

Resistance to these changes has grown: A quarter century of federal urban policy reflects this.[8] Our cities, which we had built so rapidly and with such little care and which had served so often and so well as entrepôts for immigrants and labor sheds for belching factories, were to be protected against changes that appear inevitable. The passing of the industrial era and the staunch defense of nineteenth-century city functions as well as forms are resisted by citizens for whom these functions and forms are familiar, by politicians who are dependent on the traditional spatial arrangements that define the size and composition of their power base, and by intellectuals whose search for an invariant ideal urban form presupposes that one exists in the first place.[9]

Nurtured for a generation and a half on the notion that wise public policy via Keynesian demand management rather than collective response to the exigencies of World War II rescued us from the depression, we largely refuse to abide the inevitability that appears to be associated with the passage of the industrial era. Apparently nothing so diminishes our self-image as a nation than witnessing a broad-scale societal and economic transformation without a fight.

In 1981 in the propwash of (1) the predictable 1980 census results which chronicle the continuing contraction of our largest and oldest cities while suburbs and the tiniest settlements in rural and small-town areas of the United States show zesty growth rates; (2) concern for the foundering of the nation's economy experiencing the indignities of stiff international competition; and (3) the ascendance of a political coterie intent in using federal budget cuts to bring realignment of the intergovernmental system and definition to the responsibilities of the public, private, and volunteer sectors, the New Deal juggernaut lies dead in the water. Many of the goals, and even more of the means, pursued since the 1930s have been reexamined and found wanting.

Among the many fascinating means-ends policy debates that have unfolded is the one involving the fate of our distressed cities. Even though the panoply of old cities of the industrial heartland pops into our minds, by most measures hundreds of U.S. cities located throughout the nation are experiencing distress.[10] One startlingly frank reaction to this that is being heard increasingly these days is that yes, cities are going through rough times, but it is a good thing—"a consummation devoutly to be wished." These cities are not dying; their distress accompanies a difficult transformation to the new spatial scales at which business is conducted and lives are lived. Their transformation must proceed, salved by government programs and interventions applied to ease the transition and insulate people more than places during this period of painful adjustment.

Reflecting this minority perspective and to some extent orchestrating a decade or more of voices crying in the wilderness that perhaps the thrust of our federal approach to urban policy was not only wrongheaded (compassionate, but ironically prolonging the pain) but downright obstructive of the adjustments that had to be made to allow the national economy to recover, was the urban policy report (*Urban America in the Eighties: Perspectives and Prospects*) of the President's Commission for a National Agenda for the Eighties.[11] In the storm of controversy that surrounded its being leaked to the press by Carter administration officials intent on discrediting it, there was for the first time a brisk, if brief, debate precipitated about the wisdom of hell-bent efforts to isolate the task of saving our nation's industrial era cities from rejuvenating our national economy. If nothing else, the ensuing squabble may have legitimized the seldom-encountered view that we are in the midst of social and economic changes of such relentless sweep and momentum that the wisest national policy response may well be to accommodate the changes rather than continue to resist them as we have for a half century. A month before its delivery to the president and the nation, John Herbers of the *New York Times* said of the report:

> [I]t will for the first time put the presidential imprimatur on the view that cities should be allowed to shrink drastically when they can no longer generate their own wealth and jobs, and that the dispersal of people to new suburbs and beyond should be overtly encouraged.[12]

It is the last part of Herbers's quote that pushes us beyond the grudging acceptance of the inevitability, or something close to it, of the transformation of the nation's system of urban settlements to consider the implications at several spatial scales of this perspective for the nation's land and the uses to which it is put.

Deconcentration and Land:
Rearrangements for Twenty-first Century
Urban America

Among the more interesting accompaniments of the passing of the industrial era with its implications for the structure of our nation's economy and the form and functions of our nation's settlements is the matter of land use. As our older cities, suburbs, and entire metropolitan areas thin out and growth in the nation's nonmetropolitan areas eclipses that elsewhere, the uses to which we put land either by design or by default, more so than land itself, are well worth examination. Land assumes its special role in public-policy issues, especially as it is in the process of having a prior use displaced by a subsequent one (for example, the usurpation of rural land by urban uses) or as its current or future use comes to be the focus of regulation (for example, zoning restrictions). Inherent in the processes of deconcentration and reconcentration, of course, are often troublesome transitions of land from one use to another.[13]

Today as the deconcentration processes work themselves out at several spatial scales across the nation's landscape and within the nation's economy, a variety of land-related issues have emerged. The following are examples tied to these scales: (1) the high proportions of central-city land areas that are vacant; (2) the spatial evidence of lower-density settlement and development arrangements referred to commonly as sprawl or spread development; (3) the encroachment on rural lands of urban uses, usually at the periphery of metropolitan areas; and (4) the development in traditionally undeveloped regions such as is so often encountered as the mix of our energy resources shifts. While this listing is far from complete, it enables us to examine selective land-use issues at several spatial scales. We now examine each of these illustrations in turn.

Thinning of Cities: Vacant Land and Urban Infill

A surprisingly high proportion of the land area in our central cities is vacant. For our largest cities, estimates range as high as 20-25 percent.[14] Given the traditional policy preferences for concentrated over dispersed growth and development patterns, a concern for urban infill and a supporting literature has been built up over the past decade or so. Partly to counter the lower-density-development tendencies at the periphery of cities, considerable effort has been expended to understand the dynamics by which land comes to be or stays vacant within central cities. The stated purpose is to intervene so as to reduce the comparative advantage of land at the periphery in favor of more centrally located land. To stem the tide as it were of growth out of the city has been the expressed policy goal.

Urban infill is defined as "the economic use of vacant land in already urbanized areas where water, sewer and other public services are in place" (*Urban Infill*).[15] As the cost gradients between central cities and suburbs became flatter, many observers judged that the stage was set for deflected growth to surge back into the city. The distressed central city was seen as the new frontier, overlooking the equally plausible alternative that would have growth bypass suburbs and move out even further to the edge of metropolitan areas and beyond. Even though suburbs grew more expensive and did not offer the full range of cost advantages that they had since World War II, the lower-density arrangements that were their raison d'être still made good sense.

The relatively brief preoccupation with vacant inner-city land in the mid- to late 1970s greatly stressed the importance of existing infrastructure such as mail delivery, utilities, and the like. The fact that much of that infrastructure was in great disrepair and was functioning at all in part because of the lessened demands on it was overlooked. The costs of replacing broken sewer lines, leaky water lines, badly surfaced streets, and traffic-control systems are often prohibitively high in conditions of high density. Years of disregard for infrastructure below ground took their toll as the political requirements of officeholders above ground dictated that higher-profile activities than infrastructure maintenance be the track record for running for reelection. Little attention was given to the possibility that people and business expansion may well have been leaving cities because of these well-developed service packages and the tax burdens they generated than because the services were absent or deficient.

Vacant land is not all of one piece. Much of it cannot be developed because of its dimensions; land parcels are often irregular in shape or small and noncontiguous. Much is captured in the crossfire of multiple ownership, with each owner's envisioning alternative scenarios for the city that justify their individual actions or inactions. Privately held land is often for speculation; often private landholders face the threat that a large property-tax assessment will accompany any development of the land. Land held in public hands by government or other institutions often has its uses determined by a blend of politics and economics that lead to unpredictable outcomes.

Schenk has made the useful distinction between "structurally vacant" land and "frictionally vacant" land.[16] The former is undevelopable and the latter is land that is developable but only as circumstances change to transform essentially the same land parcel from undesirable to desirable. This is essentially the same dynamic that we have seen redefine repeatedly the value of land in the primary sector of the economy discussed earlier.

The changing function of the central cities is being accompanied by a changing form. Increasingly the larger central cities inhibit residential development on the scale and in the proportions that they have experienced in the past. Fiscal constraints imposed by tax-weary voters as well as the transformation of cities from centers of production to centers of consumption have meant that city land can only with great difficulty and only for a very narrow range of prospective households be the site for new residential development. Yet a virtual building boom has been underway in even the most distressed of our larger and older cities; this portends not a renaissance but a transformation since much of the building activity has been office construction to house the workspaces of the expanding service economy just as the factory construction to house the work spaces of the manufacturing sector has exited to selected locations out of town.[17] (Between 1956 and 1978, nearly 60 percent of all new manufacturing jobs were located in non-metropolitan areas.)

As the central city transforms and increasingly comes to specialize in cultural, convention, commercial, and related activites, the thinning-out process will involve abandoned houses and factories than can no longer be economically returned to their older functions. Vacant land is less a problem, then, than a symptom of the transformation of the central city. Vacant land parcels are for the time being put to no productive uses if they are scattered, too small to enable them to accommodate the space-extensive arrangements of modern industrial processes, or prohibitively expensive due to the nature of contiguous or prospective land uses. In short, the condition of vacancy is governed more directly by the nature of the transformation of the central city in the larger regional and national economies than because of inherent properties of the land itself or public policies meant to guide or preserve specific land uses. At this smallest of spatial scales—intracity—land can be viewed as dependent on social and economic arrangements in transition.

Lower-Density Development
and Reexamination of Sprawl

At the next larger spatial scale is the familiar suburbanization process. This larger-scale-deconcentration dynamic will likely continue well on into the next century. Even the rising real cost of energy for transportation that was anticipated to redirect growth back into central cities had a more likely impact that went unappreciated. First, given other technological (for example, cars with better gas mileage) and organizational options (for example, multifamily housing in suburbs), relocation to central cities was an unnecessarily costly and cumbersome response to changing energy realities. Second, while relocation to more concentrated arrangements might make excellent sense in order to cut energy costs, reconcentration in newer peripheral locations—chunking up—is perhaps more attractive than moving back into central cities. In that way, the suburbanization process could be accommodated rather than reversed. Like the intracity deconcentration dynamic discussed previously, the suburbanization process reserves for land a role that is frequently misunderstood and underappreciated.[18]

Land at the periphery of central-city local jurisdictions is the stage for the suburbanization process which is nearly a century old. Even though it never started winning battles against the urbanization and centralization processes until the massive out-migrations of the middle class after World War II, suburban development has continually directed pressure at the vast reserves of cheap, buildable land at the city periphery. Urban sprawl, spread development, and a handful of other pejorative terms—all reflecting the value judgments of well-educated, middle-class academics, planners, and intellectuals—have been used to define a literature that serves as a cultural denouncement of the lower-density social and economic arrangements that have evolved at the peripheries of the nation's urban centers.

This decades-old perspective on suburban growth has equaled the smugness of the literary diatribes and invectives from Jefferson on through the nineteenth century that railed against the arrival of an increasingly urban and centralizing United States.

The possibility that far more order, efficiency, and opportunity could be possible at some distance from the city center has not constituted a convincing argument. The new arrangements have been opposed and resisted by a political order seeking to protect its concentrated political base while at the same time undoing it as the traditional order worked to foster economic growth and prosperity that increasingly could be pursued more easily beyond the borders of the nation's cities. It is estimated that the cost of doing business in the nation's central cities is 20-30 percent higher than the cost encountered in peripheral areas.[19] The characteristics of the new industrial technology (for example, land-extensive plants, parking lots, middle-class enclaves of single-family detached dwellings, and so on) demand access to relatively large and cheap tracts of land, which are most reliably found at the city's periphery.

How can we evaluate this lower-density development? Its success is linked to the same economic, technological, and social influences that have operated to thin out the central city. From that perspective both may be seen as part of a general process of the transformation of urban forms in response to a shift in functions performed by historical urban centers. People and jobs have moved to the urban periphery so that nearly 80 percent of those who live in suburbs work in them as well. The potential then for shortening the commute, not lengthening it (as is so often the charge against suburbanization) is great. Beale notes that there has been a reduction in commuting between workplace and home in lower-density arrangements. Workers in nonmetropolitan areas travel 25 percent fewer miles and spend 25 percent less time commuting than do workers in metropolitan areas.[20] Presumably some of this efficiency redounds to life in suburbs as well. Keyes notes that the dispersal of employment and residence holds the potential for lessening air and noise pollution and the demands placed on public infrastructures.[21]

A number of further potential and actual benefits accruing to lower-density development are considered in the President's Commission urban-policy report, and so they will not be repeated here. Suffice it to say that suburbs are here to stay. They are here because they work, and in a very real sense they no longer can be considered subordinate to central cities. Over the years the older industrial suburban cities have shown the same susceptibility to life-cycle changes as have the older industrial central cities, including a growing inability to sustain their growth. Distance diminishes under the influence of advances in linking technologies, and suburbs are created in the process. As is the case with the transforming central city, the lower-density arrangements that dominate in suburban areas reflect the technological era when the bulk of their growth occurred; the battle that many are now waging to maintain their growth simply is the predictable result of new developments enabling urban life to range well beyond the metropolitan area.

The implementation of land-use controls to contain growth in metropolitan areas springs from the same impulse as have efforts to save the dying cities, and they will probably meet with the same fate. Land is largely a stage for arranging and rearranging human activity. Controls placed on that process are legitimate if they are proposed to exempt some particular land parcel from this rearrangement for cultural or aesthetic reasons. Sufficient evidence is lacking, however, to justify the conclusion that this sprawling development is wasteful of time, energy, environmental, or other resources. Rather, like so many of the land-based changes we have discussed thus far, they may actually create these resources.

Encroachment at the Urban Frontier:
The Rural Revolution

At the next larger spatial scale the metropolitan-nonmetropolitan interface is brought into focus; now the width and breadth of the urban United States can be fully appreciated. A recent issue that inspires predictable criticism of the transition of land uses at this scale is the concern for the encroachment of urban land uses on rural lands. The media are filled with alarming stories concerning the deteriorating condition of the world's land resources as population rises. This Neo-Malthusian perspective arrays grim statistics and scenarios derived from projections concerning the footrace between population increase and food-resources increases.[22] The fact that gradually agriculture, now the mainstay of our national exports, has been the locus of many of the major revolutions of the twentieth century is overlooked. The revolution of organization and technology affecting our productive resources has demonstrated that neither is there now nor has there ever been such a thing as inherently prime farmland.[23]

Perhaps more importantly for our purposes, what has also been overlooked is that the distinction between urban and rural makes far less sense now than it ever has. Agriculture is increasingly an urban occupation, as shown by its volatile and large capital requirements; its need for managerial talents; its dependence on international, national, and regional markets and the skill of those who can negotiate them; its scale for success, risk, and failure and the technological developments that have revolutionized both crop growing and livestock breeding. Yet the very success of this sector of the economy is measured by its decline. Today agriculture comprises an ever-smaller proportion of the nation's economy as the number of farm families dwindles; the number of large agribusinesses increases; and the economies of rural areas become increasingly diversified, reflecting the fact that small towns and rural areas have for the first time grown faster than the nation's metropolitan areas.[24]

The diversity of local economies beyond arbitrary metropolitan-area boundaries indicates that the bases for nonagricultural economic growth can be found anywhere. The nation's hinterland is no longer the setting for the dwindling agrarian economy in a century-long struggle with the growing cities for its young people, capital, entrepreneurship and cultural attention. The distinctly urban characteristics of our early cities have long since left town; the spreading out of health and wealth and welfare beyond cities has reduced their comparative advantage over other areas. The transformation of the traditionally rural-agricultural economy has proceeded along with the transformation of city-based economies so as to render the distinctions among them increasingly insignificant.

Interregional Convergence: Role of
Government in Nation Building

Even though the more significant changes that accompany the transformation of the nation's economy and cities can be seen clearly *within* regions or at the spatial scale of multistate regions, a larger-scale dimension that focuses on the relative fortunes of multistate regions, fueled by the same sectional rivalries reminiscent of the War Between the States, has attracted great attention recently.[25] The West was a national growth center until about 1960, after which the mantle was passed to the South. These regions have been economic and political tag-team contenders with the industrial heartland. The experience of nation building may be grossly misunderstood when we assume that the role of national government policies in probing relatively underdeveloped territory—epitomized by the Appalachian strategy that included the highly successful Tennessee Valley Authority (TVA) experiments and rural electrification—could be reversed to protect the historically dominant industrial regions as the gaps between the West and South and the Northeast and North Central began to close.[26] The once-lagging regions have been catching up; they now serve as the staging area and incubators for the next economic postindustrial wave and are joining the heretofore dominant regions in increasing national productivity, producing cheaply and efficiently, providing jobs for Americans, and saving jobs as we face an increasingly competitive international marketplace. As we examine the regional sparring that we have seen over the past decade, we may detect certain misplaced emphases. The structural transformation of the nation's economy and the functional contraction of the nation's cities reflect changing technological developments and possibilities that have slowly modified the geographical distribution of the nation's capital and the jobs it creates, its people and the incomes they command, political power and the allegiances it reflects, and even the capacity for innovation itself. Yet the role of the federal government in aiding and abetting patterns of regional change may well be overstated. Moreover, we may misunderstand the role of national government in nation building when we assign undue importance to the purposive spatial impacts of public policy.[27] Undeniably, throughout our history, the federal government has played a major role in penetrating successive frontiers and facilitating, in turn, migrations of people and jobs from East to West, countryside to city, South to North, the Northeast and upper Midwest to the South and West, and city to suburb and beyond. However, many of these spatial tilts favoring one region over another, or even one kind of locality over another, are largely the inescapable consequences of the multifaceted role the federal government plays in the national economy. Further, once the historically disadvantaged regions were on their way toward social and economic convergence with historically advantaged regions, the process became largely irreversible.

As the once-peripheral economies attracted and retained increasingly diversified populations, growth became largely self-sustaining. Historical patterns of regional dominance were bound to change over time, and it is likely that the deliberate rewiring of federal policies to achieve goals of regional restoration would be as ineffective as it would be unwise. It is unclear whether the principal responsibility of a national government is the compensation of regions for ebbing and flowing fortunes, especially if those fortunes are comprehended in terms of relative growth rates. At a time when the vitality of the national economy is of such special concern, too great an emphasis on the principle of compensation via regionally sensitive federal policies may delay the adjustments that our national economy must make in order to stay competitive internationally.

Accordingly it may be worthwhile to examine whether or not building a regional sensitivity into federal policies by design is wise. The very notion of region is contrived and artificial; it involves grouping states that may share many characteristics, but that also differ on at least as many others. Regions have become politically manufactured symbols interjected into the political process, and it is far from clear that they are legitimate criteria for guiding the presence or process of a national government.

We must resist the temptation to translate our domestic-policy issues into regional-sectional squabbles. Increasingly, region is an inappropriate level of analysis, especially since the regional squabbles increase in intensity precisely when the historical differences among them are rapidly closing.[28] Even a potentially fractious division as energy-producing versus energy-consuming states clearly is not well served by the imposition of a Sunbelt versus Snowbelt distinction. The energy issue is a clear threat to regional solidarity since only a few of the Sunbelt states are energy producers whereas many southern and western states are energy consumers; the same is true of the Snowbelt. Further, even the locus of growth itself is poorly served by lapsing into regional explanations. As Briggs has shown, growth at the county level is better explained by proximity to amenities than by regional location.[29]

Increasingly we are seeing that economic factors in household- and business-location decisions are being eclipsed by essentially noneconomic factors including amenities, environmental qualities, and life-style possibilities. The same has been suggested for the advanced nations of Europe.[30] Neither specific regional development policies as in the European experience nor regionally sensitive policies as in the U.S. experience seem able to claim much success in themselves. The disparities among the nation's regions are being eroded without much assistance from the federal government. Accordingly:

> It seems to me that we still have to start from the importance of macro-economic forces. Sustained pressure of demand in the leading regions is perhaps the most powerful aid that can be offered to the lagging regions. Not every region can be in the lead, and so long as the spread is not very wide, regional policy as such is of subordinate importance. (Cairncross 1979:13; quoted in Bartels and Duijn 1981)

Notes

1. Council of State Governments, *Land: State Alternatives for Planning and Management* (Lexington, Ky.: 1975).

2. Hawley, Amos, *Urban Society: An Ecological Approach* (New York: Ronald, 1971).

3. Norton, R.D., *City Life-Cycles and American Urban Policy* (New York: Academic, 1979).

4. Solomon, A.P., ed., *The Prospective City: Economic, Population, Energy and Environmental Developments Shaping Our Cities and Suburbs* (Cambridge, Mass.: MIT Press, 1980).

5. Berry, Brian, J.L., and Lester P. Silverman, eds., *Population Redistribution and Public Policy* (Washington, D.C.: National Academy of Sciences, 1980).

6. Vernez, Georges, Roger J. Vaughan, and Robert K. Yin, *Federal Activities in Urban Economic Development* (Santa Monica, Calif.: Rand, 1979).

7. Lincoln Institute of Land Policy, *American Federalism in the 1980's: Changes and Consequences* (Cambridge, Mass.: 1981).

8. The President's Urban and Regional Policy Group, U.S. Department of Housing and Urban Development, *A New Partnership to Conserve America's Communities: A National Urban Policy* (Washington, D.C., 1978); U.S. Department of Housing and Urban Development, *The President's National Urban Policy Report* (Washington, D.C., 1978); ibid.

9. Lefcoe, George, "California's Land Planning Requirements: The Case for Deregulation," *Southern California Law Review* 54, no. 3 (March 1981):447-501.

10. Bradbury, Katherine L., Anthony Downs, and Kenneth A. Small, *Urban Decline and the Future of American Cities* (Washington, D.C.: Brookings Institution), forthcoming.

11. Hicks, Donald A., ed., *Urban America in the Eighties: Perspectives and Prospects* (New Brunswick, N.J.: Transaction Press, 1982).

12. "Report to Carter on Cities: Scholars 1—Politicians 0," *New York Times*, 12 January 1981, p. A17.

13. de Neufuille, Judith Innes, ed., *The Land Use Policy Debate in the United States* (New York: Plenum, 1981).

14. Northam, Ray M., "Vacant Urban Land in the American City," *Land Economics* 47 (1971):345-355; Subcommittee on the City, Committee on Banking, Finance and Urban Affairs, *Compact Cities: Energy Saving Strategies for the Eighties* (Washington, D.C.: U.S. Congress, 1980).

15. *Urban Infill: The Literature* (Washington, D.C.: U.S. Department of Housing and Urban Development, 1980).

16. Schenk, Robert E., "A Theory of Vacant Urban Land," *Journal of American Real Estate and Urban Economics Association* 6 (1978):153-163.

17. Kasarda, J.D., "The Implications of Contemporary Redistribution Trends for National Urban Policy," *Social Science Quarterly*, December 1980. Reprinted in Hicks, D.A., and N.J. Glickman, eds., *Transition to the 21st Century: Prospects and Policies for Economic and Urban-Regional Transformation* (Greenwich, Conn.: JAI), forthcoming.

18. Altshuler, A., "Review of the Costs of Urban Sprawl," *Journal of the American Institute of Planning* 43 (April 1977):209; Peterson, George, and Worth Bateman, "Effects of Metropolitan Development Pattern: A Summary Report" (Washington, D.C.: U.S. Department of Housing and Urban Development, 1980).

19. Howell, James M., "Urban Revitalization and Industrial Policy." Testimony before the Subcommittee on the City, Committee on Banking, Housing and Urban Affairs, U.S. House of Representatives, Washington, D.C., 1980.

20. "The Rural Commuter," *American Demographics*, February 1981, p. 12.

21. Keyes, Dale, "The Influence of Energy on Future Patterns of Urban Development," in Solomon, *The Prospective City*, 1980.

22. "Where Have the Farm Lands Gone?" (Washington, D.C.: National Agricultural Lands Study, 1979).

23. Simon, Julian L., "Are We Losing Ground?" *Illinois Business Review* 37, no. 3 (April 1980):1-6; Vining, Daniel R., Sr., Thomas Plaut, and Kenneth Bieri, "Urban Encroachment on Prime Agricultural Land in the United States," *International Regional Science Review* 2, no. 2 (1977): 143-156; Hart, John Fraser, "Urban Encroachment on Rural Areas," *The Geographical Review* 66, no. 1 (January 1976):1-17; Luttrell, Clifton B., "Our 'Shrinking' Farmland: Mirage or Potential Crisis," Federal Reserve Bank of St. Louis (October 1980):11-18.

24. Fugitt, Glenn V., Paul R. Voss, and J.C. Doherty, *Growth and Change in Rural America* (Washington, D.C.: Urban Land Institute, 1979).

25. Jackson, Gregory, George Masnick, et al., *Regional Diversity: Growth in the United States, 1960-1990* (Boston: Auburn House, 1981).

26. Sternlieb, G., and J.W. Hughes, eds., *Post-Industrial America: Metropolitan Decline and Inter-regional Job Shifts* (New Brunswick, N.J.: Center for Urban Policy Research, 1975); Sternlieb, G., and J.W. Hughes, eds., *Revitalizing the Northeast: Prelude to an Agenda* (New Brunswick, N.J.: Center for Urban Policy Research, 1978).

27. Suttles, Gerald D., "Community Design: The Search for Participation in a Metropolitan Society," in Amos H. Hawley and Vincent P. Rock, eds., *Metropolitan America in Contemporary Perspective* (New York: Sage, 1975).

28. Hicks, D.A., "Place-Sensitive Public Policies in the Eighties." Testimony before the Joint Economic Committee, U.S. Congress in hearings on *The Economic Report of the President: Regional Balance and Economic Policy*, February 1981.

29. Briggs, R. *The Impact of Interstate Highway System on Non-Metropolitan Growth* (Department of Transportation, 1980).

30. Bartels, Cornelius, P.A., and Jaap J. van Duijn, "Regional Economic Policy in a Changed Labor Market" (Laxenburg, Austria: International Institute of Applied Systems Analysis, 1981).

Comments

Katharine Lyall

In commenting on Don Hicks's chapter I find I am in great sympathy with some of what he is saying and at the same time resistant to some of the conclusions implied in his remarks and also in the "Urban America in the '80s" document.

I agree that our national trends affecting land use are becoming more complex, and there is relatively little that cities themselves can do to cope with them. The traditional concerns of land-use planners are no longer at the heart of the economic- and urban-development problem. For better or for ill, the day of lawyers and economists has arrived. We cannot and should not, even if we could, try to recreate nineteenth-century cities. The task of urban revitalization is a necessary but neither a complete nor sufficient condition for the task of economic revitalization.

I have some differences with the Hicksian view. Along with the underlying economic trends he has described, we have experienced profound changes in political and social attitudes, including an increased recognition of public responsibility for the poor, for attaining full employment, and for economic development at national, state, and local levels. Some demographic changes brighten the picture for declining cities, such as the startling movement of women into the labor force over the last decade and the increase in the number of two-earner households which are now the norm rather than the exception.

If the underlying economic trends are inevitable, I am not sure that the policy responses and outcomes are. The vital question raised by the "Urban America in the '80s" report was whether there is a federal role at all for declining urban areas and, if so, what it should be. The implications of the report seemed to be that if these trends are inevitable, there is nothing we can or should do, except, possibly, help unemployed people move from Detroit to the Sunbelt.

Is doing nothing really an efficient strategy? Older suburbs are going through much the same life cycle as the central cities: decline, decay, an outward movement of the population accompanied by needs for new public facilities. Is that efficient? Do we want to throw away cities as they get old and continue reinvesting in new areas? Not that we can ever stop growth or should stop it completely—but do we really want to do nothing about it? Is population redistribution politically and socially acceptable other than on a voluntary basis?

One of the difficulties in this discusison is the implicit assumption that the present urban pattern occurred by the normal workings of market forces.

This is clearly false. The present population distribution is as much the result of public policy as of market forces. A number of federal policies, past and current, have had substantial spatial impacts. After the Second World War, the development of the federal highway network and the federal insurance of home mortgages made possible suburbanization which is continuing even now. Neither the highway nor the mortgage program was conceived as an urban policy when adopted. Yet these programs favored new housing rather than the purchase of existing housing because new housing was cheapest to build in open spaces on the fringes of older cities.

Other examples of federal actions and policies that have distinct spatial impacts are the current tax codes that provide progressive subsidies for home ownership and again encourage new housing consumption over existing housing and the overconsumption of housing generally. The monetary policy we are pursuing is not spatially neutral; it strikes specific areas. The burden falls heavily on older urban areas much affected by the slowdown in housing, automobiles, and other industries.

Reaganomics does nothing to improve the plight of declining regions. Little attention, if any, is given to what the regional impacts of programs may be. Shifting service responsibilities from federal to state and local governments will especially harm areas with declining land values since their major local tax source is the real property tax. Finally, Reaganomics exacerbates social-class and racial tensions that may create increasing difficulties for cities by reducing federal responsibility for the poor who are concentrated primarily in central, older cities. In sum, we have created and in some instances have exacerbated the present urban structure with policies; should we now simply stand aside?

Discussion

Alan Schwartz: Dr. Lyall, it seems to me the proper question is whether people live in suburbs because the federal government subsidized the roads or whether the federal government subsidized the roads because people wanted to live in the suburbs and were moving there? If you believe it was the latter, then you really cannot defeat Professor Hicks's thesis by pointing out that it was government intervention that caused this.

Katharine Lyall: The original motivation for the interstate highway system was defense. Once the systems were developed, more local-road and highway construction was undertaken because the population that wanted to live there applied pressure for road construction. On other programs, it is not quite as clear in which direction the causality runs. My only point was that a number of federal policies have spatial impacts which for the most part were unintended and unanticipated: genuine spillover effects.

I agree with you that employable people move themselves. What, if any, obligation do we have to those who are not employable? The dilemma that older central cities have is that they are the repository of those folks.

Edward Rabin: I think there is a difference between strategies that help people live where they want to live and strategies that seek to keep people in the cities because it serves some other purpose. I suspect that many of the people in the decaying Northeast would like to get out. It might be a second-best alternative to say we should make their lives less unbearable by certain policies. A preferable strategy would be to help people get where they want to go.

David Shulman: A place-oriented strategy subsidizes old industries. So to put money in older areas by definition props up the older losing industries. Isn't that a detriment to economic growth in the country? A person-oriented strategy is more a winner strategy and a place-oriented strategy is a loser strategy.

Katharine Lyall: And when they all tell us they want to move to Petaluma, what do we do?

Gideon Kanner: Keep them out.

Donald Hicks: The thought that somehow government can get people to trek back into central cities or the industrial heartland of the country suggests that we have the mechanics of economic development more firmly under control than in fact we do. Cities are convinced that a wide range of services is necessary to keep people. Yet people are rushing to relatively service-primitive areas. This past decade, the fastest-growing places in the country have been the very smallest—what used to be called rural America. It is not because people want to get their hands dirty growing their own vegetables and the like. People are not seeking a rural life. The fact is they can live an urban life in the country away from other people, high tax loads, and so on. You can buy Perrier and the *National Enquirer* in every little resort town anywhere in the country.

Katharine Lyall: You should notice about this trek into the wilderness that people do not travel far beyond commuting access to a central city. They want the space, the environmental amenities, the peace and quiet, and the urban amenities that have been developed over many years. If you put a barrier across the New York State Freeway and said anybody who lives outside the city limits may not come into the city, I think you would find an incredible decline in housing prices and the willingness to live beyond the city limits.

Donald Hicks: Half of the nonmetropolitan growth did build up around existing metropolitan areas. The other half took place well away from these areas. If people still do commute, it says something about our ability to shrink the significance of place. I see an increasing willingness of households to internalize the costs of public services. They would rather buy locks than depend on the police. So I do see a significant shift from metropolitan areas, not an exploitation of them.

**Part III
Notes from the
United Kingdom**

3 Housing, Planning, Land, and Local Finance: The British Experience

Peter Hall

The United States and the United Kingdom, it has been said, are two nations divided by a common language. They are also separated by a partly common legal system, a largely common culture, and in particular by a common heritage of political and philosophical ideas. Airplanes fly frequently between them, bearing a steady flow of academics and professionals anxious to trade ideas and experiences. Academic and professional journals, likewise, maintain the constant exchange. It is a wonder, in these circumstances, that any differences remain between the two nations.

But there are nevertheless differences—and stubborn ones at that. Nowhere is this clearer than in the subject matter of this chapter. From common origins the United States and the United Kingdom have developed very different systems for housing their citizens, for planning the development and redevelopment of land, for taxing the enjoyment of land and property, and for financing the essential public services that are traditionally provided by local governments. To a much greater extent than in the United States, British governments have intervened to control or to modify market processes. They (or more precisely, their local governments, with central-government aid) have built very large amounts of public housing. They have vigorously controlled the use of land, not hesitating to deny to landowners the right to develop rural land. From time to time, they have sought to extract from individuals the gains arising from development of land. To a greater degree than in the United States, the U.K. central government has subsidized the proceeds of local property taxes from the exchequer.

Recently, however, it appears that having once diverged, the two nations may again be in process of convergence. It is the British who are on the move in a U.S. direction: selling public housing, simplifying and speeding the planning process, abandoning the attempt to extract special taxes from developers, and reducing the amount of central financial aid to high-spending local authorities. That, at any rate, appears to be the general view.

The purpose of this chapter is to ask how far this view is true. Can the United States and the United Kingdom both be regarded as the first two nations to go through the welfare-state phase and then emerge as Arthur Sheldon of the Institute of Economic Affairs has suggested will be true for

Great Britain (Sheldon 1981)? Or, despite recent developments and despite an obvious degree of similarity in the prevailing governmental ideologies in the two countries, do they still remain in some way apart?

In this chapter, we will look in turn at some main aspects of housing, planning, land, and public-finance policy. We will seek to identify particularly the changes that have been made by Thatcher's Conservative administration since its election in May 1979 and that have resulted from initiatives by Thatcher's secretary of state for the environment, Michael Heseltine. We will also speculate on further changes that might be made in the lifetime of the present administration and on the possible impact of a change in political complexion of government after the next general election that is likely to take place in 1983 or 1984.

Housing Policies

As noted, the United Kingdom is distinguished from the United States by the existence of a large public-housing sector. Originating in legislation passed at the end of World War I, in 1919, this pool of housing was built in two great bursts of activity: the first, dating from about 1920 to 1939 and mainly taking the form of single-family homes of simple cottage type on the periphery of urban areas; the second, dating from about 1950 to the present day, consisting of a mixture of cottage housing with a greater proportion of high-density, high-rise apartment blocks resulting from in situ slum clearance and renewal in the inner cities. At the end of 1979, some 32 percent of the U.K. housing stock consisted of dwellings rented from local authorities or new town corporations as compared with 54 percent owner-occupied and a mere 14 percent rented privately or by virtue of employment. This last figure had been shrinking, both as a percentage and in terms of absolute numbers, for many years: as recently as 1960, as many as 32 percent of dwellings were in the privately rented sector. So increasingly in Britain there have been two dominant forms of tenure: the owner-occupied sector, and the publicly rented sector.

But even before the advent of the Thatcher government in 1979, the growth of the public sector had been weakening. As against an average of 189,000 new dwellings a year in the 1950s and 170,000 in the 1960s, completions were still running at a near-record 169,000 in 1976. They then fell away sharply: to 105,000 in 1979, the year of the change of government. Since then, however, the figure has plummeted: In 1981, estimated starts were down to a maximum of 30,000, reflecting an overall cut in government subsidy of no less than 70 percent between 1975-1976 and the projection for 1983-1984. Birmingham, the biggest single district authority in England, completed only 800 new homes in 1980, as against an average of 9,000 a year during the 1960s; during 1981, it had funds to start only 169. The reason is the drastic cuts in public expenditure that have been imposed through withdrawal of central-government subsidies and that have resulted in many authorities virtually suspending their housing programs altogether. In July 1981, the Association of Metropolitan Authorities (AMA) revealed that 81 percent of local authorities had either frozen the letting of new contracts or had substantially delayed them. Eighteen percent of local authorities, it said, had no housing program at all or one of only one or two dwellings. Public housing, as the AMA suggested, was effectively frozen by a moratorium: as the House of Commons Select Committee on the Environment has stressed, the program has shrunk to a level not seen in peacetime since the 1920s.

Private building has not benefited from the plight of the public sector; it is suffering its own problems in the form of the general recession in the economy and the consequent lack of purchasing power, the high rates of interest on mortgage loans, and—a new factor—the sale of council housing, which creates an alternative source of housing for lower-income buyers. It is perhaps highly relevant for a U.S. audience that in the United Kingdom the building societies (the equivalent of U.S. savings and loan institutions) have traditionally borrowed money at market rates of interest and have similarly varied the mortgage interest rates payable by home buyers. In general, therefore, the building societies have never faced the kind of crisis now faced by savings and loans. But the double-digit rates of interest that have prevailed in Britain for much of the last decade have clearly inhibited some potential home buyers, and the housing markets generally are depressed compared with their peak years of the late 1970s. Private new construction peaked during the 1960s, with an average of 198,000 completions a year. Since then it has fallen away, to 155,000 in 1976 and 136,000 in 1979. Overall, by the end of the 1970s construction of new homes was running at only two-thirds of the level of the 1960s; and since then it has dropped sharply, with an estimated 110,000 starts in 1981.

Not only has the public sector been decimated by the contraction in housing starts; it has also lost, of course, from the sale of public housing to tenants and others, as a matter of public policy. This policy is generally, though misleadingly, associated with the Conservative party. It is true that sales of local-authority housing peaked—at nearly 46,000 houses a year—during 1972, at a time of Conservative government, and again after 1979, with sales of nearly 50,000 in 1980. But even in 1978, the last full year of office of the Callaghan labour government, sales were sharply on the increase, at over 30,000. To a considerable degree, it can be said that the sales represent a sharp trend toward owner-occuptership in the public at large, a trend that has been encouraged for the council-house tenants by the highly advantageous terms on which they can buy. Under the new terms announced by Michael Heseltine shortly after he assumed office, there was to be a minimum 30 percent discount for sitting tenants, rising to 50 percent in the case of tenants with more than 20 years' occupancy. This, coupled with a price freeze during the second part of 1979 and the first part of 1980, created maximally advantageous conditions for sitting tenants, and it was small wonder that they took advantage of it.

The opposition Labour party has of course criticized both the reduction in the public building program and the accelerated sale of houses. Both, labourites say, will have the effect of shrinking the public sector so that it caters only for the least fortunate members of the population who live in the least attractive housing: the equivalent, perhaps, of project housing in the United States, with all the stigma that attaches to it. Certainly, in part this seems to be Heseltine's stated intention. He has announced, for instance, that the reduced building program is to be concentrated on those members of the population in greatest need. He has abandoned the so-called Parker Morris standards for public-housing construction, which have been a condition of government subsidy ever since the 1960s. Also it appears clear, in London and elsewhere, that the sales program is disproportionately affecting the more attractive estates of cottage homes, leaving the less attractive apartment projects to house the remaining council tenants.

Still, it should be stressed that the whole process has a long way to go before it begins to approach a U.S. condition. Even with sales at 50,000 a year, it would take 120 years to reduce the public-sector stock to the same proportion of the total (3 percent) as it has historically formed in the United States. Long before that, sales resistance might be forthcoming. It must be stressed that though the British public-housing sector contains a much larger cross section of the population, in terms of income and socioeconomic status, than its U.S. equivalent, nevertheless the main stress is still on lower-income households. Of those heads of households earning less than £ 60 a week (approximately $120 a week) in 1979, no fewer than 47 percent rented from local authorities, as did 39 percent of those earning between £ 60 and £ 80 ($120-$160). Still, it should be noted that 33 percent of the first group and 44 percent of the second already owned their own homes. The scope for further movement of lower-income households out of the public sector and into the private owner-occupied one is still considerable, even if it does not shrink Britain's public housing sector to U.S. proportions.

Planning and Land Policies

In part, the downturn in private building represents a contradiction for government policy brought about by unintended—and certainly unwished for—failures in the wider British economy. For the policies of Michael Heseltine, however controversial, have been clear and consistent. They have aimed to free the private builder to build broadly when and where he wished in order to fill the demands of the market, thus compensating for the shrinkage of the public sector. To this end, immediately on coming into office Heseltine began to try massively to simplify and streamline Britain's complex system of planning controls.

The much-vaunted British planning system, however varied in detail, is essentially the same as that created by the historic Town and Country Planning Act of 1947. This fact testifies to the strong bipartisan support that strong land-use planning has enjoyed. Under the British system, the right to develop land is essentially nationalized, and payment was made for proven losses of development rights. The publicly-owned rights are then vested in the local authorities, who exercise development control in accordance with plans that they make and then regularly revise. This contrasts strongly with the U.S. system of zoning, which is based on the general police power and hence carries no presumption of compensation for lost rights. In practice it has meant that local authorities have been able to exercise fierce restraints on urban growth, expecially in the green-belt areas that ring London and the other major urban agglomerations as well as smaller freestanding cities such as Oxford or Cambridge.

However, since the late 1960s the process of planning has become considerably more complex. First, from 1968 onward a two-tier system of planning was introduced, with broad-brush structure plans providing policy frameworks for more detailed local plans. Second, from 1974 (1975 in Scotland), a new system of two-tier local government was introduced so that in practice counties (in Scotland regions) produced structure plans while the second-tier districts produced the local plans. There were, however, many complexities in this system, not least in the divided responsibility for development control. One major consequence has been extended delay in producing structure plans and having them approved by the central government as is required by law. Another has been considerable complexity and delay in the process of giving (or refusing) permission to develop, including the statutory process of appeal by those aggrieved by a denial of planning permission.

Heseltine has energetically sought to reduce these complexities and delays. First, he massively simplified responsibilities by removing from the counties nearly all their development control powers. Though the districts still had certain responsibilities to adhere to the counties' structure plans, the latter lost virtually all their powers to enforce compliance. Second, he speeded up his own department's approval of structure plans. Third, he suggested that local plans should henceforth be prepared only for areas where significant development would take place. Fourth, he streamlined the development-control procedures by allowing a substantial proportion of minor works (the extension of a dwelling by up to 15 percent, of industrial buildings by up to 20 percent) to occur without planning permission at all, save in special cases requiring specific consideration (such as conservation areas). At the same time, he began to charge for the grant of planning permissions although the proposed charges were greatly reduced after protests by builders' associations. Fifth, he went beyond this by proposing that henceforth control over details of design should in effect be removed. (This proposal ran into much opposition, and has been modified.) Sixth, he simplified the appeals procedures by allowing his own inspectors to determine a higher proportion of cases (now up to 95 percent) without the need to go to him for approval. Seventh and perhaps most significantly of all, he called on all planning authorities to guarantee a five-year supply of building land. Also he underlined this by modifying the structure plans for the highly controversial area west of London (between the cities of Reading and Aldershot and Basingstoke) to house another 80,000 people, despite the rooted opposition of residents and local councilmen. Extensions of the green belts, he made it clear in doing this, would no longer be approved; land that the counties had been holding in interim green belt status, sometimes for as long as twenty years, would now have that status withdrawn.

The implication of all this was clear. From now on, urban development in Britain would proceed on lines that were similar to U.S. ones. The constraints on the private builder would be removed. Suburbanization would be the general order of the day. Public housing would play a strictly subordinate role in dealing with the problems of the especially unfortunate. The general presumption against development, so rooted in British urban policy ever since 1947, would cease.

However, in practice this represented a change in degree rather than in kind. Strict controls were to remain in the agreed green belts and in conservation areas. Further, the stress on growth west of London only confirmed a policy enunciated in a regional plan of as long ago as 1970, which had identified this as one of five major growth areas in Southeast England and which the government of the day had accepted. Therefore it could be argued that Heseltine was not undermining the 1947 system; rather, he was enabling it to work more expeditiously and more effectively.

One means to this end followed traditional Conservative policy lines. The 1980 Local Government, Planning and Land Act rescinded the previous Labour administration's 1975 Community Land Act. The latter act represented the third successive attempt of a Labour government[1] to intervene in the process of land supply and in the capture of development gains. This time the means were novel—the transfer of development land to local authorities—but the essential philosophy was the same as before. It was to remove the supply of development land from the private market and put it firmly in the public domain. Though the 1980 act returned development land to the market, it did retain one feature that indeed had characterized Conservative approaches to the land problem since the early 1970s: development land tax, a special capital-gains tax levied on sale of development land, remained in force. In practice, therefore, the Conservatives now admit, as previously they did not, that gains in value on development land do represent a form of betterment arising at least in part from public action and so meriting public recapture. This element of land policy, at any rate, now seems to be firmly bipartisan.

New Development Concepts: Urban Development Corporations and Enterprise Zones

The Thatcher administration has, however, made two real innovations in development techniques, both of them specifically intended for application in Britain's depressed inner urban areas. As the riots of summer 1981 underlined, Britain shares with the United States a common set of problems in the rapid demographic and economic decline of its older inner cities and in the consequent high levels of unemployment and deprivation in those areas. During the decade from 1971-1981, preliminary returns from the 1981 census have revealed, more than 1.5 million people have deserted the major British cities: Greater London lost 750,000 people, while Manchester, Liverpool, and Birmingham each lost between 90,000 and 100,000. The previous Labour administration, in 1977, had announced a major policy initiative to deal with this problem: a set of central-local government partnerships in the worst-hit areas, administering a greatly increased urban-aid grant. These partnerships used their money in a great variety of ways, some concentrating on job-creation schemes, some on community groups and recreational developments (Hall 1981, pp. 94-95). The Thatcher strategy has been different. Though the partnerships and the urban-program grants have continued, they have been badly affected by public-expenditure cuts; the new emphasis has been on promotion of a very rapid rate of economic and physical development through two new policy initiatives.

The first of these were the Urban Development Corporations (UDCs), established under legislation of 1980 to take over the planning responsibilities of local government in the two nearly derelict dockland areas of London and Liverpool. In both of these, containerization and the subsequent downstream shift of gravity of the port had created very large areas of land ripe for development close to city centers. The local authorities involved (several in each case) had set up mechanisms for redevelopment but relatively little impact was to be seen on the ground. This was Heseltine's opportunity to impose on these areas a radical solution, earlier urged upon him (in the London case) by the now-defunct South East Economic Planning Council: UDCs, modeled on the example of the corporations that had built Britain's new towns, which would operate with a good deal of commercial freedom and a minimum of central- or local-government interference to produce a mixture of commercial, industrial, and residential developments in their areas. This idea of new towns intown, far from appealing to local-community groups, excited vehement opposition which, in the case of the London UDC, led to a protracted hearing before a House of Lords Select Committee and delayed the final transfer of power until June 1981. But soon after starting work, the London UDC was announcing ambitious plans for a combination of commercial development and private housing on its 5,000-acre area; these plans were greeted with predictable rage by local area labour councils. Strangely enough, while all this was happening Heseltine was busy ordering the existing new towns to divest themselves of their commercial assets and to wind themselves up, in most cases, as soon as practicable.

The other initiative was perhaps even more radical, at any rate in original conception. It was for a series of enterprise zones in which normal planning and other regulations would be lifted so as to provide a kind of laboratory for the kind of free development which—so it was alleged—had aided the economic rise of such new economic powers as Hong Kong and Taiwan. By fall 1981 ten of these had been designated in various parts of urban Britain; all but one were in inner urban areas, the exception being a new town (Corby) that had lost the steelworks that had been the foundation of the local economy. However, in the process of designation the concept had been considerably diluted. The zones were exempt from Development Land Tax (the special capital-gains tax that is levied on development of land); firms coming into them would enjoy 100 percent capital allowances for industrial and commercial premises; these buildings would be exempt from local property taxes (rates, in British terminology), the government making up this shortfall; and they would have greatly simplified planning and building controls. However, they would not be free of other controls such as those on environmental pollution, health and fire, and highway access; and in some of the zones, the local authorities even continued to try to control aspects such as height of buildings and type of permitted land use. So in practice, it was doubtful whether they could have a major impact in encouraging new enterprise. Rather, the risk was that they might merely encourage existing local firms to relocate, with no lasting benefit to the entire urban economy. It is perhaps significant that of the first 200 inquiries received at Swansea, the first zone to start operations, the biggest single group represented firms already established in the local area. But with the oldest enterprise zone established only three months at the writing of this chapter, any judgment on the success of the concept would be grossly premature.

Local Authority Finance

No other area of Thatcherite policy has been more controversial inside the United Kingdom than the new system of central-government support and control of local authorities, which was initiated with the passage of the fiercely contested Local Government, Planning and Land Act of November 1980. This long and highly complex act—itself only a fragment of an even longer measure that had had to be abandoned—inter alia established the UDCs and ended the previous Labour government's Community Land Act. But its most important part fundamentally recast the system whereby central government subsidizes the expenditure of British local authorities through the so-called Rate Support Grant (RSG).

Evolved over many years through a painful process of trial and error, the RSG during the 1970s was based on a complicated formula that took account both of the resources of local authorities and of their special needs for assistance. It was much criticized by experts for its cumbrous quality and for the rough justice it administered, but few found anything superior. Heseltine, pursuing an election-campaign promise, pushed through a measure—the 1980 act—that drastically simplified the award of the grant and totally altered its incidence. Henceforth, all local authorities would receive a block grant based on a standard cost of providing local authority services. Authorities that exceeded this cost would be penalized by a withdrawal of part of the grant; the additional cost, which previously could attract a grant, would thus be thrown totally onto the rates.

The results of this change were soon felt in the cities, which at the end of March 1981 were announcing an average rates increase of 26 percent as opposed to a mere 11 percent increase in the rural areas. In inner London the average increase was no less than 40 percent, in outer London 30 percent. These increases reflected spending that was still much in excess of the standard cost target. For all local authorities in England, the budgets were 9.4 percent over target, but this concealed huge differences: for the metropolitan counties (that is, the large urban agglomerations) the average was 27 percent over target and for the London boroughs it was 23 percent. The record was set by the east London Labour borough of Tower Hamlets, which exceeded its norm by 88 percent. Many boroughs were therefore reckoning on the unprecedented step of supplementary rates demands, but by this time Heseltine was said to be contemplating further legislation to stop them from penalizing commercial and industrial property owners.

Heseltine had a model for this. Already by the summer of 1981, Scots legislation—the Miscellaneous Powers (Scotland) Act—permitted the secretary of state for Scotland, whose role was equivalent to that of secretary of state for the environment in England, to cut the RSG of any local authority whose spending he considered excessive or unreasonable. In August 1981 George Younger, the Scots secretary, put these powers into operation by cutting £ 47 million from the Labour-controlled Lothian Regional Council, one of the larger Scots local authorities. The effect was to cut the weekly RSG by nearly half. This was in response to the council's refusal to make any cuts in its budget. It was expected that two other authorities, Stirling and Dundee Districts, also would be fined in the same way.

These powers are particularly interesting because they are coupled with another, not available to the English secretary of state: the power to stop local authorities levying supplementary rates to make up for the cuts. A consultation paper, due to be published by Michael Heseltine, was likely to propose similar powers for England. These would throw the whole burden of rates increases on to domestic ratepayers, and then only after a referendum or reelection of the council; and the size of any increase would be limited. At the end of August 1981 several English authorities, including the Greater London Council, had announced supplementary rate demands to be levied in fall 1981. But any legislation introduced by Heseltine could have no effect until the start of fiscal 1982-1983 in April 1982 at earliest.

Toward a Verdict

It is not easy to draw up a balanced verdict on the British experience and its U.S. relevance. Britain is a highly centralized country with a long history of central-government interference in local affairs and with a much more highly developed welfare state. It is also a country sunk in deep and general economic recession, in which the wealth necessary to support a high and rising level of public services is no longer available. Further, as in the United States, in Britain profound shifts are occurring in the location of people and economic activity. Even had a Labour government been elected in 1979, the strong suspicion remains, public expenditure cuts would have been the order of the day. These would have been most severe in the inner cities, where the economic base is contracting while much of the social burden remains.

Nevertheless the arrival of the Thatcher government seems to have had quite radical effects. The cities have received a reduced share of the RSG and they have received clear warning that if they seek to compensate for this by raising their own property taxes, they will face major obstacles. The so-called Shire counties and their district authorities have received a bigger share, partly reflecting the fact that, at least in certain parts of the country, they are being asked to take a positive attitude to the fact of rapid growth. In other words, until recently the Conservative policy has encouraged rapid suburbanization through owner-occupied housing at the expense of the public renter in the major cities. That trend may be halted or at least slowed as a result of the riots of summer 1981, but the best guess is that the changes will be little more than cosmetic: designed to have maximum visibility at minimum central-government cost. The one significant change may prove to be that the cities once again receive a slightly larger share of the RSG, but any shift in this direction is likely to be marginal.

The obvious question must be: To what extent would a change of government mean a reversal of the trends described in this chapter? The answer is not as obvious as it seems. Opposition parties, however much they may dissent from the other side of the House of Commons gangway, have a curious habit once in office of stealing some of the previous administration's clothes. A Labour government, in the circumstances of the 1980s, also has an urgent vested interest in controlling total public expenditure, and local-authority spending is a significant part of that total. In these times, any government, is likely to have to trim public-housing programs as part of that general retrenchment. What is more likely is that under a Labour government the spatial incidence of the cuts, and of the remaining government aid, would be different. More would go to the big cities that provide much of Labour's diminished electoral support, whereas less would be directed to the suburban Shire Counties around them. Overall, it is unlikely that Labour cuts in social programs such as housing would be quite as savage as under the Thatcher government.

Nevertheless the continuing changes in the geography of Britain are unlikely to be reversed. The outflow from the cities is almost certain to continue, though perhaps at a diminishing rate. A nation deeply struck by recession is likely to grasp at any kind of growth, and growth is most likely to occur in the suburban and exurban rings between London and Birmingham, Birmingham and Manchester, and London and Bristol. This will require any government to devise policies to provide infrastructure for the necessary housing and other development in those areas. No British government in the 1980s, whether Conservative or Labour or Liberal-Socdem, is likely for long to resist encouraging private building for sale and the necessary land policies that go with it. Growth is also going to necessitate adequate aid to the local authorities in those areas for the extra burdens they are going to shoulder. For a Conservative administration, riots or not, the choice of priorities is relatively easy. For a Labour administration and perhaps for a Liberal-SDP one, it will be harder; but the logic of development may force an answer.

Notes

1. The two earlier attempts were the financial provisions of the original 1947 Town and Country Planning Act, rescinded by the Conser-

vatives in 1953-1954, and the 1967 Land Commission Act, rescinded in 1970.

References

Hall, P., ed. *The Inner City in Context: The Final Report of the Social Science Research Council Inner Cities Working Party.* London: Heinemann Education, 1981.

Sheldon, A. *Wither the Welfare State.* London: Institute of Economic Affairs, 1981.

4

Lessons From Experience: A Review of Britain's Land Policies

Donald R. Denman

Six Lessons

Peter Hall has given us a comprehensive and concise account of present land policies in Britain and of the earlier versions that lead up to them. In one sense these policies are peculiar to Britain and its circumstances; in another, more important, sense, the policies make common cause with land issues here in the United States and, indeed, wherever people and governments struggle with the problems of modern civilization.

Over the years, we in Britain have learnt many lessons from changing and abortive land policies. There is sufficient common cause between the United States and Britain to suppose that these lessons could be of interest and perhaps of help. Professor Hall has told you the stories, my purpose and privilege is to try and turn these stories into parables. These lessons may be interpreted in several ways. For me, experience of the British land policies over the postwar decades to the present has presented six precepts as follows:

1. Know what you are doing.
2. Do not be positive.
3. Let a tax be a tax.
4. Realize that red tape can be untied.
5. Remember the time.
6. Remember that *micro* is stronger than *macro*.

Know What You Are Doing

Citizens in a free society should know how they stand before the law; this is the rule of law. When a government acts arbitrarily through its officials, or policy loses its purpose, or the law is used to confound the law, we are on the highway to confusion, if not to bondage.

In Britain there is much to show from the experience of our land-use planning policies that we can become so hedged in by forms and procedures and a mass of intricate law as to assemble a machine without a purpose. Our enterprise zones and urban-development areas of today and the earlier new-towns policy show, along with other special departures in land policy, that whenever in the United Kingdom the government wants to see land resources put to a definite and predetermined use, it has to bring in special laws. Why is this so when we are possessed of a much-hearlded planning policy? The answer can only lie in one of two directions: Either our land-planning policies are directed to other ends or they are directed no where in particular.

The truth lies with the second of these alternatives. Nowhere in the vast body of law, which in Britain gives power to the planning authorities, is the purpose of planning stated. We simply do not know what we are planning for. There are as many answers to questions about the purpose of land-use planning as there are top planners responsible for the job.

We appear to have succeeded in our planning policy. Indeed, we have done so, for our plan is to have a plan, and we have thousands of them. In the bargain we have decayed and abandoned city centers, urban sprawl, and most, if not all, of the horrors and blemishes that planning policy from 1947 onward was designed to combat. The latest modification of planning structures under the Local Government, Planning and Land Act, 1980 aims to decentralize planning downward to the district councils and has not altered the underlying indeterminacy. The law itself still does not describe the purpose of the plans its legislates for. Admittedly, in recent days the secretary of state for the environment, Michael Heseltine, has shown an awareness of the need for purpose and direction by suggesting that the new local plans should be restricted to areas with specific and patent problems. Manifestly, the whole tenor of the new laws that set up enterprise zones more or less free of planning controls and urban-development areas under the control of their own authorities with power to plan the areas to directed ends in place of orthodox planning is an indictment of the purposelessness of that orthodoxy. In Britain we have structure plans, development plans, and local plans but in no way can the private citizen tell whether the planners are doing their job properly and keeping to the legally sanctioned intentions for the plans. Because planning permission rests ultimately on the arbitrary decisions of the planning authority, the indetermination is the more confounded and the citizen more than ever bewildered to know what is expected of him. The lesson from this is that it is possible, over many years, to conjecture and implement a planning policy without a purpose other than to have planning for planning's sake. In short, after forty years we do not know what we are doing.

There are other instances where British land policies of recent years have sanctioned arbitrary powers of government and left the citizen defenseless against state action. The government may know what it is doing but the private citizen is in the dark.

The danger is all the more acute when the arbitrary power of government is not the main aim of policy. So often that power is a side consequence of a main thrust toward an urgent end. The government acts in a kind of blindness; look, for example, at what happened in Britain under the Community Land Act 1975. The government intended to vest all urban land suitable for development in the hands of local-planning authorities: the vesting process was paramount. Consequently, the authorities were given power to take compulsorily all land which they thought suitable for relevant development. This was a fundamental departure from tradition and practice. Tradition required compulsory powers to be conditional upon the need to achieve objectively prescribed and demonstrated purposes. Here, under the legislation of 1975 we have authorities being authorized to proceed on the ground of subjective judgments. The authority has but to say, we think the land suitable for development; they do not have to establish that it is so suitable. The landowner and citizen have no grounds upon which they can contest the action. The government has taken power to acquire land for acquisition's sake.

There are numerous examples where the execution of land policies in Britain has permitted government authorities to acquire land for one purpose and then condone its use for another, a process euphemistically referred to as appropriation. Again, the citizen loses track of what the government is doing. A high proportion of land now held by local authorities and government corporations (especially in the inner cities) was acquired for specific purposes now long forgotten, certainly for different uses to which the land is now put (or the nonuse for that matter). Because this is so, the present government is requiring all local authorities to compile registers of the land held by them and to dispose of what is not needed for the purposes that prompted their acquisition. Likewise the new towns have been commanded to sell off their land. It was necessary to take the land in the first place to establish the new town. The job has now been done and there is no need for the land titles to continue with the corporations or, indeed, for the existence of the corporations themselves. So it is, at the present time, that government can simultaneously empower the new UDC to take land and instruct the old corporations of the new towns to sell out. At least the citizen knows what the government is doing; its actions are consistent with the intentions of prescribed law.

Do not Be Positive.

The foundation statute of Britain's planning policy for land has for two generations been the Town and Country Planning Act, 1947. None can deny that this piece of legislation was and still is a monument to legislative achievement and that it has been successful in setting up planning machinery of the most comprehensive and complex form. For many years it was significant socially and constitutionally: It gave new life, vigor, and identity to the planning profession. So much was this so that the planners through the powers of the statute became mesmerized into thinking that the ultimate control over land use lay with them and the planning process.

For many years planners and politicians were deaf to those who in no way opposed planning yet, and for good reason, pointed time and again to the ultimate power of decision over land use as lying inevitably with the land owner, public or private. The property right was the sole positive power—to do or to leave undone.

Slowly but most surely in Britain this fundamental truth has penetrated the minds of politicians and planning philosophers. Positive planning (by which is meant the power both to plan and to do) became from the mid-1970s a cause célébre. For planning to be effective positive planning makes sense. But events have shown how the pursuit of its logic can lead directly to land nationalization and all that that entails for national and political disaster.

The Labourites in Britain were the proud architects of the Town and Country Planning Act, 1947. Much was expected from the comprehensive use of its passive, prohibitive development control. Now it is the Labour party who claims that the passive control has failed. The purpose now is to achieve positive planning and by the only means possible: by making the planning authority the owner of all development land. Such was the intent of the Community Land Act, 1975, and such is the intent of current Labour party policy. A recent statement from the party reads:

> Land and planning policies are inextricably mixed. Planning without control of the land becomes merely negative development control. For planning to be positive the direction of the key resources in development—above all land—is essential. Our ultimate aim is to restore to the people the full benefits of their land; the basic policy of the Party is, the public ownership of all land.

If land nationalization is an objective of government land policy, bringing together planning power and property power makes sense. The lesson from Britain is that if land nationalization is to be eschewed, then care must be taken not to talk unguardedly and at random about endowing planning authorities with powers of positive planning. This is not to say that it is in the interests of planning and the planners for ways and means to be found for cooperation between those holding property powers—the landowners—and the planners. There are planning policies on the continent of Europe where such cooperation has been achieved. But the achievement keeps the planner to his skills and the landowners to their independence.

Britain nearly effected a full-scale land-nationalization policy by proclaiming the aims of positive planning. The unwary citizen can be led to espouse the cause of positive planning not knowing that by his affiance he has opted for land nationalization.

Let a Tax be a Tax

As we all know, radical political economists have for a hundred years or more been agitated by the problem of land values; land values, as J.S. Mill contended, rise as the landowner sleeps. Something of the increment should in fairness be given to the state by fiscal means.

But this enduring problem has in our day acquired a new and more formidable shape. The advent of the public control of land use has added gravity to it. Radical thought now contends that increments in land value that arise from changes in land use are benefits created by the community (whatever that might be). If, so the argument runs, a builder is willing to give a price for a building plot higher than the price a farmer would give for the same land and the owner of the plot is deprived of his right to put a building on it by the operation of public control and hence of receiving its value for building purposes and later there is a change of mind in the public authority and permission to build is given, the right to receive the market value of the land for building has somehow been created by the community and hence should belong to that abstraction.

It is not our purpose here to explore and expose this untenable contention; the argument against this has been made in other places and time enough. What we are concerned with here is the fact of the argument and that on the strength of it radical governments in Britain have based their land policies. Our experience in Britain shows that by basing a land policy on taxes, the citizen becomes confused between land reform and fiscal policy. If the confusion were simply academic, we might be merely curious. The distinction, however, is practical. A tax is a fiscal impost and, as such, has important implications. The confusion was most stark in Britain in the mid-1960s under the Land Commission Act, 1965. The government of the day, a radical one, had set up a land commission with wide powers to acquire land for planning and redistribution at prices that deprived the landowner of much of his development value. Where land was the subject of private transactions, vendors of the land were similarly deprived by charging them a betterment levy. Rates varied but the ultimate intention was in the long run to extract 100 percent of development value and the acquisition of all development land by the land commission.

The extreme event never happened. The betterment levy, however, bore most grievously upon charities whose incomes depended on land wealth. The government was challenged on this question and pleaded with to give the normal tax concessions to the charities. Grace was refused on the ground that the levy was not a tax; it was, said the lord chancellor of the day, an instrument of land reform, a means of transferring from private hands to public hands benefits of development that belonged to the community. The betterment levy was, in short, a vehicle of land reform.

As is well known, Britain's House of Lords cannot hold up or oppose a finance bill. When the government contended that betterment levy was not a tax, the Upper House immediately extracted all references to the levy from what was then the Land Commission Bill and sent the tattered remnant back to the House of Commons. Later, the government was forced to yield to the righteous claims of the charities. When the government was asked to make its alleviations restrospective, however, it argued that this could not be done because the betterment levy was a tax, and tax concessions could not be retrospective.

If the view is held that all increments in land value due to development of the land and changes in land use are created in some hidden way by the community, then logically it is justifiable to render unto the state what belongs to it, indeed to grant the full 100 percent of value. To impose a tax on development value, however clumsy and in breach of the canons of taxation it may be, is not to imply that the government accepts the argument that development values are generated by the community anymore than imposing an income tax implies that personal income is earned by the community. The present administration in Britain has, like its predecessor, levied a Development Land Tax. The tax is in every respect a true tax, much reduced from the earlier levels and continued as a matter of expediency. As a tax the impost is innocent of any endorsement of the radical notion that development values belong to the community. Taxes should remain as such and should not be contrived as a means to effect a land reform.

Red Tape Can Be Untied

When the government set the centralized planning process going in wartime Britain and brought it to full adulthood in 1947, none could have foreseen what it would mean for industry and commerce nor have imagined the centrifugal growth upon growth of a new bureaucracy in the departments of government and throughout local government. The early idealists had never comprehended how cardinal was the land factor in shaping development, investment, and enterprise. Throughout the 1970s studies were made (such as the Dobry Report) to judge how far, if at all, the red tape that bureaucratized the business world in the name of planning control could be unravelled. Every attempt, every planning act seem to strengthen the binding cords into a closer knit. Planning cost industry and commerce dear in time and money and wasted opportunity. In 1975, to make matters worse, the community land scheme brought control of the land market into an associated planning process.

Against this background, we should see and try to understand the present government's novel experiment of setting up enterprise zones. As originally conceived, the enterprise zone was not devised as a way of helping the rundown areas of Britain's inner cities. The idea came from those who were trying to find clear pathways for the business world, untrammelled by planning control and other forms of state surveillance. Tory party policy, spelled out in *The Right Approach*, hinted at proprietary companies—that is, companies with special status to give them exemption from specific controls and taxes. The enterprise zone shifted the incidence of privilege and benefit from the operator to the place of operation. Once in government, Tory policymakers saw in the enterprise zones an additional means of helping the areas in the cities that were suffering from economic and physical decay: thus translated into policy, these zones are regarded as an important feature of the government's program to rejuvinate depressed areas. Ten sites have been formally designated and management schemes adopted. The sites are not all in inner-city areas but each lies in a problem area of one kind or another.

There is no universal pattern. In most zones the land is owned by the local authority or other public body, but there are zones (notably Belfast in Northern Ireland) where the bulk of the land is privately owned. Enough time has not yet passed for this experiment to be examined and judged. Anyone visiting the enterprise zones today, however, cannot but be impressed by the lively enthusiasm of the officials in charge. There is a spirit of challenge abroad; it is the very enthusiasts whose powers of control over the detailed development of the sites have been reduced almost to the simple administration of bylaws. In the enterprise zones the bureaucracy has been overcome and business is free to make decisions in a way not known in Britain for forty years or more. Should the United States consider tightening its grip on public control over land use and, as some fear, tie up economic expansion in regulations, the message from Britain is that red tape can be untied.

Fears have been expressed with special vigor on the radical side of British politics that the enterprise zones will be but another example of using new cloth to patch old garments and thus could cause further deterioration. An enterprise zone might draw active and profitable firms from the surrounding industrial areas and thereby leave vacuums for decay and unemployment to enter in formerly stable places. Only time will tell. There are enterprise zones in such areas as Swansea and Corby where the zone is located in the outer expanding districts. If successful, these zones have no immediate industrial areas to rob and could well draw industrial and commercial development to the towns they serve.

Of course the enterprise-zone policy is at present only experimental and as such it can throw up the unexpected. Examples are readily found in the attitudes and activities. In Swansea, for instance, a certain official was genuinely puzzled to know how to manage an industrial estate without the imposition of planning controls. Low-grade development could put off prestige factories and discourage investment. This official was a man in his forties and had never known the laissez-faire world of the 1930s. When the use of restrictive covenants as a means of estate management was suggested to him, he displayed a genuine relief. Clearly, prolonged controls can rob us of the ability to respond to freedom.

Another example of the unexpected was found in the Tyneside enterprise zone. Here private companies with more than one factory are rationalizing their factory ownership. Old factories, because of the enterprise-zone privileges can be sold and the proceeds directed into the construction of new ones. Such a beneficial rearrangement was not possible until tax concessions, planning release, and other benefits made available to the enterprise zone, had induced purchasers to take up the old sites.

Remember the Time

The enterprise-zone legislation and policy illustrate the principle that where a policy is highly charged with political risk (such as in Britain, ruled by the electoral fortunes of contending political parties), the time that must elapse to give a policy a fair trial may not be available. Enterprise zones in their present form and under a government that gave them parentage, are limited to ten years. Ten years, however, in a parliamentary democracy can see many changes of political chance. There is no power (short of agreement with the government's opponents, whose turn for office may follow next) to secure the privileges of an enterprise zone for ten years to those who have entered upon the zone in good faith today.

Nowhere is this risk factor more apparent in the realm of land policy in Britain than when a government attempts to modify the operation of rent control. The rent acts with us have a long, almost unbroken history going back to 1915. The first rent act was passed to deal with the wartime housing shortage. Since then there have been wars and rumors of wars but in the main the days of peace have outnumbered the days of conflict. Yet the rent acts remain, now strengthened and now modified but never repealed. In Britain, the rented private sector on our housing scene has fallen to its lowest percentage. Nevertheless, the control of house rents is passionately espoused by the political left wing. Rent control today is a political football;

the latest housing legislation, The Housing Act, 1980, has attempted to break the deadlock. New tenancies—shortholds and assured tenancies—can now be created outside the range of the rent acts. The policy is a sane one, but it is not likely to stand a fair trial. Shortholds have been a possibility now for a year, yet only 3,500 shorthold tenancies have been entered into; the landlords, not the tenants, are reluctant. The landlords are apprehensive that the benefits assured to them today will be taken from them tomorrow on a change of government. The future repeal of the shorthold legislation could find tenancies created today and free of rent control, fettered by control before the tenancy ends.

Land policies more than any other activity of government in Britain are prone to suffer instability from changes of government. This aspect of our democratic scene is touched upon here because so often land policies have failed, not because they are inherently weak or ill-conceived but because they have never had a fair trial. Opponents of the present government may well be able, in the future, to point to the failure of the housing tenancy reform and also to the enterprise zones. The indictment would claim that they failed to win support. Indifferent support might well be truly demonstrated, but the lack of response would not stem from aversion to the policies but from fear of the threat to disallow them on change of government. Not all politically highly charged land policies are rendered impotent by the prospects of change of government support. A policy currently beneficial can be taken advantage of and its merits demonstrated; only those policies whose outcomes need time are at the mercy of misjudgment. I put this lesson to you from our experience, lest over here you should judge a policy rightly to have failed but blame failure on the policy instead of upon its opponents and their threat to cut it down before its time.

Micro Is Stronger than Macro

The postwar years from the 1940s have in Britain as elsewhere been the era of the macroeconomists. These latter-day collectivists take their cue from Maynard Keynes, who first taught economists to look at the economy of a nation in one piece. Economic growth should be demand led; demand management is a task for central government. It meant ensuring a propensity to consume, a step in the demand management program that might, and almost certainly would, require an expansion of the money supply. Thus Western economists fell into the habit of assuming that if we got the macro planning right, the rest would follow in due order. Response at the micro level was disregarded. This new attitude in the realm of economic planning affected land-use planning and the attitude of its devotees.

On this score there was no excuse for the growing malaise of Britain's inner cities. Order the land-use categories in relation to customers' demand as measured on the macro scale and plan the life and advance of the city accordingly. What went wrong? We must presume that no planning body ever made a blueprint for the wasteland in Liverpool or Nottingham or elsewhere, yet the wastelands do exist.

British experience emphasizes that the micro dimension is crucial and must be understood. In the realm of land-use planning, the macroeconomic approach is the prerogative of the land-use planner. Micro actions remain with the individual, the company, the public body—in short, the independent landowners. Nevertheless, it is at the micro level that vital, telling decisions are taken; this is well illustrated from the findings of a recent research project undertaken in Britain for the Department of the Environment by the Department of Land Economy of Cambridge University. The aim was to learn what was delaying the building of houses by the private sector in the inner and middle areas of the city of Nottingham. Surveys were made of 379 sites covering in all 1,770 acres in an area to the west of the inner city and in the inner city itself. In both places some 60 percent of the sites were judged to be suitable land for building houses. The desire that housing should be developed on these was widely expressed by the attitude of the planning authorities (the macro judgment) and by builders, developers, and even financiers. Yet the sites remained neglected and undeveloped; the explanation for this was found with the landowners. Sixty-nine percent of the sites were owned by the city council and 80 percent of these were deliberately kept out of the housing market by the council who owned them. A very high percentage of the sites remaining in private ownership were likewise not available to the market. Thus at the micro level the vast majority of landowners, public and private, had intentions for the use of the land that ran counter to the desires and judgments of the planners working as they did at the macro level. The micro-level decisions prevailed. This case study bears out the general theme and reiterates that micro is stronger than the macro.

Note Bene:

Most assuredly there are other lessons by the score to be gleaned from our experience of land policies on the other side of the trench but these that I have selected have stood out for me above the others. Whatever the other lessons may look like, these I commend to you as worthy of thought, for in one way or another they must surely be pertinent to your policies either now or in the future.

References

Denman, D.R. *The Place of Property*. Berkhamstead, Herts, United Kingdom: Geographical Publications, 1978.

Denman, D.R. *Land in a Free Society*. London: Centre for Policy Studies, 1980.

Nicholls; Turner; Kirby-Smith; and Cullen. *Private Housing Process*. London: InnerCities Directorate, Department of the Environment, 1980.

Norman, L. *Effect of the Housing Act 1980 on the Private Sector*. London: Chartered Surveyor, April 1981.

Operation Expansion Britain Committee. *Getting Britain Moving*. London: Aims, 1980.

Steen, A.D. *New Life for Old Cities*. London: Aims, 1981.

Discussion

Maureen FitzGerald: I would like to ask both Professors Hall and Denman where they would place the achievement of the British new towns: specifically, what influence that attempt to disperse the population had. I am often asked by Americans if Britain's new-town policy was a success and I would like to have an authoritative opinion from two rather different points of view.

Peter Hall: I think they have undoubtedly been a success. The ones around London have been more successful than the ones in the less economically favored parts of the country. They have been such a success precisely because they channeled and organized the outward movement of the population. They have been extremely attractive to industry that was taking place anyway, including quite a lot of industry brought in by multinational corporations. That illustrates for me that planning policies that complement trends can also help shape them and create a physical expression that is efficient and also good environmentally, providing extremely good living conditions for very large numbers of people who would not otherwise have had them. So they have been a success, I think, on almost all fronts.

Donald Denman: I would agree in one sense. But I think the question is, why were they established in the first place? As far as I remember, they were established in order to relieve the congestion from the inner cities. They indeed have been a success. The inner cities are now irrelevant.

Otto Hetzel: I wonder if you could compare the enterprise-zone theory in England with its development in the United States.

Peter Hall: I have the greatest difficulty understanding what the present policy emanating from Washington on enterprise zones actually is. I have read the relevant paragraph of the state of the union message very carefully at least four times. But the original idea that I put forward in 1977, in a purely theoretical way, was for something more radical: a set of free-trade zones with totally unrestricted movement of capital and labor into them. I did not expect any government to buy that idea, and it was not bought. Instead, we have a watered-down version that provides in effect a set of financial incentives plus a dismantling of planning controls which itself is not complete. Other controls, such as building, health, and safety regulations, are retained. In effect, the enterprise zones have become a new version of British regional policy—rather small zones in which there is a very favorable financial package. I see no reason why zones so defined should really encourage much totally new enterprise. They may attract a movement of firms across boundaries into them from other zones. That may be a good thing if they are relieving unemployment and coming from areas where there is greater pressure on the local economy, although there is not much pressure on the local economy in Britain anyway. They may do some good nevertheless, but they are not addressing the central question of the creation of new enterprises. That, I think, is where the U.S. debate should be focused.

Frank Jones: My question is for Professor Denman. You made a very telling point that it is curious to have a policy that does not state what the purpose of the policy is. I wonder, either with respect to city planning or nonplanning, if you can tell us a little bit about what the policy ought to be.

Donald Denman: I'm not a planner.

Frank Jones: That's right. So what is the purpose of nonplanning?

Donald Denman: How do you know nonplanning should have a purpose anyway? Seriously, my criticism of our planning policy is that we have not defined what we are planning for. It all started in wartime with three great reports, each of which advocated a central planning authority, but each for a specifically different purpose. When the government came to implement those reports and then to set up the central planning authority, the purpose advocated was expressed in three different, and sometimes contradictory, ways. I think that certainly we in Britain are moving into a time when environmental issues define a criterion for planning. I think the answer to your question is that we ought to plan for environmental or ecological balance.

**Part IV
Reagan Energy and
Environmental Programs**

Comments

Edwin M. Smith

Is federalism in the context of environmental issues and energy development a term of convenience rather than an article of faith for the current administration? When states have adopted positions consistent with the Reagan perception of proper environmental policy, the administration has not hesitated to abandon the doctrine that governments that govern least invariably govern best. But the Department of Interior has been quick to encourage offshore petroleum development despite the concerns expressed by California state officials. Recent experience with Outer Continental Shelf (OCS) Lease Sale No. 56, off the coast of northern and central California, amply illustrates the pattern.

Authorized under the Outer Continental Shelf Lands Act Amendments of 1978 (OCSLA), the lease sale was initially proposed in November 1977 by the Carter administration. In October 1978, 243 lease tracts were selected by the Department of the Interior, the federal agency responsible for the leasing process. One hundred and fifteen of these were located slightly north of Point Conception in an area known as the Santa Maria Basin. The coastal area nearest the basin supports important fisheries and provides habitat for the California sea otter, a species listed as threatened under the Endangered Species Act of 1973. Substantial controversy was generated between the federal government and the state of California. Just prior to the 1980 presidential election, some of this controversy was resolved by the deletion of the most sensitive tracts, those located off northern California; however, the Santa Maria Basin conflicts remained unresolved.

The halting efforts at compromise came to an untimely end with the appointment of James Watt as secretary of the Interior. He immediately reinstated the controversial northern California tracts. When a political firestorm resulted, Watt postponed sales of the northern tracts but simultaneously rejected the state's proposal to delete selected tracts from the Santa Maria Basin. Watt cited the predominance of federal over state interests.

California brought suit against Secretary Watt, alleging a number of statutory violations, including the Coastal Zone management Act of 1972 (CZMA), which was intended to encourage cooperation between the federal and state governments in coastal activities, particularly those relating to energy development. Shortly after California filed suit, and apparently at the behest of Watt, the National Oceanic and Atmospheric Administration (NOAA), the federal agency responsible for supervision of state coastal management plans under CZMA, promulgated regulations exempting OCS leasing from statutory requirements that federal action directly affecting the coastal zone be consistent with the state management plan.

The United States District Court for the Central District of California reversed Secretary Watt, finding violations of the CZMA and severely chastising NOAA for the promulgation of self-serving regulations that reversed more than five years of settled policy. NOAA had previously maintained that leasing was required to be consistent with state plans. Discussing the congressional intent to encourage cooperation between the federal and state governments in coastal-management policies, Judge Pfaelzer found that Secretary Watt had violated the spirit of the law in those instances where he had not actually violated its letter. The court enjoined the leasing of those selected tracts proposed by the State for deletion from the Santa Maria Basin. Subsequently, Congress forced NOAA to withdraw the offending OCS leasing regulations as inconsistent with the purposes of the CZMA.

If the New Federalism is intended to represent an attitude of federal deference to state control whenever possible, the California offshore oil controversy shows the limits of the policy. It is possible for OCS development where the Reagan administration sees no appropriate state role. It is not clear whether the federal government is willing to compromise any of the policy directions that it perceives as in the national interest.

One indication of a willingness to compromise may already have been manifested in the withdrawal by Watt of a number of tracts located within the highly sensitive Channel Islands Marine Sanctuary. Since California has already manifested its opposition to the Santa Monica Bay tracts, this lease sale may offer additional data with which to test the importance of the New Federalism to the resolution of state-federal conflicts that involve environmental and natural-resource issues.

5 Reagan Energy and Environmental Programs: Implications for State and Local Governments

Dale L. Keyes

The Reagan administration's speed in translating campaign rhetoric into public policy is impressive, if not universally popular. Unleashing the sleeping giant and removing the federal government from the backs of industry have been powerfully expressed through broad-scale policy changes and the revamping of major regulatory programs. Returning power to the states also has proven to be something more than a campaign slogan, as a substantial shift in federal-state responsibilities is now underway in several federal programs. These changes are nowhere more evident than in the energy and environmental areas where decontrolling energy prices and reducing development subsidies, releasing federal land for mineral exploration, relaxing environmental regulations, and, in general, streamlining the regulatory apparatus all promise to redefine basic energy and environmental issues. This chapter explores the changing nature of energy and environmental problems under the Reagan administration and the implications these changes hold for state and local governments.

Energy Issues

Greater reliance on the private market for energy production and consumption suggests three major policy changes at the federal level: decontrolling the price of fuels, withdrawing federal subsidies for new energy technologies, and releasing more federal lands for mineral exploration. Shortly after his inauguration Reagan removed remaining price controls on crude oil and refined-petroleum products. Accelerated decontrol of natural-gas prices is under consideration. Major federal aid for synthetic-fuel demonstration projects has been scaled back, although the administration's decision to support three commercial developments and the Synthetic Fuels Corporation's loan-guarantee programs contradict a purely free-market approach. Finally, the administration has decided to relax what may have been an energy supply-side constraint—that is, the slow release of federal land and offshore territory for mineral exploration and production.

Price Decontrol

Removing federal controls on the price of crude oil and refined products has forced these commodities to be priced at their scarcity value. This value reflects the cost of obtaining marginal crude supplies—the OPEC price—plus the cost of refining, transporting, and cleaning the fuels where necessary. Not only did decontrol produce an immediate price increase in petroleum products (7 percent in the average cost of all refined products), the price of partially substitutable fuels such as coal has also risen. Moreover, the pending removal of price controls on natural gas should allow its price to equal that of distillate oil on a heat-content basis, other factors being equal. Recovery of economic activity in the United States and elsewhere likely will stimulate energy demand and subsequent price rises for all types of fuels.

For state and local governments the most immediate consequence is an increase in operating expenses. However, fuel costs remain a minor budget item for most governments (generally less than 5 percent of expenditures).

Of perhaps greater political if not economic consequence will be the effect of fuel price increases on low-income households. Many families in northern states currently spend well over one-fourth of their income on fuel-related expenses. Price rises will decrease their purchasing power for other goods and services. For some, increased fuel bills will mean heatless dwellings. With a simultaneous reduction in federal weatherization and energy-assistance programs, pressure for state and local action will mount. The form that this action may take will vary among communities but could involve temporary-shelter programs as well as direct fuel-cost subsidies to low-income families.

Less direct responses to fuel-price increases may appear in the form of locational and building style changes within urban areas. Some have speculated that a scarcity of fuel supplies combined with rising energy prices will force most urban residents to seek more centrally located dwellings and, typically, to choose townhouses or apartments—building styles that are more energy efficient. Likewise, more energy-conscious employers will site new plants closer to residential areas or nearer to transportation corridors. The net result would be more compact and dense urban areas, or at least ones more highly focused on key transportation corridors. But urban residents and employers have several options for reducing energy use short of changing locations. Upgrading building insulation and buying more efficient automobiles or trucks are the most obvious. Simply buying a smaller home or car of the same style would also achieve energy economies. Assessments of these and other options suggest that a major reshaping of the urban United States is simply not in order. For example, the nationwide decrease of 10 percent in energy used for transportation between 1978 and

1980 can be accounted for in large part by improvements in average vehicle fuel efficiency, which totaled 13 percent between 1973 and 1979. This is not to imply that city and state governments can ignore the land-use implications of energy-price increases. Clearly, zoning ordinances and development financing practices should facilitate the expression of market responses. Likewise, state and local transportation and land-development planning should be highly coordinated. But proactive attempts to achieve more compact urban forms or to accommodate an "urban implosion" are not necessary or advised.

Rising energy prices increase revenues to energy-producing states through royalties and severance taxes. These revenues and the resulting interregional flows of money are so substantial that economic warfare among states has been threatened. Oil and gas revenues for the top eight energy-producing states have been estimated at over $200 billion for this decade. Since these taxes are keyed to the total value of exported fuels, revenues will increase proportionally with energy-price increases. The constitutionality of these taxes has been challenged in Maryland, a state with limited energy resources, and by public utilities. Initial judgments have upheld the rights of producing states to levy these taxes but have narrowed their applicability.

Finally, rising oil prices will encourage development of alternative fuels. Whether current prices are sufficiently high to justify the large risks and capital investments required for new-technology development is not known. Changes in federal policies regarding alternative fuels, described in the following discussion, also will be influential.

Reduction in Supply Subsidies

The appropriate role for the federal government in sponsoring research and development in an unfettered free-market economy is a limited one. Accordingly, the Department of Energy (DOE) is restructuring its research and development (R&D) program around exotic, long-term, high-risk technologies. Projects that show appreciable near- or medium-term potential must find support in the private sector.

Conceptually, this should slow the rate of alternative-fuels development. Firms that require public financial support for demonstration plants would have to delay or cancel their plans. In reality, substantial federal subsidies will continue in the near future.

First, in a complete reversal of his initial position, Regan recently approved $3.12 billion in loan guarantees plus purchase commitments for 20,000 barrels per day of jet and diesel fuel in support of three major synfuel projects: Union Oil's Parachute Creek oil shale project; Tosco's and Exxon's Colony oil shale project; and the Great Plains coal gasification project. Likewise, the Synthetic Fuels Corporation is proceeding to evaluate applicants for its first $20 billion of loan guarantees. However, seven DOE demonstration projects have been denied further funding and current activities are likely to signal the end of federal R&D subsidies in this area.

The effect of this partially scaled-back program must be measured against the most likely scenario under a Carter administration in order to gauge the net effect on state and local governments. Table 5-1 provides development estimates of synfuels in 1980 under two scenarios. The actual production levels in 1990 are likely to fall between these estimates, with the specific level of cuntion of world oil prices, the cost of capital, the severity of environmental constraints, and the portfolio of projects supported by the Synthetic Fuels Corporation. Clearly, the potential for reduction in the pace of synfuel development during the rest of this decade is substantial.

The effects of this potential reduction will be played out in terms of impacts on local communities. Most of the synfuel projects will be sited in western states, especially Colorado, Utah, Wyoming, and Montana. Depending on the magnitude of these projects, their demand for scarce resources and their ability to employ surplus local labor, the net impacts could be either positive or negative. In the case of most western communities, however, the state and local perceptions are decidedly negative. An influx of construction workers and operating personnel swelling local populations will create social, environmental, and fiscal challenges for affected communities. For example, the shale-oil production levels shown in the second scenario in table 5-1 are estimated to attract about 70,000 additional people to Colorado's Piceance Basin, or about four and one-half times the basin's current population. Stresses placed on regional water supplies loom as the most significant natural-resource effect. Although total water supplies have been judged sufficient to sustain up to 3 million barrels

Table 5-1
U.S. Synfuel Development Estimates for 1980

Projects	Production (barrels/day of oil equivalents)	Number of Plants
Currently (1979) Planned Projects		
Shale oil		12
	0.9 million	
Coal synfuels		19
Carter's Goals		
Shale oil		
	2 million	40-60
Coal synfuels		

per day of shale-oil production in the upper Colorado region, competing water rights and legal constraints on interbasin transfers could cause severe conflicts locally. Potential degradation of air and water quality could pose additional problems.

At the very least, slowing the pace of synfuels development will allow state and local governments more time to accommodate population growth and increased resource demands. A less ambitious federal support role for the synfuel industry also may reduce the cumulative impact of development and the number of communities adversely affected. Additionally, a slower pace of development affords the opportunity to learn from first-generation activities and, through facility design and public-infrastructure changes, to reduce or better accommodate the impacts of synfuel development. Managing this growth industry has assumed added importance now that the federal government's impact grant program has been terminated.

Expanded Leasing of Federal Land

As the owner and landlord of over 750,000 square miles of land in the continental United States and about 1.8 million square miles of OCS territory, the federal government controls extraction rights to vast quantities of minerals. Only a tiny fraction of this area has been made available for lease sale. Arguing that a restrictive federal leasing policy has distorted free markets in fuels, Department of Interior (DOI) Secretary Watt has initiated a total restructuring of the department's leasing programs. The results have already been dramatic (especially for Californians). Watt acted in March 1982 to offer for sale several tracts off California's northern and central coasts. Public reaction was overwhelmingly negative, with many criticizing Watt for a callous disregard for the environment. Since the expedited offerings had been accomplished by ignoring provisions of the CZMA, California successfully challenged Watt's action in federal court. All California offshore tracts in Lease Sale No. 53 have now been withdrawn. However, DOI has appealed the court's decision and has issued new regulations under the CAMA that exempt the DOI's OCS leasing activities from the previous requirement that federal activities affecting the coastal zone be consistent with state coastal-zone-management plans. If not vetoed by both houses of Congress, these new regulations would allow lease sales without regard to state requirements for environmental impact assessments or other reviews. Only when exploration of drilling were to begin would an impact evaluation be necessary. Moreover, the DOI has proposed to conduct sales on a regional rather than tract-by-tract basis. In concept, this would make the lease sales more attractive to bidders since the precise locations of oil and gas deposits in frontier areas are unknown. Unfortunately, this plan also would necessitate the assessments of potential environmental impacts on a region-wide basis, with site-specific analyses conducted only after the location of drilling sites is known. The DOI has already set a one-year record for OCS territory leased (2 million acres) and revenues generated ($9.8 billion). The new proposals promise to greatly expand these efforts.

A similar restructuring of the terrestrial mineral-leasing policies is underway. The DOI soon will decide on a new direction for the oil-shale leasing program. One option is to lease four additional tracts under the current prototype program. This would double the 20,000 acres currently under lease for the purpose of encouraging innovative production technologies. Alternatively, the DOI could proceed with the permanent program designed to increase the area in production manyfold. This option would allow for larger-scale operations and could exacerbate boomtown problems. The DOI supports legislation now before Congress that would increase the maximum size of each lease and would allow companies to hold up to three leases simultaneously. Significantly, however, the DOI has agreed to additional language in the bill which requires the secretary of interior to consult with governors, local officials, or tribal leaders before issuing a lease. If their recommendations are not accepted, the secretary must publish an explanation in the *Federal Register*. If this language survives congressional debate, the sharp edge of an expanded oil-shale program would be blunted. In any case, Secretary Watt's acquiescence to western states' demands for a more substantial role in oil-shale-leasing decisions marks a softening of his states-rights position implied by his OCS leasing initiatives.

Also under consideration are more liberal lease-sale approaches to coal- and oil-bearing lands. As an example, the Department of the Interior recently filed documents in federal court to reopen a coal-mining case settled by former Secretary Andrus. This involves the declaration of certain lands near Bryce Canyon in Utah off limits to coal mining. This land is currently under lease but mining on a portion of the tract was deemed a threat to visibility in the National Park. Despite the fact that the power plant for which the coal was to be mined now appears unlikely to be built, Watt will pursue this case since he sees it as precedent-setting. His goal is to remove all unnecessary environmental encumbrances to accelerated energy development.

In a similar vein, the DOI has moved to initiate mineral leases in several wilderness areas, the Bob Marshall Wilderness Area in Montana being perhaps the most celebrated case. The House Interior Committee cancelled this action by declaring an emergency situation under the Federal Land Policy Management Act. However, future use of the act's emergency provisions will be curtailed by a recent court decision. Furthermore, Watt has announced his intention of unilaterally releasing for mineral exploration wilderness lands found unsuitable for wilderness designation, an action that promises to raise the ire of environmentalists and several members of Congress. On the other hand, Watt has assured Congress that new lease sales in existing wilderness areas will only occur after an environmental assessment and thirty to sixty days notice, and only if there is an overwhelming national need.

But are restrictions on the availability of federal land a significant supply-side factor? There is no clear answer. Offshore petroleum and gas production now account for about 9 percent of crude oil and 24 percent of natural gas produced domestically, despite the fact that less than 2 percent of the federal OCS has been leased to date. Additional tracts hold great promise for new discoveries. But even here, the rate at which newly leased territory can be explored is limited by available equipment and trained personnel in the near term. The fact that currently leased oil-shale lands are not fully under development indicates that current and projected economic conditions are only marginally favorable to the industry. In fact, termination of construction of the Cathedral Bluffs oil-shale facility was recently announced by Occidental and Tenneco. The argument for terrestrial oil and gas is a bit more compelling since domestic production has been falling for several years. But only 20 percent of the total land area of the United States is under production or exploration, and the exploratory vigor evidenced by the petroleum industry appears much more sensitive to the price of crude oil than to the availability of federally owned lands. For example, the number of completed oil wells doubled between 1979 and 1981, largely in response to oil-price decontrol. With respect to coal, few would argue that we face a shortage of supply. (Mining activity has yet to begin on almost half of the 522 tracts leased since 1976.) Opening additional federal land could decrease transport costs for specific customers but is unlikely to affect the total quantity of minable coal.

The implications for state and local governments of a more liberal leasing policy are expected to be limited and highly site-specific. Of greatest concern will be new tracts or parcels near environmentally sensitive areas or in remote locations lacking adequate public facilities. Combined with a lower federal profile in environment affairs (see the following discussion) and a reduced flow of money from federal to state treasuries, the resulting burdens on state and local governments could be substantial.

Environmental Issues

Overregulation of the private sector and federal usurpation of state responsibilities are the twin precepts guiding the administration's current reevaluation and restructuring of the environmental regulatory apparatus. Evidence is abundant on all fronts: recommendations for changes to the Clean Air

and Clean Water Acts, administrative rule-making and program management in both the air and water areas, and the development and implementation of hazardous-waste regulations.

Air Quality

The Clean Air Act Amendments of 1977 are now seen as perhaps the most
ambitious and pervasive set of environmental laws in history. Not only were
standards for new pollutants and more stringent standards for conventional
pollutants either established outright or mandated for review by the Environmental Protection Agency (EPA), specific penalties for recalcitrant
communities and individual companies were established. For example, if a
state could not demonstrate attainment of ambient air-quality standards by
the required deadlines to EPA's satisfaction, a ban on the construction of
new facilities could be imposed. If future attainment could not be demonstrated for automobile-related pollutants, costly inspection and
maintenance programs for all automobiles in the affected communities were
required. Failing the adoption of an inspection and maintenance program,
EPA was empowered to withhold all federal highway and sewer funds. Individual companies that missed pollution control compliance deadlines were
to be fined an amount equal to the cost savings realized from the delay.
Although the previous administration was reluctant to use all of these enforcement rules and in every allowable case, they were employed against
especially recalcitrant states and companies and used as a threat to many
others.

The present administration has relaxed several of these regulations.
First, construction bans are unlikely to be authorized in the future. Second,
although state or local inspection and maintenance programs already mandated will be retained, imposition of these requirements elsewhere will not
be pursued at the present time. Third, EPA Administrator Gorsuch is pursuing a policy of cooperation and negotiation with industry, thus making
imposition of noncompliance penalties most unlikely.

The EPA has also moved to ease siting and pollution-control requirements for new and expanding plants. By liberalizing the definition of
what constitutes a new source of emissions and by allowing companies to
trade emissions among individual sources within a plant (the so-called bubble approach), these companies have ways to meet emission limitations even
in urban areas that currently do not meet air-quality standards. Moreover,
states and local communities are being encouraged to experiment with innovative, market-based regulatory systems that promise to reduce the total
costs of meeting air-quality standards. Portland, Chicago, Philadelphia,
and Boston are examples of cities currently evaluating the utility of market-
based approaches such as emission fees, marketable air-quality rights, and

emissions banking. A preliminary investigation of market-based strategies in Chicago suggested that the least-cost approach to meeting a stringent nitrogen dioxide standard could be perhaps $100 million less than the cost of the typical uniform-regulation approach.

Finally, EPA has begun both to streamline administrative requirements and to transfer Clean Air Act enforcement responsibilities to the states. These actions should: (1) reduce the time required to develop state implementation plans and the frequency of plan revisions; and (2) provide much greater state discretion in planning and enforcement processes. In addition, a high priority item on Gorsuch's agenda is to expedite the delegation to the states of the Clean Air Act's program for new source performance standards and national emission standards for hazardous air pollutants. This will likely place a greater financial burden on the states for air-quality monitoring and enforcement at a time when federal grants to the states are being reduced.

In addition to these administrative and rule-making changes, the Reagan administration at first issued general guidelines for legislative changes to the Clean Air Act and now supports a bill introduced by Representative Luken and others. If passed, this bill would accomplish the following:

1. Deadlines for attaining air-quality standards could be extended from 1982 or 1987 (depending on the pollutant) to 1993 on a case-by-case basis.
2. The Prevention of Significant Deterioration provisions would only be retained for pristine (Class I) areas.
3. The state implementation-planning process would be streamlined by (a) requiring plan adoption within a reasonable time rather than nine months after national air-quality standards are adopted or revised, and (b) reducing the need to revise the plan for every change in control orders issued to emission sources.
4. Federal sewer and highway funds would no longer be used as sanctions against states, and construction bans would be enforced only in unusual circumstances.
5. Penalties for companies that do not comply with control orders would be discretionary.
6. Automobile inspection and maintenance programs would be required only in large urban areas that show air-quality readings at least 50 percent above the standards.
7. Automobile-emission standards for carbon monoxide and nitrogen oxides would be relaxed.

The Administration also favors extending the time nonferrous smelters can avoid compliance with control orders beyond the current 1988 deadline, which is especially significant for the depressed smelter industry in the West.

Although passage of this bill is not assured, pressure for a leaner, less stringent act with a decentralized implementation scheme clearly is building.

Water Quality

Many of the recent trends that have surfaced in federal air programs apply equally well to EPA's water programs. New industrial regulations (technology-based effluent standards) will be less stringent than they would likely have been under the previous administration, and some existing rules are being relaxed (for example, imposition of treatment requirements for plants discharging to a municipal wastewater plant have been delayed). Intraplant and interplant trading of effluent constituents (the water bubble approach) also is under active consideration. In addition to increasing state responsibility for monitoring and enforcement (and this includes increasing reliance on state as opposed to metropolitan or regional organizations), some movement toward allowing greater state discretion for establishing ambient water-quality standards is evident. The latter step could lead to the elimination of uniform-treatment standards for all plants within an industry, since the degree of treatment would depend in part on the assimilative capacity of the receiving water body. This effect plus variations among states in ambient water-quality standards themselves could produce state bidding wars for polluting industries.

The opportunity soon will be available to codify several of these changes in amendments to the Clean Water Act. EPA Deputy Administrator Hernandez has indicated that changes desired by the administration will be detailed within the next few weeks Additional requests are likely to focus on: (1) relaxation of deadlines for achieving technology-based treatment standards by selected industries, and for attaining fishable and swimmable waters everywhere; and (2) extending the life of water discharge permits beyond the current five-year period.

In addition to these administrative and potential legislative changes, a major revamping of the wastewater treatment-facility construction-grants program is underway. President Reagan has just signed a reauthorization of the program which substantially reduces future federal obligations (from a total of about $90 billion to $36 billion by the year 2000). Annual authorizations will be $2.4 billion until 1985, and, starting in October 1984, the program will undergo significant restructuring:

1. Funding will be focused on construction of treatment plants (or innovative treatment approaches) and major sewer lines (interceptors) only. Construction of smaller sewer lines and renovation of sewer networks can only be funded from the states' discretionary funds.

2. Excess treatment capacity to accommodate future community growth will no longer be funded with federal money.
3. Municipal treatment plants will have until 1988 rather than 1983 to achieve secondary levels of treatment.
4. All states are encouraged to assume operation of the grants program.

The realities of lower federal-funding levels, greater state responsibilities, and greater state discretion will likely produce new points of stress within state and local systems for planning and administering these activities. The premium for improved quality control will be heightened considerably, and procedures such as those employed by New Hampshire (annual reimbursement of locally raised capital) may become the rule.

Hazardous Wastes

Although each of the pollutants addressed in the Clean Air and Clean Water Acts are in some sense hazardous, the term *hazardous wastes* refers to liquid and solid by-products of industrial operations that are corrosive, explosive, flammable, or toxic. This obviously encompasses a wide range of waste materials, the specific number being a function of the exact definitions of the characteristics just given. The threat of environmental pollution (especially groundwater contamination) from improperly disposed wastes and the realization of that threat at such sites as Love Canal in New York and Valley of the Drums in Kentucky led directly to enactment of hazardous-waste legislation.

The primary laws are the Resource Conservation and Recovery Act (RCRA) and the Comprehensive Environmental Response, Compensation, and Liability Act (Superfund), although portions of the safe Drinking Water Act and the Clean Water Act are relevant as well. RCRA authorized EPA to establish reporting and facility-operation standards for existing and new hazardous-waste generators, transporters, and disposers. Superfund provides revenues (through a tax on the oil and chemical industries) and response actions (including legal options) in the case of abandoned dump sites and emergency spills of hazardous materials. Together, these laws promise to impose significant financial burdens on all but small firms that generate, handle, or treat hazardous wastes. As a direct result of RCRA, these firms can be expected to seek locations near an approved storage/treatment/disposal site and away from residential areas.

The Reagan administration has declared the regulation of hazardous wastes to be its top environmental priority. As part of this emphasis, Administrator Gorsuch has undertaken a complete review of the RCRA implementation actions including all interim guidelines and standards. Based on initial results of this review, EPA will attempt to ease the financial burden on affected parties by relaxing some requirements and declaring others optional at the discretion of the states. For example, EPA has decided to issue RCRA permits for the normal operating life of treatment and disposal facilities and to allow expansion of existing facilities without prior approval. Similarly, EPA has withdrawn rules for financial responsibility applicable to treatment facilities. Gorsuch is now hinting that the mandatory insurance requirements should be left to state discretion.

RCRA also provides a formal process by which states can assume facility permitting and control authority. EPA is expediting applications for both interim and final authorization. This will allow states to issue permits for existing and new treatment and disposal facilities, to enforce the cradle-to-grave manifest tracking system, to set postclosure financial accountability rules, and to enforce the regulations. States also are expected to assume major program management and financial responsibility for site cleanup under Superfund and to undertake research on hazardous-waste cleanup techniques.

In addition, many states are addressing the key missing ingredient in RCRA: treatment- or disposal-facility siting. Given the shortage of current facilities, the licensing requirements for new ones, and the opposition to facility plans generated by local residents, overall program success may turn on the state's ability to site new facilities. Some states such as Maryland maintain a highly proactive role in the siting process; candidate sites are evaluated and ranked, top-rated sites are selected for development (with local zoning preempted, if necessary), and state-owned and -operated facilities are built. Other states such as Utah will use public ownership only if adequate private facilities are not available. Still others such as Wisconsin become involved in siting at the conflict-resolution stage, in this case by creating a special board to arbitrate disputes among the various private parties.

Unfortunately, the federal pool of money to help fund these state activities is small and growing smaller. Moreover, the Superfund legislation preempts any state-level hazardous-waste-site cleanup fund based on an industrial tax scheme. As alternatives, states are selecting user fees, general revenues, or facility bonds to finance their programs.

Summary

The winds of change blowing from Washington are swirling around state capitals. Some energy and environmental policy changes will reduce state administrative requirements while others increase those responsibilities. Some may create new environmental, social, or economic problems while others will lower the likelihood of adverse impacts. Most will increase state prerogatives, but a few will preempt state options.

Several changes in energy policy appear to be mutually offsetting. The deregulation of oil and eventually natural gas will encourage the development of synthetic fuels. To a much lesser extent, the leasing of additional shale-oil- and coal-bearing lands owned by the federal government may have the same effect. Reducing federal support for demonstration projects, on the other hand, will retard at least the pace of synfuels development. The net effect likely will vary by state.

Making available more land and OCS territory for energy exploration and production also threatens to create new environmental-energy conflicts. The administration justifies these actions on the basis of the overriding national interest in energy production. At the same time, the states are being asked by EPA to assume primary responsibility for administering and enforcing the major federal pieces of environmental legislation, with state rights used as the primary rationale. Clearly, the states will have wider discretion in designing and implementing air, water, and hazardous-waste laws, except, perhaps, as applied to energy-development projects on federal land.

Finally, the states will be expected to assume a much larger share of energy-development and environmental-protection costs. Energy-impact subsidies are no longer under consideration by the federal government, and wastewater facility construction grants will be scaled back. Grants for program administration also will be reduced. To compensate for the twin burden of increasing responsibility and decreasing financial backing, states must turn to energy-severance taxes (now augmented by price deregulation), user fees, general revenues, and special bonds.

Comments: Public-Resource Management under the Reagan Administration

Richard D. Lamm

Dale Keyes's chapter regarding the impact of President Reagan's energy and environmental programs is quite comprehensive. Keyes illuminated a fact of life that Westerners live by: that is, the federal government has a massive influence over land use, economic development, and environmental quality throughout our states.

Keyes raised the issue of oil-shale development and demonstrated the extent to which a federal decision to subsidize the industry influences developmental patterns in Colorado. Following passage of the Energy Security Act in 1980, shale companies became extremely optimistic as talk prevailed of eight shale plants in the state. The prospects were overwhelming, not only from an environmental standpoint but also with regard to social and economic impacts. The Reagan administration has been more cautious and is looking for less risky investments. Therefore, it is likely that only the two projects supported under the Defense Production Act will move ahead.

The present situation is not bad for Colorado. While Coloradans support the demonstration of commercial feasibility of shale, a more moderate growth scenario will give us the ability to absorb the growth and to test the two shale technologies. We are keenly aware, however—with 80 percent of the high-grade shale under federal ownership, and with 80 percent of that locked in formations within Colorado—that another round of gas lines could produce federal action designed to produce oil from shale at any cost. Therefore we live in a constant state of uncertainty, knowing that the potential for federal intervention over land use and environmental conditions is enormous.

One further observation regarding Keyes's analysis of what is likely to happen within the Reagan administration is appropriate. We must acknowledge that the current fiscal situation will continue to dominate all policy discussions with the exception of national defense. Had the $19 billion provided by the Energy Security Act for synfuels been on budget, certainly the program would have been eliminated.

Public Land and Resource Law

There is no more historically rich and profound area of public policy than
that of public land and resource law. Throughout this century, Congress
has provided a full and precise body of resource laws through which a fundamental principle has emerged: Public resources should be managed in a
manner that benefits a broad spectrum of present and future generations.

While resource-utilization issues have been very controversial, there has
remained over the decades an unbroken linkage of this principle. Throughout presidential terms and through enactment of significant resource law,
the philosophy has provided that government has a responsibility to manage
resources for the broad interest of the public. Gifford Pinchot coined the
very simple saying: "The greatest good for the greatest number for the
longest time."

President Theodore Roosevelt chastised the nation for not exercising
appropriate management control: "In a word, we have thoughtlessly and,
to a large degree, unnecessarily diminished the resources upon which not
only our prosperity but the prosperity of our children and our children's
children must always depend."

Implicit in the principle of public-resource management is a proper role of
government as the steward, as the manager, and as the public's agent in the
allocation of its resources. The Reagan administration seems anxious to break
this policy tradition and transfer heretofore public responsibilities to the
private sector. There is no need for the relationship between government and
the private sector to be adversarial; in order for both sectors to function properly, a high level of cooperation must be established. However, the roles cannot
be confused. The private sector can no more assure protection of the public interest than government can force the marketplace to function efficiently.

Some have characterized the policies of Secretary James Watt as a huge
swing of the pendulum in resource management. Yet on examination, this is
not necessarily convincing. A new philosophy is being proposed by many influential people inside the administration and close to key members of Congress. This philosophy seeks to have the marketplace determine how public
lands are managed. In its clearest form, the new approach seeks simply to
hand over public lands to the private sector: to sell off our national heritage
to raise funds to cover budget deficits and pay off the national debt. This
philosophy goes under the name of privatizing federal lands. Privatizing is
more than another swing of the pendulum: It is an effort to take the pendulum off the clock! In dealing with the specifics of federal resource policy,
it is important not to lose sight of this fundamental philosophical threat to
the public lands.

The following anecdote illustrates the point. A prisoner on an honor
farm passed the guards every day with a wheelbarrow full of hay. Each time

he passed through the gate, the guards would carefully examine the hay, probing for stolen items. They knew the prisoner was stealing something. As hard as they tried, they could not discover anything in the hay. Well, as you probably know, he was stealing wheelbarrows!

In forums such as this book it is proper to raise the fundamental issue of whether or not basic public policy is being dismantled. The hallmark report of the Public Land Law Review Commission issued in 1970 clearly set forth government's management responsibilities. The commission first sought to reverse a policy of lands disposal and held that public lands "whose values must be preserved so that they may be used and enjoyed by all Americans" generally should be held in federal ownership. The commission went on to detail sound management responsibilities of the federal government.

The comprehensive congressional rewrite of public resource law, Federal Land Policy and Management Act of 1976 (FLPMA) sharply and soundly reaffirmed the wisdom of the commission. FLPMA declared that public lands should not only be retained in federal ownership unless it was clearly determined that disposal would serve the national interest, but, more importantly, the act reembraced the concept of conservation. Thus in 1976 Congress reaffirmed that public resources should be utilized in a manner that best meets "present and *future* needs of the American people."

Goals of Public-Resource Management

1. Revenue. Utilization of public resources is designed to return a *monetary profit* to the U.S. Treasurey. Alexander Hamilton was the first to raise the idea of using public land to provide public revenue. While this goal has been reaffirmed throughout our history, it has by no means been the exclusive purpose for the utilization of public resources. As recently as 1976, Congress cautioned that considerations beyond the greatest economic return should drive public-resource decisions.

2. Subsidy. Federal land and mineral holdings have been used throughout the ages to *subsidize* congressionally approved activities seen as consistent with the public interest. The very settlement of the West through homesteading and railroading land grants represented a clear policy decision to use the public domain for the economic benefit of a specific few and the advance of public interest. Thomas Jefferson reflected this priority: "Whenever there is in any country uncultivated land and unemployed poor, it is clear that the laws of property rights have been so far extended as to violate natural rights."

Priorities of subsidizing individual interests obviously shift over time. Provision of low user fees for livestock grazing on public lands represents another conscious policy determination that a single interest should benefit from the public domain.

3. Conservation. Resource conservation has been a fundamental goal of lands management for many years. Major John Wesley Powell in 1879 viewed western resources as a capacity that could be used by future generations if there were ever a resource crisis.

The goal of conservation in resource management has several dimensions. First, the concepts of multiple use and sustained yield provide a goal of stretching the available resource base out over time to benefit future generations. Secondly, the goal of conservation embodies a philosophy of balancing competing resource uses so that a broad spectrum of utilization is achieved. The fundamental policy exists that a wide variety of resource uses be achieved regardless of whether they return an equal profit to the Treasury.

4. Preservation. Public lands have also been managed in a manner to preserve certain values in the national interest. The most dramatic commitment to the preservation of unique land resources was enactment of the Wilderness Act of 1964: "It is hereby declared the policy of the Congress to secure for the American people of present and future generations the benefits of an enduring resource of wilderness."

More recently, FLPMA reaffirmed the goal of managing certain public resources—not for profit, not for productivity—but to preserve "the quality of scientific, scenic, historical, ecological . . . archeological values. . . ."

5. Environmental Protection. The goals of public resource management go beyond simple good business management. It appears that Congress had every intent of seeing that the public's resources were managed in a model fashion. For example, the Public Land Law Review Commission asserted that those who use public land should conduct their activities "in a manner that avoids or minimizes adverse environmental impacts and should be responsible for restoring areas to acceptable standards. . . ." The commission's recommendations imply that separate, distinguishable, and sometimes higher standards should exist in the protection of the public domain. This notion was reaffirmed by the passage of FLPMA, particularly in its section requiring the secretary to give priority to the designation and protection of areas of critical environmental concern.

6. Public Participation. The value and necessity of public participation in public management decisions have been viewed for years as a fundamental aspect of prudent resource management. The report of the Public Land Law Review Commission was clear on this topic, providing several recommendations to improve the public's participation in the use of their resources. What the commission recommended, the Federal Land Policy and Management Act of 1976 conferred as law. Not only did FLPMA require a high level of public participation, but it further mandated that federally owned resources be utilized in a manner consistent with state and local land-use plans and policies. The consistency requirement held that it was in the public interest that local and regional values be honored in the pursuit of national goals. This concept was not designed to further the profitability of federal resources; it expressed a basic concept of harmony. That is, that to the extent practical, the federal government should manage its resources in harmony with local values and policies.

Taken together, these six public-resource goals imply a sophisticated management responsibility on the part of the federal government. They indicate that while the private sector's utilization of resources is fundamental to the success of the system, values beyond those of the marketplace must control the use of public lands.

Obviously public resources have long provided sustenance to private industry and played a significant role in marketplace economics. However, our laws have sharply distinguished between public and private lands. In the case of the public domain, profitability and marketplace values are balanced with other public values such as resource conservation and preservation of unique characteristics as well as the value of environmental stewardship.

The new philosophy of privatization runs counter to these six principles. There is certainly nothing wrong, and nothing new, about selling small tracts of excess lands. But consider what is being discussed in Washington.

There are serious proposals to liquidate as much as 100 million acres of public land in order to generate additional revenues to balance the federal budget. *Public Land News* quoted an aide to Senator Paul Laxalt (R-Nev.): "We're talking about selling off a lot of BLM lands. . . . We're going to have to do something to get the nation on a firm financial footing. . . . You can make an analogy to business. When a business gets in trouble, it sells off excess capital. Some of these public lands are excess capital."

William Niskanen, a member of the President's Council of Economic Advisors, called for a radical change in the present system of public lands management. One of Niskanen's proposals was to also privatize or sell off the public lands.

The law of the land, however, will not allow for such a radical shift in resource policy. But there is a lot that can be done, within current law, to move us far along toward privatizing the public land. For one thing, a secretary of the interior can dismantle his department's management capability by drastic and ill-considered budget cuts. He can shut the public out of key management decisions so the full range of public values need not be considered. Also a secretary can lease vast areas to private interests on easy terms, and that is what Secretary Watt has tried to do in his first year in office.

Reduction of the Capacity to Manage

The operative responsibility of the DOI is to manage multiple resources in a manner that highlights and balances the individual and, at times, competing goals. The ability to manage requires a technical and planning capacity to know the consequences of individual actions and how they relate in fulfilling or detracting from the goals of public-resource law.

This has been the first area of attack by the president and his administration. Under the guise of streamlining the planning process—a general concept endorsed by the western governors—proposed changes in the Bureau of Land Management (BLM) planning process go far beyond the removal of unnecessary red tape. The proposed regulations would allow BLM to abandon much of its comprehensive planning responsibilities. If adopted, BLM would not have the capacity to adequately assess the cumulative aspects of resource decisions nor the impacts of such actions on nearby nonfederal resources. While reductions in the BLM budget have already reduced its essential planning staff by 50 percent, further budget cuts under consideration will strip the agency of a vital management capacity.

Reduction of Public Input

Despite the well-publicized attitude of the Reagan administration to provide state and local governments with greater responsibilities, the DOI has taken several moves to weaken the ability of state and local governments to have input to federal-resource decisions. In an earlier draft of its coal-leasing regulations, the unique regional coal-leasing teams were rendered virtually useless. The regional teams represent a forum for efficient interaction of local, state, and federal government officials. Following objections by the Western governors, the department recanted and proposed another set of regulations, this time supporting continuation of the coal teams.

At the same time, the administration is proposing draft regulations that would countermand the spirit and letter of FLPMA regarding the consistency of federal-resource decisions with state and local land-use plans and policies. As Governor Bruce Babbitt of Arizona stated, "the proposed revisions reduce the role of the states to that of a bystander."

Not only is the administration taking action to reduce state and local governments' roles in federal-resource decisions, but it is also significantly impairing the ability of the public to participate in these critical matters. Again, proposed revised regulations aimed at modifying FLPMA substantially reduce the opportunities for public participation in the planning process.

Abandonment of Traditional Leasing Objectives

Secretary Watt's philosophy of resource leasing underscores the fundamental philosophy of this administration. In its most simple form, Watt views leasing as an unnecessary barrier to the private-sector's access to public land and resources. For a number of decades, leasing was open, haphazard, and speculative. The decade of the 1970s brought reform and the end of the open leasing era, the latter part of which saw court action, delay, and frustration. Reform legislation such as the Coastal Zone Management Act (1972), the Coal Leasing Amendments Act (1976), and the Outer Continental Shelf Land Act (1978) was enacted to balance the need for energy production with other important state and national interests. Congressional intent clearly was to see that leased federal resources were diligently developed and the Treasury received a fair return. In short, leasing for leasing's sake was replaced by a process in which individual management goals are to be applied so that resulting development balances various values.

Watt's laissez-faire approach to leasing runs counter to that objective. Soon after he became secretary, Watt described his approach to leasing as follows:

> Instead of having the Department of Interior determine which tracts of land would be best mined, we want to rely more on the marketplace, which has more wisdom in allocating the resources than does the federal government.

The administration has overruled recommendations of almost every regional coal team concerning the amount of coal to be leased, even in the face of strong evidence that industry would be unable to bring the leases into production. Several environmentally sensitive areas off the California coast have been targeted for oil exploration and development; oil and gas leasing in wilderness areas is under consideration. In each of these cases, there have been objections to overleasing on the part of governors or congressional committees. The administration's record during its first year clearly has been one of consistently seeking to enlarge the scope of leasing.

In the recently released coal-leasing regulations, the administration has announced a new policy to guide decisions about how much coal should be leased. In the future, the department will lease enough coal to meet the demand for reserves. Does this mean that DOI would return to the disastrous policy of leasing anything industry wanted? It is hopeful that DOI will back off and return to the more balanced and reasoned approach of leasing coal to meet demand for production that was developed through several years of painstaking negotiations under Secretary Andrus.

The department's rush to lease vast areas for coal or for oil and gas exploration in wilderness areas is simply not supported by the facts of the situation. Recent studies have shown that the 1.4 percent of our land area in wilderness in the continental forty-eight states contains a correspondingly small amount of oil and gas. If there are ample prospects for exploration elsewhere, why should we disturb our small and fragile wilderness?

As for coal, there is overwhelming evidence that industry already has leased much more coal than can be sold in the foreseeable future. According to a December 1981 study by the Office of Technology Assessment (OTA), coal production from mines on federal land already under lease could increase by 300 percent over the next decade, if the demand were there. OTA reports that the extent of demand, not the availability of leased coal reserves, is expected to determine the amount of coal that will be produced from existing federal leases.

A critical question is whether new federal leasing is necessary. A January 1981 Department of Energy Western coal survey indicates that demand in most cases is below capacity with or without new federal leases. For example, the demand forecast for Wyoming's Powder River Basin coal is approximately 50 million tons below capacity without additional federal leases. While there may be specific local instances where demand exceeds capacity, regionwide it is safe to say that overcapacity will exist well into the 1990s. This is not to suggest that leasing should be halted. We in Colorado have supported a reasonable, paced approach to coal and oil-shale leasing that meets industry's demands while conserving public-resource values on less desirable and more environmentally sensitive tracts and minimizing boom-town growth problems.

In the case of oil shale specifically, we support the offering of a multimineral lease to test the concurrent development of other minerals geologically associated with oil shale. We also support the design of a permanent oil-shale-leasing program that must include a strong state/local government role and serious consideration of the environmental limits to development. Colorado, however, does not support its implementation, especially at a time when there is no indication an industry hindered by poor economics and technology problems is prepared to use such broad access to the resource. Once the program is designed, we can then consider whether there is an immediate need for more oil-shale leasing or whether sufficient land is already available to industry.

The problem with overleasing is not only that it is unnecessary but also that it makes it difficult for the DOI to manage its lands prudently. Extensive leasing, in the absence of a similar level of demand or need for production, prevents the comprehensive planning envisioned by the Public Land Law Review Commission and by FLPMA. When decisions of rate, pace, and location of development are ceded to the private sector, public-resource goals such as conservation, multiple use, and environmental protection are similarly left to the marketplace. It should be obvious that the marketplace cannot advance individual investments while at the same time balancing the public interests.

Taken together, dismantling of the DOI planning capability, reduced participation by the public and by state and local governments, a hurry up, lease it all approach to leasing, and the elimination of critical environmental standards represent a fundamental and radical departure from the principles that have guided public resource use for decades. It is not clear whether these radical initiatives will be successful. DOI has been pressured to postpone oil and gas leasing in wilderness areas for at least a year and to postpone excessive leasing off the California coast. There are indications that DOI is considering restoring a strong voice for states in the coal-leasing process. There may be similar retreats from the dismantling of the BLM land-use planning system and from the new policy of leasing as much coal as industry feels it needs to hold.

Recent reports that the administration is considering significant sales of the public domain to assist in balancing the present federal budget are shocking. It runs counter to the spirit of the Public Land Law Review Commission, to the Federal Lands Policy and Management Act, and contrary to the very basic principle of public-resource management.

Privatization of the public lands or the more subtle forms of President Reagan's and Secretary Watt's policies of allowing the marketplace to dictate land-management decisions, if successfully implemented, would lead to an uncoordinated and conflicting land and resource pattern throughout the public-lands states. If the marketplace becomes an exclusive factor in resource management, resources could be squandered as dominant uses obliterate other legitimate utilizations of the public domain. Developmental scenarios inconsistent with state and local plans may cause yet another set of land-use problems.

Perhaps the more likely outcome is not a victory for the new economics of privatization but rather continual, escalating conflict over how public lands are managed. This conflict will be debilitating to all parties at interest and will not help industry to discover the minerals and produce the mineral and energy resources that our economy needs.

As various aspects of the administration's programs are debated, a very real possibility exists for political chaos and polarization.

1. The private sector will be placed in the awkward position of either supporting the pure marketplace approach of the administration, thus alienating many state and local governments, or disavowing the very administration that is attempting to bolster production.
2. Many Western governors who support accelerated resource development along with proper safeguards will find themselves in a position of having to oppose development because their constituents had insufficient input to development decisions—decisions that because of improper planning may threaten local communities.
3. Public-interest groups, whose leaders have been chastised by the Heritage Foundation, will abandon all sensible efforts to compromise and will merely focus their energies upon the courts.

The result will be a period of uncertainty for industry, for the states, and for the U.S. public that will be unprecedented in the history of public-lands administration. At a time when production must be prudently accelerated, we will be locked in a most negative and detrimental battle—one that we cannot afford to wage, let alone lose.

Discussion

Ira Lowry: Government Lamm, would you have more confidence in the wise management of public lands if it were turned over to the states?

Richard Lamm: No. I vetoed the Sagebrush Rebellion as did most of the Western governors. The idea is politically naive and counterproductive. State legislatures are subject to short-term pressures to sell public lands far faster than the DOI, no matter who is running the Interior.

Arlo Woolery: Governor, by what criteria should we evaluate government's performance as a land manager? In the private sector we do have criteria for performance but, from what you have said, you must have rather different standards in mind for evaluating public-sector performance. How would you approach the job of drafting the standards by which public-land management might be judged?

Richard Lamm: I wish I could respond directly to that question because it is very thoughtful. We have had experience mostly with cost-benefit ratios. They work adequately for water projects, but wilderness would never pass a cost-benefit test. The best we can do is to promulgate a comprehensive list of sometimes-conflicting preferred values. You cannot use a profit-maximizing or a cost-benefit approach. Finally, you must make a value judgment as to whether an administration is adequately protecting the public domain.

Arlo Woolery: That becomes quite subjective. For the management of collective goods, I would think, we need some agreed measurement.

Frank Mittelbach: Governor, you spoke about differences in values: conservation goals versus resource development. I hear you say that we should concentrate our resource-extraction activities in a few areas and not create so much turmoil. The problem is if you want to create a market, presumably you are looking for competition to get correct pricing. How do you reconcile efficiency with other goals?

Richard Lamm: If all the coal leases were owned by a handful of companies then you would have a persuasive argument for leasing additional lands. But in our state, coal leases are owned by hundreds of private speculators. Anyone who wanted to start a coal company would have no trouble buying current leases. So I think the demands of competition are already satisfied, and preservation interests should be given greater weight at this point.

Marlee Coughlan: Mr. Smith, public involvement is receiving less attention these days. I heard you say that the law requires comprehensive public involvement. I wonder if you can comment on it.

Edwin Smith: Just as with coastal zoning, the statutes provide a skeletal structure that is fleshed out by regulations.

Marlee Coughlan: Governor Lamm, are you hopeful the public will be involved?

Richard Lamm: No. I think that we are going to see decreased public participation.

Edwin Smith: One great embarrassment that Los Angeles had on OCS lease sale 68 was that in the hearings in Long Beach only about twenty people appeared to speak. Notices had been sent to over four hundred people. With that kind of public response, participation provisions matter very little because no one is going to be around to listen.

George Lefcoe: Is OCS 68 the one that would bring oil rigs to Santa Monica Bay?

Edwin Smith: With the current proposed lease sale between Palos Verdes and Point Dume there will be eight tracts twelve to twenty-five miles outside Santa Monica Bay. The leases that are thirteen miles off Highway 101 toward Santa Barbara are clearly visible, so I would expect that from the Palisades the platforms would be visible all the way around Santa Monica Bay.

Deni Greene: We are seeing a Seaweed Rebellion among coastal communities. Secretary Watt ignored state and local recommendations on offshore leasing.

Jack Spahn: I have a question for Dale Keyes. Given that there is a need for liquid hazardous waste-treatment plants, do you think we are going to see either state or federal regulations because local politicians cannot handle siting these facilities in their own areas?

Dale Keyes: The trend is toward state-level siting efforts. A multistate regional approach also makes sense. EPA is under a court order to promulgate rules for landfill operations that will, among other things, provide minimum standards for state regulations.

Fred Kahane: What do you think the land-use impacts are going to be of EPA's not funding sewage-treatment plants for any excess capacity?

Dale Keyes: The philosophy is that the federal government should not subsidize growth. Funding will have to be provided by state or local arrangements.

Leroy Graymer: Mr. Keyes, how much evidence do we have that EPA is urging the use of market-type mechanisms for environmental protection?

Dale Keyes: The Office of Policy Analysis has established a regulatory reform group, a holdover from the Carter administration. EPA has held a series of seminars, in Philadelphia most recently, trying to advertise the economic efficiency gains from a market-based approach. They bring us firms that have successfully traded emission controls within or among plants in an attempt to proselytize the advantages. They are advertising their intention and seem to be moving in this direction.

Trixie Johnson: Would you comment on the Reagan policies on nuclear power and the impacts on state and local governments?

Dale Keyes: The Reagan administration is a promoter of nuclear power. However, I do not think it is going to make a difference in the number of power plants built. Whether it is a viable source of energy in the next ten to twenty years depends on economics. The fact that two partially built plants in the state of Washington have recently been put in mothballs tells me that is does not make economic sense and I do not think that any action on the part of the Reagan administration is going to change that very much.

Part V
Financing Public Services and
Facilities

Comments

Bruce Howard

Mr. Peterson's chapter is part of a new wave of scholarship about life after Propositions 13, 2½, and other taxpayer pressures on government revenues and spending. This new approach presents itself as simultaneously more optimistic and more realistic. After a dreary stretch of critics simply crying over the spilled milk of fiscal crisis, many new studies, including this one, at least attempt to describe the interesting shapes of the puddles.

In this chapter, Mr. Peterson's particular focus is that perennial favorite of fiscal doomsayers: underfunding of public infrastructure. The traditional story line on public infrastructure reads like an old B movie. State and local officials faced with higher costs and lower revenues are tempted to slice away at such low-profile time-bomb expenditures as infrastructure maintenance: sewers, roads, and so on. While each foregone stitch may necessitate nine down the road, the drivers down that road will be the next generation of politicians, officials, and taxpayers. So, the story concludes, we need special institutional structures or check to prevent short-sighted politicians (and taxpayers) from systematically underfunding the unglamorous but essential programs of infrastructure maintenance and repair.

Mr. Peterson's chapter presents a quite sane and stimulating view. In essence, he suggests that perhaps observers have exaggerated the inadequacies of the political process to maintain infrastructure while at the same time underestimating the costs of institutionalizing controls of infrastructure budgeting. Relating to the exaggeration point, Mr. Peterson argues that we should reexamine many of the Cassandra claims that infrastructure is dangerously neglected. In many cases, he notes, frightful statistics of inadequate infrastructure are functions of outdated go-go year projections and goals for growth. Scaling down our boom-time expectations may reveal that infrastructure is adequate for current needs and even for some conservative growth. Similarly, he argues that many of our deterioration projections are themselves outdated and in need of reexamination; for example, he suggests that many old pipes age more like Cary Grant and Kate Hepburn than like you and me.

As for the costs of institutionalizing controls on budgeting, Mr. Peterson warns that public officials, especially during times of fiscal crisis, need budget flexibility to serve the complex mix of social and political needs demanding their attention. At least at the extreme, it would indeed be absurd to see municipal workers nonchalantly patching potholes while uncontrolled fires raged nearby.

Mr. Peterson admits his position is one that is won or lost in the trenches of the footnotes. He raises largely empirical questions, and we must wait to see the real numbers before embracing or dismissing his approach. In fact, Mr. Peterson appreciates this quite well and with his research group has embarked on an intense and comprehensive empirical study of the real infrastructure situation. While many empirical studies often demonstrate little more than the source of funding for the enterprise, the empirical studies outlined by Mr. Peterson are clearly needed. We must know more about the empirical reality of infrastructure needs before we can say whether or not we are meeting them, or need meet them, and how. It is always appropriate to examine the examiner's questions before conceding that we have flunked. Mr. Peterson suggests that, at least in the world of roads and sewers, we may be pleasantly surprised.

6 Rebuilding Public Infrastructure: The Institutional Choices

George E. Peterson

In the last few years the nation has discovered its infrastructure problem. In this country, most of the ordinary public investment supporting household and business activities is undertaken by state and local governments. For at least a decade and a half, real levels of capital spending by these governments have fallen, and the capital share of state-local budgets has declined. Capital spending in 1980 accounted for little more than half the share of state and local budgets than it did during most of the 1960s (see table 6-1). The downward trend in capital commitment is especially apparent in the country's large cities and even more pronounced for capital maintenance spending than for investment outlay.

Taken by itself, this shift in budget allocation might not be cause for concern. It is, after all, the function of government to adjust spending patterns to citizen demand, and much of the 1960s' demand for public capital facilities (for new school and university buildings, for the interstate highway system) has now been satisfied. The decline in capital spending, however, has been accompanied by ample signs of erosion in the condition and performance of the urban capital plant.[1] The need to rebuild the nation's public infrastructure has become a journalistic and political article of faith in many quarters.[2]

Like any suddenly popular proposition, the need for infrastructure rebuilding has spawned exaggerations. One such item is the implicit presumption that every aged and deteriorating element of the public capital stock should be restored to its original condition or improved to meet contemporary standards. As economic activity and population decline in some parts of the country, it is inevitable that the extent and quality of the physical support systems should also decline. A handful of cities have tried to plan deliberate shrinkage of their road, bridge, and underground network systems. Most have allowed the condition of their facilities to deteriorate through cutbacks in maintenance and replacement. As regrettable as this deterioration may be to local residents, it often parallels deterioration in private capital facilities and current-service provisions by local governments. No part of local life has been spared the consequences of economic decline.

The costs of restoring the state and local capital plant to good condition have large implications for this country's de facto land-use policy. Tradi-

109

Table 6-1
State and Local Capital-Expenditure Trends

Fiscal Year	Gross Capital Investment (billion 1972 dollars)	Capital Spending As a Percent of Total State and Local Expenditures
1960	$21.8	27.1
1965	29.6	26.8
1968	36.8	28.7
1970	32.9	21.8
1975	31.2	18.0
1976	28.2	15.9
1977	26.1	14.4
1978	27.5	15.7
1979	27.5	15.7
1980	26.8	15.4

Source: Gross capital investment figures from the Bureau of Economic Analysis. Total expenditures from the "National Income and Products Accounts, State and Local Sector," published in the *Special Analyses, Budget of the U.S. Government*, FY 1982, Table H-10.

tionally, one of the principal economic arguments for targeting aid to cities has been the wastefulness involved in abandoning, or underutilizing, the inherited stock of public capital while duplicating these facilities in new locations. But if the costs of preserving old capital plant are as large as they now appear to be, the efficiency advantages of steering new development to make use of it are correspondingly lower. It is far from clear, in fact, whether the congested streets, weight-posted bridges, and frequently fully utilized treatment plants and sewer lines of old cities have excess serviceable capacity that could absorb private development without construction of new supporting public facilities. For these reasons, the geographic patterns of infrastructure repair and upgrading, as well as those of new construction, are likely to strongly shape future economic activity.

This chapter is divided into three parts. The first section considers the magnitude of the capital needs gap. It seems to be an iron law of social behavior that needs outrun the resources available to fill them, and the currently perceived backlog of public investment requirements is no exception to this rule. In the end, a large part of this gap will have to be closed by reconsidering investment standards in light of the costs of achieving them, or else the gap will remain unbridged.

One set of questions raised by the capital-investment backlog and the depreciation that has given rise to it is: Has the quality of capital services truly deteriorated, or is the present concern a product of new attention to the issue, reinforced by newly mandated (and higher) performance standards. And how variable is the capital-performance record across different parts of the country? We at the Urban Institute are now engaged in establishing a historical and city-specific benchmarking of capital condition and service performance. The second section provides a glimpse of the empirical base that has emerged.

The needs and standards approach to capital requirements is clearly inadequate. The third section discusses institutional considerations. The choice of how much to spend for capital improvements is a public decision, where the claims of public capital facilities must be weighed against the other claims on government budgets and against the claims of private households to keep income in the private sector. The capital-investment problems of the next decades are better understood not as a gap that must be filled but as a series of budgetary and institutional choices. Institutional choices are involved because there are certain structural features of the political and budgetary processes that seem to work against the claims of public capital preservation. The consequences of deferred maintenance or postponed repairs ordinarily are not visible for several years, making these items a favorite target for budget reductions in times of fiscal strain. Bridges do not vote, and therefore they make for a less persuasive political constituency than government employees or the recipients of current government services.

This reality creates a possible tilt in political decision making: a tendency to underinvest in capital and undermaintain existing plants, in the expectation that most of the costs will be borne by the next generation of taxpayers or at least the next generation of political leaders. Capital facilities have been better preserved in cities where they have benefited from special institutional protections. Where capital systems are managed by independent authorities, facilities are in better condition and capital investment plans are better financed. Capital plant also has fared better in cities that are run by professional managers and in places where capital financing is guaranteed by taxes dedicated exclusively to capital maintenance or repair. Without these special arrangements, the claims of capital preservation have come under intense budgetary pressure.

Whether the apparent bias against capital upkeep in ordinary political institutions is great enough to warrant the loss of budgetary flexibility that comes from establishing special institutional barriers is one of the key questions to be decided in rebuilding the nation's capital stock.

The Capital-Needs Gap

An understanding of the nation's capital-investment choices must begin with an assessment of the currently estimated needs gap. Most of the components of this estimate come from federal studies. The federal government regularly compares standards for different facilities with actual capital-stock conditions or performance. The amount of investment that would be required to upgrade existing capital facilities to achieve the federally specified standard is treated as a needs gap, which in the past the federal government has usually helped to finance through categorical capital grants.

The standards and needs approach has been applied to many capital functions. The large municipal wastewater-treatment program is based on performance mandates written into the Clean Water Act. The federal government carries out biennially a study of wastewater investment needs to meet federal standards. The most recent published survey (1978) places the needs backlog at $106 billion, and preliminary data from the 1980 survey reports remaining eligible needs of $119 billion.[3]

Regular needs assessments of the costs of achieving federal-capital-facility standards also are conducted for bridges and roads and highways. In these cases the standards are not mandated for local compliance but are guidelines used in determining eligibility for federal-capital assistance.

The extent of the imbalance between the capital financing needs established by federal needs assessments and current capital spending and federal-aid levels is shown in table 6-2. The third column shows the capital needs backlog, as estimated by official federal studies. With few exceptions, these needs exclude the claims of new capital projects; they represent the backlog involved in upgrading existing facilities to current standards. The fourth column indicates the level of federal capital assistance provided for these capital purposes in fiscal 1980. The fifth column shows projected fiscal 1981 federal aid, and the final column, total state-local capital spending. To discharge the needs backlog, as well as continue ordinary new construction, would require more than doubling real annual capital commitments in the state and local sector.

It is as certain as economic and political events can be that the United States will not choose to make this degree of commitment to public capital upgrading. A reexamination of the standards that generate the reported needs therefore is in order. The federal government is now in the process of reviewing capital standards in the United States, with a view to relaxing or removing those standards that are too costly to attain or whose fulfillment the federal government is unwilling to help finance. Congress has already stricken investment necessary to control flooding from needs eligibility for EPA grants. The administration's current legislative package would eliminate several further categories of need under the Clean Water Act from eligibility for federal assistance. These include investment needs to correct infiltration and inflow problems with old sewer pipe, to replace old collection systems, and to provide separate facilities for handling stormwater runoff and wastewater discharges. The costs of correcting combined wastewater and stormwater overflow alone account for approximately one-fourth of the estimated capital needs in sewer systems.

Table 6-2
Federal Capital-Needs Estimates Compared to Current Funding Levels
(in billions of current dollars)

Infrastructure Category	Period	Coverage	Total Needs	Fiscal Year 1980 Federal Outlays	Fiscal Year 1981 Federal Authorizations	Total 1979 Capital Spending by All Levels of Government
Highways	1980-1995	Capital investment required to maintain existing highways at minimum-condition standards. Does not include interstate completion costs.[a]	336.6 to 362.8[b]	8.7	8.9	15.7
Bridges	Current backlog	Capital investment required to rehabilitate or replace deficient bridges on and off the federal-aid system.	41.1[c]	0.76	1.3	Included above
Sewerage	1980-2000	Capital investment required to meet water-quality goals in existing federal law and to accommodate population growth.	119.[d]	4.3	3.3	5.6
Transit	1982-1991	Capital investment required for rehabilitation of bus and rail systems and to accommodate projected passenger growth.	49.3[e]	2.3[f]	3.5[f]	1.6

Water

[a]Interstate completion costs were estimated to be $50.75 billion in 1980. Source: U.S. Dept. of Transportation, "1981 Federal Highway Legislation: Program and Revenue Options," June 26, 1980.

[b]Source: U.S. Dept. of Transportation, "The Status of the Nation's Highways: Conditions and Performance," January 1981. For a discussion of minimum-condition standards (as determined by engineering performance and safety standards), see p. 136-148. Highway capital needs reported here cover bridges on the federal-aid highway system.

[c]Source: U.S. Dept. of Transportation, "Second Annual Report to Congress, Highway Bridge Replacement and Rehabilitation Program," March 1981.

[d]Source: U.S. Environmental Protection Agency, "1980 Needs Survey: Cost Estimates for Construction of Publicly-Owned Wastewater Treatment Facilities," February 1981.

[e]Source: American Public Transit Association, preliminary results of 1981 capital-needs study.

[f]Includes transit operating aid that may be used for capital purposes at the option of the transit system.

In other areas, too, needs standards are under review. Over one-half of all bridges eligible for federal aid from the bridge program are deficient because of inappropriate deck geometry—that is, the fact that a bridge is narrower than the approaching highway.[4] This is always a structural inconvenience, but whether it represents a need for capital expenditure depends upon the traffic density and economic demand for the bridge.

In the same vein, states and localities have begun reevaluation of capital standards. These include requirements that establish minimum square footage of school space per pupil in order to qualify for state school-construction aid, and earthquake standards which, if enforced literally, would render obsolete large parts of the public-building inventory in such states as California. At the local level, individual governments have found that the planning goal of replacing all water pipe as it reaches a given age (sixty years in Buffalo, seventy-five years in Newark, ninety years in Boston) is too expensive a standard to be financed through present resources. A reevaluation of the link between pipe age and pipe failure is being carried out in these and other cities, with the goal of finding less-costly replacement rules. Studies in New York City have revealed that a water-pipeline-replacement strategy that targets on pipe segments with the highest probability of failure can accomplish the same reduction in breaks as a replacement strategy based on age alone that costs three times as much.

In short, it now appears that a large part of the public investment-needs gap in the United States will be closed, not by increasing investment levels and discovering new sources of capital financing, but by lowering capital standards to meet budget constraints or adopting more cost-effective replacement strategies. This introduction of cost considerations into public investment goals has the effect of converting capital investment from a pure planning and legislative standards basis to an economic-demand basis.

Although lowering federal needs standards is one part of a realistic adjustment to budget constraints, it can create special problems where performance goals have been written into law and are binding upon state and local governments regardless of the availability of federal aid. A reduction of needs standards, if limited to federal-grants legislation alone, has the effect of shifting a much larger share of the costs of compliance with federal mandates to the state and local sector. It also shifts to state and local governments the responsibility for deciding how much of their budgets to devote to capital improvements—a choice that requires far more information about the current condition of the public capital plant than we now possess and greater understanding of the consequences of different levels of future funding and maintenance.

Capital Condition and Capital Performance

Most of the debate over public infrastructure has occurred in an empirical vacuum. While this on occasion has improved its liveliness, it has detracted from its practical usefulness.

Without systematic information, it is imposible to determine whether the colorful anecdotes about the collapse of the West Side Highway or about ruptures in water-main systems are dramatic illustrations of a pervasive capital deterioration or are spectacular exceptions to the general rule. It is impossible even to know whether the quality of service rendered by capital facilities is getting worse or whether normal events suddenly are gaining unusual publicity.

The Urban Institute is now completing a comprehensive study of capital condition, capital investment and maintenance spending, and capital stock-performance trends in sixty-two randomly selected cities. Although the full results of this study are not yet available, an earlier examination of capital-stock conditions in twenty-eight cities indicates the type of information that is being collected. Moreover, enough of the information is now in hand to allow qualitative characterization of the findings, which are ventured in the following discussion.

Are Capital Condition and Capital Performance Getting Worse?

For some (mostly large, northern) cities and for some capital functions, this question can unambiguously be answered "yes." Deterioration in mass-transit facilities is perhaps the most acute example. Figure 6-1 illustrates the extreme worsening of transit breakdowns that has occurred in New York City and Philadelphia in the last few years. Not only are breakdowns far more frequent now than in the early 1970s, but the rate of performance decay has accelerated alarmingly. Specialized studies in both Philadelphia and New York indicate that capital deterioration (of buses, rail lines, rail vehicles, traffic signals, and switching equipment) is directly responsible for the largest part of the leap in failure rates. Reversing this capital deterioration is by no means inexpensive. The capital plan recently adopted by New York State for the New York City transit system calls for the expenditure of six billion dollars over six years in a catch-up effort. The cities shown in figure 6-1, however, are extreme examples of transit deterioration; they are not representative even of the big-city universe.

For other elements of the nation's public-capital base, there are signs of general and significant deterioration. The nation's interstate highway system, for example, is reaching the end of its originally planned life. When repairs are postponed or maintenance deferred, as has occurred under budget pressures, deterioration occurs at an accelerated rate. Between 1978 and 1980 alone, the percentage of the interstate-highway system classified as in poor condition, the lowest rating, doubled to 8 percent. A general lowering of road-surface quality occurred throughout the interstate system. Deterioration has been most severe in those states like Pennsylvania that have the oldest interstate road links and have had the most drastic cutbacks in maintenance and resurfacing rates.

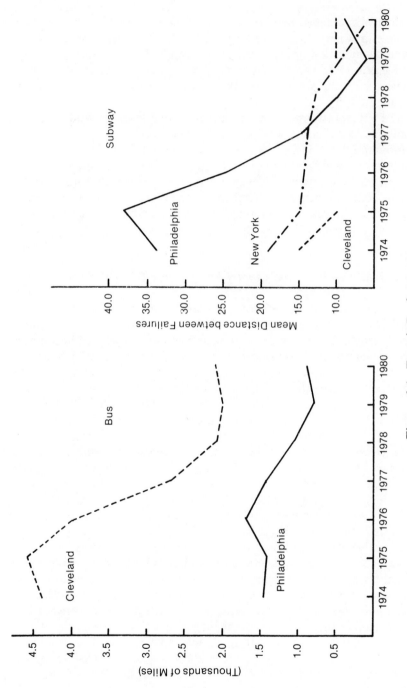

Figure 6-1. Transit Performance

In contrast to the largest cities' transit systems and to the interstate-highway system, no general worsening of sewer and water capital facilities is evident. Water-treatment standards have been upgraded by federal law, creating the large reported backlog in this field. Acute concern has been expressed by Northeast and Midwest lobbying groups over the massive costs involved in replacing the old water-distribution networks of these states. It is true that in several cities, the majority of water pipe is now more than eighty years of age. For a few scattered sections of the Trenton and Philadelphia systems, wooden pipe is still in use, which has ruptured under the water pressure needed to meet today's demand. Looking at the last decade of experience of cities as a group, however, or even that of old and northern cities, one sees no general trend toward increased water-main breaks, leaks, or other problems with water-distribution systems. In a number of cities, in fact, the oldest portions of the water network continue to outperform more recent installations.

For still other capital functions the last decade appears to have brought a substantial improvement in capital conditions. Bridges are perhaps the most conspicuous example. The adoption of the federal bridge-replacement and -rehabilitation program required the first national inventory of bridge condition. This inventory revealed that the nation's bridges were in worse condition than had been recognized. However, the new federal monies devoted to subsidizing bridge repairs have resulted in large increases in spending on bridges in most cities. Table 6-3 illustrates the growth that has occurred in selected cities. Such investment has improved bridge conditions even though the backlog of remaining investment is impressive.

The recent record of capital condition, then, is mixed. The general decline in state and local-sector capital spending has not prevented a reallocation of capital funds that has actually increased outlays within many functions for repair and preservation purposes. These trends have arrested the deterioration that comes automatically with age and use. The principal problems today are not those of across-the-board deterioration in public capital facilities. Rather, they are targeted problems: geographically targeted in that capital decay is concentrated in large cities, old cities, cities with a history of budget strain, and cities without special institutional protection for capital and targeted by function as well. A few categories of capital stock—highways and mass transit—are demonstrably getting worse at a rapid rate; some others, such as bridges, have capital-investments requirements that, while not getting worse, are large and previously unrecognized; and still other categories, such as water treatment, have needs that were created mostly by society's adoption of new standards of performance.

Geographic Patterns of Capital-Stock Condition

Although the capital conditions of individual cities are highly variable, certain patterns do emerge. Tables 6-4 and 6-5 illustrate these systematic differ-

Table 6-3

Comparison of Bridge Condition with Growth in Bridge Contracts

City	Annual Average Bridge Contracts 1965-1971 (in thousand 1967 dollars)	Annual Average Bridge Contracts 1972-1978 (in thousand 1967 dollars)	Percent Change- 1965-1971 Average- 1972-1978 Average	Deficient Bridge Miles (percent)
Louisville	28.1	326.7	1,062	4
St. Louis	128.9	1,161.9	800	42
Atlanta	207.8	1,198.5	477	8
Pittsburgh	242.6	1,230.7	407	27
Minneapolis	269.2	692.1	157	17
Cincinnati	49.5	745.8	140	4
Denver	444.8	680.9	53	39
Detroit	1,180.5	984.3	(17)	34
Kansas City	513.8	376.1	(27)	12
Cleveland	584.3	392.1	(33)	45

[Note: *Deflator* is Construction Cost Index in *Engineering News Record*, March 1979 (1967 = base year).]

Sources: Federal Highway Administration, computer tabulation of obligations for all bridge projects using federal funds for fifty major urbanized areas on an annual basis from 1964 through July 31, 1978.

ences in performance records. Table 6-4 shows that water loss from cities' distribution systems varies systematically with the city's economic condition, age of housing (used as a proxy for age of the capital infrastructure generally), as well as by region of the country. Like any other performance measure, this one must be used with caution when interpreted as an index of capital condition. The degree of attention that a city will give to repairing or preventing leaks in its distribution system is a function, in part, of the adequacy and costs of its water supply. During the temporary drought conditions in both California and New Jersey, water authorities turned far more aggressively to leak detection and repair.

Table 6-5 illustrates a general capital problem that older cities face. They must spend more to maintain their facilities, even though performance levels and condition remain inferior. This difference is explained both by the older age and greater need for physical repair and by the higher costs confronted in such cities. In table 6-5 we see that maintenance spending for wastewater-collection systems in the Northeast cities is far above average, yet maintenance has been cut back, and routine maintenance actions (like cleaning of pipe) are less complete. Capital-performance levels also are inferior and promise to deteriorate more in view of maintenance reduction.

Institutional Differences in Capital Condition

Of probably greatest interest are those differences in capital conditions and performance that are related to institutional responsibilities for operating

Table 6-4
Estimated Water Leakage by City Grouping
(*based on twenty-eight cities, 1974-1978*)

City Grouping	Leakage as a Percent of Water Production
By distress index	
Severely distressed	10.8
Moderately distressed	7.8
Not distressed	6.3
By age of housing	
Old	11.4
Middle-aged	8.4
Young	6.3
By region	
Northeast	11.7
Midwest	9.2
South	7.7
West	5.7

Source: The Urban Institute.

and maintaining capital facilities. There is very little a city can do (except express chagrin) about its age or even its economic condition. It has considerably more choice about how it will organize responsibility for capital functions.

It is an institutional fact that, on average, capital facilities receive more attention when they are insulated from the general budgetary and political process. Sewer and water systems operated as independent authorities spend more on capital replacement, have better maintenance practices, and have capital facilities in better condition than sewer and water systems that are operated as part of the city's general operations. The reasons are not difficult to fathom. Independent authorities are free to set their own service prices. These are established to cover the costs of capital depreciation or capital replacement and maintenance as well as current operating costs. As a result, service rates tend to be substantially higher than in city-operated systems, where political pressures keep pricing low and where capital and maintenance budgets are the residual items that get squeezed to balance the budget. Independent authorities also have the right to raise prices and thus can guarantee to investors a reliable stream of revenue that can be used as security for revenue-bond issues.

The uncertainties to which city-operated utilities are exposed become most acute during periods of fiscal crisis. At these points, the cash reserves

Table 6-5
Condition and Performance of Wastewater-Collection Systems

Grouping	Cleaning/ 1,000 Miles of Pipe	1978 Maintenance Spending/ 1,000 Miles of Pipe (dollars)	1975-1978 Change in Maintenance Spending, (percent)
Region			
Northeast	142	1,001,274	−13
Midwest	134	542,736	2
South	162	390,426	12
West	1,310	379,855	25
Age of housing stock			
Old	89	809,131	−7
Middle-aged	667	456,127	2
Young	210	371,966	25

Source: The Urban Institute.

that utilities maintain for maintenance and investment purposes can become too tempting to resist. In the mid-1970s, when its general operating deficit became acute, the Philadelphia City Council simply passed a resolution declaring that the cash reserves of the water system were excessive and transferred $25 million to the general fund to help finance the city's general-operating-fund deficit. Buffalo's water system has been one of the most beleaguered in the nation. The city's investment requirements are cited as a number one exhibit in Northeast attempts to lobby for federal capital assistance for modernizing urban water-distribution systems. Yet in 1972, when faced with a budget crisis, the city of Buffalo passed a law requiring the annual transfer of $2.6 million from the water system to the general fund. This action virtually eliminated capital repairs and maintenance in the water system. A similar course was followed in Cleveland prior to that city's bond default.

Such raids on capital reserves are merely the most dramatic sign of the difficulties of operating capital facilities within the general city government. Postponing capital spending and maintenance is one of the few budget-cutback alternatives open to cities that does not have immediately visible consequences. For that reason, it is government's favored strategy. Examination of recent major budget reductions in New York, Boston, Cleveland, Oakland, and other cities shows that in each case capital items are the largest share of cutbacks. The *only* aggregate budget item actually reduced in dollar terms by California localities after Proposition 13 was the capital item.

Other institutional differences also are apparent from the data on capital-stock condition and performance. Cities managed by professional managers by and large have better maintenance records and better capital-replacement histories than cities run by strong mayors or city councils. This difference in policy toward capital preservation seems to be one of the few policy differences that can be attributed to political structure, now that a generation of research looking for such differences has been completed. One can interpret this difference as implying either that politicians' perspectives are tilted toward the short term, at the expense of neglecting the longer-run future, or that because professional managers' advancement comes through peer recognition of their efforts to discuss and resolve long-run difficulties, they tend to seek out opportunities to strike statesmanlike postures. Probably both explanations have an element of truth.

Finally, the dedication of specific tax-revenue sources to capital investment and maintenance has fostered spending for these activities. For years, the dedication of federal and state gas taxes to highway construction sustained capital spending. A number of communities have developed plans that earmark parts of the local sales or income tax for capital purposes. Like capital-replacement pricing and the establishment of special authorities, the earmarking of a dedicated tax source for capital purposes removes capital facilities from the general competition for budget priorities.

Institutional Choices

If the only urgent purpose of state and local governments were to sponsor rebuilding of public infrastructure, the record speaks clearly to the institutional arrangements that would be most successful. The budgetary claims of capital preservation and capital improvements would be protected from general budget competition by special institutional devices, such as independent authorities responsible for operating capital facilities on dedicated tax revenues that secure long-term financing.

A number of state and local governments have been moving in precisely this direction. An unprecedented spate of institutional reorganizations, or proposals for reorganization, has accompanied the new recognition of capital-investment backlogs.

Several cities spun off their sewer and water systems as independent authorities, with the intention of placing their capital-improvements plans on firmer footing. The city of Boston in 1977 ceded its sewer and water system to a newly established, independent Sewer and Water Commission. In its first year of operation, the commission raised water rates 16 percent and sewer rates approximately 246 percent. The increased revenue has allowed the authority to launch a $200 million capital-replacement program. The significance of the timing is enchanced by Massachusetts's passage of Proposition 2½. One of the first steps of the city of Boston in reaction to the fiscal pressure exerted by Proposition 2½ was to eliminate all capital projects not already underway—an action that would have scrapped the city's plan for water- and sewer-system renewal under the old institutional arrangements. Many of the effects of closer attention to capital condition are already visible. The number of miles of sewer line cleaned each year has more than doubled from the mid-1970s, sewer line repairs have increased more than 50 percent, and the ratio of unmetered water lost somewhere in the distribution system has fallen each year since transfer of the system to an independent authority.

The city of Cleveland, in drawing up its capital-reinvestment program, also reorganized its water system to create legal barriers that would prohibit future cash transfers to the city's general fund and to establish a legal obligation to raise service prices to the extent necessary to repay revenue bonds and carry out the city's capital program. Such legal protections were necessary in order for the water system to regain access to capital markets. The city's capital-spending program calls for a twenty-fold jump in capital outlays for the water system.

In both New York and New Jersey state governments have taken the lead in creating (New Jersey) or proposing (New York) new, statewide water authorities that will establish statewide capital-renewal plans for water systems and require local water systems to adopt pricing structures that provide adequately for the maintenance and investment called for in these plans.

Adoption of specially dedicated taxes has also become a favorite strategy to finance capital rebuilding. Cleveland launched its capital plan by securing a municipal income-tax increase. Although such a tax increase had been rejected repeatedly by Cleveland voters, once the proceeds were tied specifically to debt repayment and new capital investment, the business community took the lead in pressing for its adoption. The referendum proposal carried by a wide margin in the fall of 1980. Florida is now debating a one-cent increase in the statewide sales tax, whose proceeds would be earmarked exclusively for capital. Seattle and Kansas City, among other cities have recently adopted, or proposed, similar tax increases dedicated exclusively to capital repair.

Capital rebuilding, of course, is not the only laudable purpose of government. The current pressure on government budgets has set off an unrestrained scramble for special institutional authority or specially dedicated taxes for every governmental purpose imaginable. In sum, these efforts to unbundle the public budget, by financing each government function separately and making its expenditures a function of independent-revenue sources rather than a general-expenditure decision, threatens to greatly limit the flexibility of general-purpose governments. It renders far more difficult the establishment of government priorities.

The creation of new impediments to government choice making, especially when designed to boost expenditure levels for a given function, can be justified only if the existing political system unduly biases expenditure outcomes against that function. It seems clear that governments in the recent past have singled out capital and maintenance for budget cutbacks. Whether this is a permanent feature of general government—and demands an institutional remedy—is much less clear. The fact that New York City, Pittsburgh, Cleveland, the state of New Jersey, and other governments have greatly augmented capital outlays in the last five years, and have received strong public support for doing so, suggests that the public may have more tolerance for the long view than generally acknowledged. An open public debate over the appropriate rate for capital spending in local government budgets would seem preferable to the multiplication of special institutions designed to protect capital against ordinary budget trade-offs.

Notes

1. George E. Peterson, Nancy Humphrey, Mary Miller, and Peter Wilson, *The Future of America's Capital Plant* (Washington, D.C.: 1982). For more extreme assertions about the state of decay in public capital infrastructure, see Patrick Choate and Susan Walter, *America in Ruins* (Washington, D.C.: Council of State Planning Agencies, 1981).

2. See, for example, "Time to Repair and Restore," *Time* magazine, April 27, 1981, and "State and Local Governments in Trouble," *Business Week*, October 26, 1981.

3. U.S. EPA, "1990 Preliminary Draft Strategy for Municipal Wastewater Treatment" (Washington, D.C.: January 1981), p. 15.

4. Federal Highway Administration, *Annual Report to Congress, Highway Bridge Replacement and Rehabilitation Program*, February 1980, p. 7.

7

Financing Public Education in the Wake of Federal and State Spending Cuts: Crisis and Opportunities

E. Gareth Hoachlander

Until recently, responsibility for financing public education in California was shared more or less equally between state and local governments. Proposition 13, however, radically altered this arrangement and effectively transferred complete financial responsibility for schools to the state level. One result has been a rapid decline in support for public education. That decline is most evident in the level of spending for K-12 education, which will be declining even more rapidly when the full effects of federal cuts are felt next year. There is also evidence of waning political support as interest grows in various voucher proposals, tuition tax credits, and other proposals for abandoning the public schools.

In this chapter we analyze the changes in spending for public education in California. We argue that the rapid decline in the purchasing power of public schools will increase demands for radical changes: either the privatization of public education through vouchers and tax credits or a major reorganization of public education that returns some local taxing power, breaks up very large school districts, and expands parents' choice of schools.

Historically, the responsibility for financing public elementary and secondary education in the United States has been shared by federal, state, and local governments. The federal role has traditionally been minimal, never amounting to more than 8.5 percent of total expenditures and declining slowly from that maximum since 1974. Although ultimate constitutional responsibility for providing public education rests with the state level, states have usually delegated much of the administrative and financial responsibility to local school districts, of which there are some 16,000 throughout the country. Although the local contribution to education revenues has been steadily declining since 1942, the local share (mostly property taxes) still amounted to about 48 percent of total receipts in 1978-1979, and most local school districts enjoyed substantial control over their ability to raise and spend money for education.[1]

Until recently, public education in California closely resembled this national pattern. Elementary and secondary education was delivered through more than 1,000 school districts that, on the average in 1977-1978, contributed more than half the total funds expended on public education in grades K-12.[2] Proposition 13, however, radically altered school finance in California, effectively transferring complete financial responsibility for schools to the state level and initiating a period of rapid decline in support for public education. That decline is most evident in spending for education in California, but there is also evidence of declining political support as interest grows in various voucher proposals, tuition tax credits, and other proposals for abandoning the public schools. In short, Proposition 13 has brought about an extraordinary transformation in California's public schools, the consequences of which have received rather little public attention. In this chapter, we set forth some of the major changes, their consequences for the quality of public education in California, and their possible implications for further changes in school finance and education policy. In the first section, we examine what has happened to the financing of public education and the effects this has had on the purchasing power of local school districts. The second section discusses two of the most popular proposals for dismantling the public education system: tuition tax credits and vouchers. The third section discusses three possibilities for innovation within the public system: renewed local financing, redistricting, and expanded choice.

Proposition 13 and the End of Local Control of Schools

Proposition 13 occurred in the midst of a lengthy process of school-finance reform in California, a process that was still incomplete when Proposition 13 took effect in July 1978.[3] Responding to the constitutional principles established by *Serrano* v. *Priest*,[4] the California legislature had designed a system of revenue limits and restrictions on increases in educational spending designed to eliminate the effects of local-property-wealth disparities on school expenditures per student.[5] This system, established by AB65 (Chapter 894, Statutes of 1977), was in place before Proposition 13, but the legislation had not yet achieved the fiscal neutrality among school districts that would narrow large disparities in tax rates and per pupil spending. Consequently, when Proposition 13 took effect, large inequalities in expenditures per student remained among local school districts. In 1977-1978, expenditures per unit of average daily attendance ranged from as little as $854 in Tres Pinos Elementary to as much as $4,291 in Chawanakee Elementary.[6] Even among the large urban districts, the spending differences were substantial. San Francisco, for example, spent $2,333 per ADA, while Sacramento spent only $1,664.[7]

Proposition 13 removed any chance of achieving fiscal neutrality short of complete spending equality across all school districts. To see why, it is important to understand what *Serrano* required. Contrary to the popular view, the case did not require equal expenditures per student among all school districts; rather it required that all expenditure differences related to differences in local wealth be reduced to less than $100 per student.[8] Simply stated, the decision required equal spending for equal tax effort. However, local districts willing to tax more would be permitted to spend more. In the language of school-finance reform, this system of equal expenditures for equal tax effort is known as district power equalizing, and in 1977-1978, the legislature appeared to be moving slowly in that direction.[9]

Proposition 13, however, foreclosed this option. In effect, the initiative converted a host of widely varying local property tax rates into a single statewide tax of 1 percent of assessed value. Moreover, no local jurisdiction had a clear claim to any portion of this rate, and the task of dividing up the revenue generated by the 1-percent rate fell to the legislature. The local property tax had been converted into a state property tax, with the legislature enjoying virtually the same control over this source of revenue as it did over revenues generated by the sales and income taxes. For most practical purposes, the only revenue-raising power left to local governments, including school districts, was the power to levy user charges.

With local taxing power effectively eliminated, the legislature was left with only one option for financing public education: full state funding. With the exception of some insignificant charges for school lunches and some school supplies and extracurricular activities, there is no longer any local contribution to revenues for K-12 public education. True, approximately 25 percent of the property tax is earmarked for elementary and secondary education, but to call this local revenue is a fiction that disguises the loss of local control over taxes. In no district is this 25-percent portion sufficient to cover the full costs of public education, and the shortfall is covered with revenues from the state's general fund. The legislature could easily substitute sales and income tax revenues for property tax revenues, using the full 1-percent property levy to help fund noneducation expenditures.

With full state funding the only option for financing public schools in California, the legislature was confronted with a dilemma. On the one hand, it faced large inequalities among local school districts in expenditures per student. When these inequalities could be termed *local,* the result of local choices over taxing and spending, the differences could be politically justified. Moreover, prior to Proposition 13, district power equalizing provided a legal approach to permitting spending differences. With full state funding the only remaining option, allocating different amounts of state aid per student to different school districts would be difficult politically and was likely to be challenged in court. On the other hand, state revenues were inadequate to allocate additional funds to education in order to level up low-spending districts. Even with the state surplus of $5 billion, Proposition 13 had created a $2 billion shortfall in total state and local revenues. Consequently, allocating equal expenditures per student to all school districts could be achieved only by drastically cutting expenditures in the higher-spending districts, a step that if taken immediately would throw local schools into fiscal and political chaos.

As a first step toward resolving this dilemma, the legislature chose to cut spending in all school districts from 9 to 15 percent of expenditures per student in 1977-1978. Districts with the highest revenue limits would incur the maximum 15-percent cut, while districts with the lowest revenue limits would incur the minimum 9-percent cut.[10] A formula was designed to determine the size of the cut for districts with revenue limits in between the minimum and the maximum. As additional funds became available in future years for education, all districts would receive some increase in revenues per average daily attendance, but the percentage increase would be larger in districts with the lowest revenue limits.[11] Thus over time, expenditures per average daily attendance would be equalized, and the state would move, albeit very slowly, toward compliance with *Serrano*.

In effect, then, the legislature locked into place the spending inequalities existing in 1977-1978, and local school districts, lacking any significant revenue-raising powers of their own, have since been powerless to influence the level of financial resources available to their schools. With the exception of a few small, high-income districts that have been able to mount private fund-raising efforts, California's 1,044 school districts have become wholly dependent on state revenues and the approval of the legislature for school funding. Ironically, an initiative, whose backers so strongly reviled centralized government and the ability of the California legislature to manage public affairs, stripped public education of all local fiscal autonomy and handed it completely to the state.

For a state that once proudly vied with New York for the honor of the nation's finest public-school system, the result has been devastating. As displayed by table 7-1, statewide expenditures for K-12 education measured in constant dollars (that is, adjusted for the effects of inflation) have declined by more than 15 percent since 1977-1978. This decline has been tempered somewhat by a concommitant decline in average daily attendance, but even expenditures per average daily attendance have declined by about 12 percent since 1977-1978. In terms of expenditures for education as a percent of personal income, California fell from about 4.9 percent in 1977-1978, or twenty-three among the fifty states, to 4.5 percent in 1978-1979, or thirty-seven, behind such states as Mississippi, Alabama, and Arkansas.[12]

Table 7-1
Revenues for K-12 Public Education in California

	1977-1978	1978-1979	1979-1980	1980-1981	1981-1982
Revenues (constant dollars)	9,485.4	8,722.8	8,639.2	8,526.3	8,014.7
Decline from 1977-1978 (percent)	—	8.0	8.9	10.1	15.5
Revenues per Average Daily Attendance (constant dollars)	2,012	1,981	1,979	1,905	1,786
Decline from 1977-1978 (percent)	—	1.5	1.6	5.3	11.2
CPI (California) (constant dollars)	186	204	234	260	287

Source: California State Department of Education.

For many of California's large urban-school districts, the decline has been even more dramatic. Table 7-2 displays the trend in general purpose revenues per average daily attendance for the eight largest cities in the state. General-purpose revenues include base-revenue-limit income, federal-impact aid, state-urban-impact aid, and miscellaneous local revenues.

Table 7-2
California's Eight Largest School Districts General Purpose Revenues Per Average Daily Attendance, K-12
(constant dollars)

	1977-1978	1978-1979	1979-1980	1980-1981	1981-1982
Los Angeles	1,483	1,480	1,443	1,337	n.a.
Percent change		− 0.2	− 2.7	− 9.8	
San Diego	1,468	1,531	1,455	1,411	1,222
Percent change		+ 4.3	− 0.9	− 11.3	− 16.8
Long Beach	1,545	1,446	1,348	1,323	1,248
Percent change		− 6.4	− 12.7	− 14.4	− 19.2
San Francisco	1,940	1,736	1,737	1,606	1,340
Percent change		− 10.5	− 10.5	− 17.2	− 30.9
Oakland	1,728	1,591	1,522	1,458	1,402
Percent change		− 7.9	− 11.9	− 15.6	− 18.2
Fresno	1,364	1,386	1,348	1,310	n.a.
Percent change		+ 1.6	− 1.2	− 4.0	
Sacramento	1,516	1,484	1,506	1,421	1,326
Percent change		− 2.1	− 0.7	− 6.2	− 12.5
San Jose	1,530	1,444	1,428	1,374	1,273
Percent change		− 5.6	− 6.7	− 10.2	− 16.8

Source: Murdock, Mockler, and Associates, 1010 Eleventh Street, Sacramento, Calif. 95814.

Excluded are revenues for federal and state categorical programs such as special education, bilingual education, mandated state costs, and regional occupational programs. Thus general-purpose revenues are probably the best estimate of the total resources available for the regular education program. Hardest hit is San Francisco, which in terms of constant dollars has experienced a decline of over 30 percent in general purpose revenues per average daily attendance since 1977-1978. Four other cities—San Diego, Long Beach, Oakland, and San Jose—have each experienced declines exceeding 15 percent. Because all of these cities have had large declines in enrollments, the declines in total general-purpose revenues have been substantially greater than the declines per average daily attendance. Consequently, school boards have been forced to ruthlessly cut the regular education program.

Early indications of the magnitude of state funding for education in 1982-1983 show no signs that the erosion of school spending will abate. Faced with a deficit that may exceed $1 billion, Governor Brown has promised to make no cuts in the K-12 program, but inflation will continue to eat away at the school's purchasing power. Moreover, the effects of cuts in federal programs will begin to be felt severely in 1982-1983. Federal education programs are forward funded, meaning that funds appropriated for fiscal 1981-1982 are not spent by schools until the 1982-1983 school year. Final appropriations for federal education programs have not yet been made, and the administration is urging cuts of 30 to 40 percent from last year's levels. Should the administration succeed, total revenues for education in California will decline another 2 to 3 percent (federal funds are now about 8 percent of K-12 revenues in California). Because they depend more heavily on federal aid than most districts, three of the major cities—Oakland, San Diego, and San Francisco—will have declines 4 to 5 percent in total revenues if the administration obtains the maximum reduction it is requesting. Moreover, it appears that the annual enrollment declines that some California cities have been experiencing over the last five to ten years have now bottomed out and that average daily attendance will begin to grow again at a modest rate of about 1 percent per year.[13] Consequently, diminishing federal aid will have to be spread over a larger number of students.

It is important to remember that the effects of these reductions in spending have now been accumulating for some time, and their effects on the quality of public education are beginning to tell. Most one-time emergency responses have been exhausted. It is estimated that, statewide, schools have accumulated over $1.5 billion in deferred maintenance.[14] Expenditures on textbooks, supplies, and equipment have been severely curtailed. In many districts, students are not permitted to take home textbooks because the books must be shared with students in other classes. In many urban and rural schools, and a substantial number of suburban ones also, there is not a single computer to be found—despite the recent rhetoric on the importance of the three Cs (calculating, computing, and communicating). Most school-board members feel increasingly powerless to cope with such problems. They take the full brunt of teachers' and parents' frustrations but have no authority to seek the resources that would improve their local school systems. Indeed, so unappealing is serving on local school boards that there are now over four hundred vacant positions throughout the state, and ever-larger numbers of prospective board members run for election unopposed.

In short, even if the governor can protect public education from any new cuts in state spending, with the continuing effects of inflation and reductions in federal assistance, it is likely that in 1982-1983, California will be spending approximately 15 to 20 percent less per average daily attendance (when measured in constant dollars per average daily attendance) than it was in 1977-1978. In some of the large urban districts, the reductions will be even greater. For example, it is possible that next year San Francisco will have about 40 percent less per average daily attendance than it did in 1977-1978. Hundreds of other districts will have from 20 to 30 percent less than what they were spending prior to Proposition 13.

As the fiscal squeeze on public education in California continues to tighten, pressures will increase for some kind of relief. For some, the apparent solution is to abandon public education altogether, and they will be arguing strongly for tuition tax credits or vouchers. For others, the tradition of public education is important to sustain, but only if additional resources become available, preferably at the local level with some restoration of the link between responsibility for local spending and local power to raise revenues. Both approaches, private and public, are worth considering.

Privatizing Public Education

For those who recognize a legitimate interest of the state in supporting education but who completely despair of the state's ability to operate the schools efficiently and effectively, the most attractive alternatives to present arrangements for funding public education involve either tuition tax credits or vouchers. Both ideas have been around for some time. Adam Smith was one of the earliest advocates of vouchers for education, and the idea was later promoted by Thomas Paine.[15] More recently, Milton Friedman has been among those touting vouchers, and John Coons and Steve Sugarman are probably the most articulate contemporary spokesmen for the idea.[16] Tuition tax credits, while not enjoying such a long and illustrious history, are at least as old as the personal-income tax.

Both approaches share a number of common principles and features. Both place resources directly in the hands of the parent or student and, depending on the plan, may extend virtually unrestricted choice over schooling, including the right to instruct one's own children. Proponents of both types of plans typically place great faith in the ability of the market to achieve efficient allocation of resources. Both believe that the combination of expanded choice for consumers and competition among suppliers of education will whittle away, if not outright destroy, the cumbersome bureaucracy that has grown up around much of the public-education system. Both types of plans, in their generic forms, offer the state a substantial amount of flexibility in determining the level of public financing and the degree of the state's involvement in setting standards for admissions, curriculum, and staffing of eligible schools. However, there are important differences between the two approaches, and the specifics of each need to be clearly understood.

Tuition Tax Credits

Tuition tax credits are very popular with the Reagan administration and have been unofficially proposed as a possible substitute for the present involvement of the federal government in elementary and secondary education. The basic notion is quite simple. Parents or students are allowed to claim a specified percentage of tuition payments as a credit toward income taxes. Most plans set a limit on the maximum credit that may be claimed in any one year. For example, in the legislation now before Congress (S.543), the credit is limited to $250 in the first year of the program and would rise to $500 a year thereafter. [17] Designing a sensible tuition tax-credit plan requires settling four major issues: (1) what types of schools will be eligible to participate in the plan; (2) what constitutes acceptable tuition; (3) whether a credit resulting in a negative tax liability will lead to a cash refund; and (4) the amount of the credit and its public cost.

1. **Eligibility.** The recent furor that surrounded the Reagan administration's decision to reverse the well-established policy of denying tax-exempt status to schools practicing racial discrimination underscores the volatility of this aspect of any tax-credit plan. Most proposals disallow credits for payments to schools that discriminate on the basis of race, color, or national or ethnic origin. But there are other eligibility issues on which there is less consensus. Eligibility of religious schools, for example, is controversial and may not even be constitutional. Exclusion on the basis of sex also generates controversy and, should the Equal Rights Amendment (ERA) eventually pass, might also be unconstitutional. Other eligibility con-

cerns include accreditation, certification of teachers, and whether a core curriculum ought to be required. Most proponents of tax credits shy away from extensive eligibility restrictions, but often find they must compromise this position to gain political support.

2. **Defining Tuition**. Most plans struggle with what kinds of payments to schools will constitute creditable tuition; payments that include someone's transportation costs for a semester in Europe, for example, are likely to be politically embarrassing. In S.543, the definition of tuition excludes payments for books, supplies, equipment for courses of instruction, meals, lodging, and transportation.[18] Notice that the definition of creditable tuition raises clear equity issues. Excluding transportation, for example, solves the problem of the semester abroad, but it also discourages an inner-city family from opting to send their children to school in the suburbs or in a distant part of the city. Similarly, exclusions may indirectly encourage school administrators to levy substantial charges for excluded items in order to discourage attendance by low-income youth. Thus the definition of tuition may influence the cast of the student body in different types of schools. However, writing legislation that makes fine distinctions between what is acceptable and what is not is no simple task and may not be enforceable without substantial regulation, a feature that most proponents of tax credits would like to avoid.

3. **Refundability of a Negative Tax Liability**. Probably no aspect of a tax-credit plan has greater implications for the equity of the plan than the question of whether a negative liability is refundable in cash. In S.543, a negative credit is not refundable, and this effectively restricts the benefits of the plan (2 × $250 in the first year) to families of four with incomes in excess of $7,500. To enjoy the full benefit of the credit, a family of four would need an income in excess of $11,000. In the second year of the plan, when the credit rises to $500 for each child, a family of four would need an income in excess of $14,000 to enjoy the full benefit of the credit. Clearly, unless the credit is refundable, large numbers of low-income families are excluded from the benefits, and their numbers increase as the size of the credit rises. Moreover, these income figures apply to a federal plan. At the state level, where the income-tax liability may be typically 10 to 20 percent of the federal liability at any given income level, the full benefits of a credit of any size would accrue only to the very well-to-do. Why, then, do plans usually preclude refundability? Very simply, cost.

4. **Amount of the Credit and Public Cost**. Three variables will affect the cost of a tuition tax-credit plan: (a) the percentage of tuition that is creditable; (b) the maximum credit that may be claimed; and (c) whether

the credit is refundable. S.543 allows parents to credit only 50 percent of tuition payments.[19] As long as the maximum amount of the credit is low, the percentage of tuition creditable makes little difference. Everyone will be eligible for the maximum. But as the size of the maximum credit increases, the cost of the program can be controlled somewhat by reducing the percentage of tuition that is creditable. Presumably the rationale for such a policy is to encourage greater outlays for education. However, since the balance of tuition must be paid out of personal income, a reduction in the percentage of tuition covered will be borne more heavily by low-income families. Finally, refundability will greatly affect the cost of the plan. Sponsors of S.543 estimate that it will cost about $4.3 billion annually.[20] If the credit were refundable, the cost could be easily three times as much.

Despite the enthusiasm of the Reagan administration and some members of Congress for tuition tax credits, the notion has yet to prove politically popular. Obviously, strong supporters of public education, such as the teachers' unions, vigorously oppose such plans, fearing that they will produce a mass exodus to private schools. However, support from private schools is often lukewarm, if not absent completely. Many private-school administrators fear that tax credits could easily lead to increased government interference in their affairs. Given that private-school enrollments are up about 25 percent over the last decade, many private-school administrators see no reason to risk the problems that tax credits might generate.[21]

The latest proposal to introduce tuition tax credits was resoundingly defeated by voters. Last November [1981], residents of Washington, D.C. rejected a proposal for a $1,200-per-pupil tax credit by a margin of nine to one.[22] Interestingly, opposition ran very high in northwest Washington, the most affluent section of the city. The most frequently cited criticisms of the plan were that the credit benefitted the wealthy more than the poor and that it would damage the city's schools and other services by creating a severe drain on the city's treasury.[23] Although the Washington outcome may not be typical of voter attitudes everywhere, the defeat was a major setback for those advancing tax credits as an alternative means for financing public education. Consequently, interest may be increasing in another alternative: the voucher.

Education Vouchers

Advocates of education vouchers would have the state distribute funds for education directly to parents and students rather than to schools. Voucher recipients would then be free to select the school that best met their preferences for education, and as schools competed to meet the various demands of education consumers, presumably almost everyone's satisfaction with the educational system would increase. Although in some respects very similar to a tuition tax credit that is refundable, most voucher plans have a number of features that distinguish them from tax credits. Probably most important, voucher plans usually seek to provide a level of public support sufficient to purchase at least an adequate level of education.[24] Thus instead of reimbursing a percentage of tuition, up to some specified level, a voucher plan will cover the full cost. Consequently, voucher plans are much more expensive than tax credits and are usually intended to replace entire public-school finance arrangements. Therefore, they are seen as more appropriate for state policy, where major responsibility for education lies, rather than for federal programs.

In considering vouchers as an alternative to present arrangements for financing public education, it is important to understand that there is no generally accepted, single approach that has well-understood consequences for education. With the exception of a very modest experiment limited to public schools in Alum Rock, California, the United States has no experience with vouchers.[25] Consequently, predicting the outcomes of various voucher proposals is necessarily speculative and must consider carefully a number of important aspects.

1. **Base Amounts and Supplementation.** Almost all advocates of voucher plans for K-12 education agree that the state has an obligation to provide for all children an amount of money sufficient to purchase at least an adequate level of education. Unfortunately, what constitutes an adequate level is not easily determined. For example, should the sum be sufficient to cover the costs of elective courses, extracurricular activities, special counseling, remedial instruction, high-cost technical instruction, or special facilities (for example, swimming pools, gymnasiums, auditoriums, and so on)—some of these, all, or none? Should the amount take into account regional differences in the costs of providing various types of educational inputs and reflect differences in teacher-salary scales, costs of construction and maintenance, and so on?

Some plans beg the question of what should be properly included in an adequate education and instead establish the base amount as some percentage of what the state presently spends per student. Thus a recent proposal for a voucher initiative in California pegged the voucher amount at 90 percent of the current statewide average expenditures per unit of average daily attendance.[26] Such an approach seems more concerned with limiting the cost of the proposal than with struggling with the difficult question as to what the state is obligated to provide. Thus if one knows the size of the existing private-school enrollment and if one can estimate the number of students who will abandon the public schools for given levels of voucher funding, one can attempt to set the voucher amount at some fraction of the state average that is likely to produce no additional cost to the state for education. As long as the amount is less than the existing average amount per student, the state will make money on every student who leaves the public system, and these savings may be used to finance private-school students who previously received no state aid.

Assuming the base amount can be agreed upon, an equally troublesome question involves whether to allow parents to supplement the voucher with additional payments to schools. Permitting supplementation clearly benefits the wealthy, and one runs a high risk of creating a school system that is highly segregated by social class. Proponents of supplementation argue that such a system would probably not differ greatly from the existing public system where residential location effectively sorts public school students by social class. Moreover, denying supplementation will either reduce all education to a common level of mediocrity or will lead to devious schemes to get around the restriction. It would be extremely difficult, for example, to deny parents the right to supplement some kind of basic education with additional opportunities from other institutions that might grow up to provide a variety of specialized instruction from piano lessons to Mandarin.

One approach to permitting supplementation that does not so strongly disfavor the poor permits low-income families to purchase voucher supplements at prices below the voucher's market value.[27] Thus a family of four earning $10,000 a year might be asked to pay $100 for a voucher supplement worth $500, while a family earning $20,000 might be asked to pay $300, and a family earning $40,000 might be asked to pay the full amount. More difficult to administer than a system that prohibits supplementation or one that does not subsidize supplementation, the approach could nevertheless be adopted without great difficulty in any state with a broad-based personal-income tax. Some attention must also be paid to preventing the black market in vouchers that could develop if some simple precautions against transferability are not instituted. In short, equitable methods of supplementation can be devised, but they increase the plan's cost, sometimes very substantially.

2. School Standards and Admission Requirements. The same issues of eligibility that arise regarding tax credits apply to vouchers, and most plans deny vouchers to schools practicing racial or ethnic discrimination. However, some voucher proposals go much further than tax-credit plans in regulating participating schools. A primary concern is admissions policy. Successfully competing for students in the newly created education market would depend greatly on a school's ability to demonstrate excellence. However, what constitutes excellence is not well understood, and it is feared by many educators that competitive pressures will encourage schools to demonstrate educational excellence by admitting only excellent students. To prevent this creaming, some voucher plans provide that schools must admit any student who applies and that schools that are oversubscribed must admit by lottery.[28]

Another important facet of admissions concerns the attendance areas of existing public schools. For example, a voucher initiative recently proposed for California permits school districts to designate some or all of their public schools as voucher schools; however, the initiative retains existing school-district boundaries and does not require districts to admit students from other districts.[29] Thus the affluent city of Piedmont, which is completely surrounded by the city of Oakland, would be free to participate in the voucher plan while maintaining schools that are closed to Oakland residents living only a few blocks away. Expansion of choice for the residents of Oakland is therefore rather illusory.

3. Coordination with Categorical Funding and Other Administrative Issues. A central tenet of most voucher advocates is that vouchers would greatly reduce the administrative bureaucracy that is present in much of public education. This may be wishful thinking, for there are a number of tasks the state would be forced to assume once the existing structure of district administration is dismantled. First is the problem of achieving compatibility of a voucher system with various federal categorical programs for compensatory education and for handicapped students. Pressures for consolidation notwithstanding, current indications are that Congress will continue to operate at least two major categorical programs that retain the general objectives of ESEA Title I and P.L. 94-142 (The Education for All Handicapped Children Act).[30] A large number of diagnostic procedures and other special services now performed by school districts would need to be taken over by the state. Similarly, the state would become completely responsible for administering compulsory attendance laws, nondiscrimination provisions of state and federal law, and the like. Instead of dealing with a relatively small number of school districts, a state the size of California would be forced to deal directly with several-thousand schools or millions of school children. Making the necessary administrative changes is not impossible, but a successful transition will depend on much more careful consideration of the problem than has yet been demonstrated by any of the voucher plans to date.

In short, while vouchers raise a number of attractive possibilities for returning to parents and students a substantial degree of lost control over schooling, the plans also raise a number of difficult questions that have yet to be answered satisfactorily. The many unresolved problems have caused proponents to move slowly, but it is likely that the next two to four years will see a number of serious proposals put forth for public consideration. That likelihood has stimulated others to pursue possible innovations within the public system, and we now turn to briefly considering three of those possibilities.

Innovations within Public Eduation

For many concerned with the current state of public education in California, the problems posed by tax credits or vouchers have no likely political resolution; yet these same people readily acknowledge that the level of public frustration with the schools is reaching crisis proportions. Of paramount concern is the growing sense of powerlessness expressed by many parents to influence local education practices, and at least three ideas are beginning to take shape that might help to return a modicum of control over local schools and a sense of involvement in educational affairs. These include: (1) new possibilities for local control over incremental financing; (2) redistricting; and (3) increased choice within the public system. Ironically, insofar as these constitute real opportunities, they arise mainly because of the newly centralized control the state presently enjoys over public education.

New Local Sources of Revenue

Given California's history with tax and expenditure limitations, it will surely seem to some that proposing new local taxes for education is at worst hopelessly naive and at best wishful thinking. However, there are indications that some communities are willing to vote new local taxes if a strong case can be made that local services are deteriorating. Thus a few communities have voted special taxes for libraries, as well as for police and fire services.[31] Moreover, as Proposition 13's 2-percent limit on assessment increases (until the sale of property at which time the parcel is reassessed at full market value), greatly diminishing the tax bill of many residents relative to inflation, local voters are likely to feel that new taxes are more affordable.[32] There are, however, two major obstacles to voting new local revenues for education.

First, there is the problem that under existing school finance arrangements in California, any increase in local revenue must be used to offset state aid under the base-revenue limit. Not only does this provision completely discourage raising new taxes for education, but it also discourages seeking many kinds of efficiency in existing operations. Thus, for example, many districts operate a number of severely underutilized schools, but since revenue from the sale or lease of these schools would simply offset base-revenue-limit income, there is little incentive to close inefficient schools.[33] Second, there is the problem that, even if the offset provisions of current school finance law were altered, *Serrano* would require at the very least that new local taxes produce equal amounts per student for equal effort. From the point of view of local school districts, both of these problems are insurmountable, and they correctly perceive that any attempt to raise additional funds for education would be pointless.

Both problems, however, are within the reach of state policy. First, removing the offset provisions is a simple legislative matter. The provisions were originally instituted to enable the state to make progress toward the expenditure equalization required by *Serrano*. As long as districts had local-property-taxing power, the spending of wealthy districts had to be restricted in order to achieve compliance. However, Proposition 13 has completely equalized local-property-tax rates and removed local control over this source of revenue. Moreover, the vast majority of California's school districts have now been brought within $100 to $200 of equal expenditures per student.[34] The disparities will continue to narrow as inflation erodes the base-revenue limits of the previously high-wealth districts. Hence there is little reason to prohibit local districts from adding on to base-revenue limits from local sources of income, provided such sources could be power equalized to meet the dictates of *Serrano*.

By power equalized, we mean that all districts must be guaranteed an equal amount per student for an equal tax rate. Prior to Proposition 13, power equalization as a solution to *Serrano* was opposed because it necessarily involved a substantial redistribution of resources from property-wealthy districts to property-poor districts. It was common to find disparities of assessed value of a factor of ten to fifteen to one among school districts, and equalization of the relationship between spending and tax effort would therefore involve the state's recapturing a significant amount of local revenue.[35] Proposition 13, of course, has eliminated the property tax as a source of new revenue, but local sales taxes and local income taxes remain viable possibilities.

In some respects, a local add-on to the sales tax is probably the more acceptable of the two possibilities. The state has previous experience with local sales taxes, and voters are generally more willing to vote a regressive local tax rather than a progressive local tax. However, the local disparities in sales-tax base per capita are even greater than former disparities in property-tax base per capita, and a policy that continued the present practice of returning local sales taxes to the district of origin would surely be challenged under the *Serrano* principle.[36] Thus if the sales tax is to be a legally acceptable source of local revenue for schools, the state would have to depart from past practices and allow local districts to levy a tax against a statewide guaranteed base. This is not an insurmountable problem but runs the risk of opening the entire local sales tax (that is, that which is currently levied for local expenditures on nonschool services) to political and judicial scrutiny.

Surprisingly, of the three major tax bases—property, sales, and income—the income-tax base per capita displays the smallest disparities among local jurisdictions, rarely exceeding four to one. Consequently, allowing districts to levy locally voted income taxes for schools might escape legal challenges. Moreover, for a rather modest cost, the state could avoid all legal action by establishing a guaranteed yield per pupil in income-poor school districts.

What are the prospects that school districts would be successful in obtaining voter approval of an income-tax add-on for elementary and secondary education? Although levied in other parts of the country, local income taxes are unprecedented in California. Clearly, a strong case would have to be made for additional support for public education. The appeal would probably be most convincing in the smaller districts where residents know one another and could be more confident that the funds would be spent effectively. These are some of the same districts that have already mounted successful fund-raising campaigns for private donations to the public schools, and a local income tax would provide a means of simply making this effort official and tithing the free riders who took advantage of the opportunity to escape the costs but enjoy the benefits of collective action. In short, success would most likely depend on being small, and in this respect, the large urban districts would be placed at a distinct disadvantage. Thus if the ability to levy an equalized local income tax were to be truly accessible to all, it is likely that the state would have to provide for the dissolution of the state's larger districts into smaller units that would have a greater chance of achieving political consensus on increased local spending for schools.

Redistricting

Of the 1,044 school districts operating in California during 1976-1977, only 36, or less than 4 percent, had total average daily attendance of more than 20,000.[37] Yet these 36 districts accounted for nearly 40 percent of total average daily attendance in the state. One district, Los Angeles Unified School District, accounted for nearly 15 percent of the state's average daily attendance. In short, approximately half the state's elementary and secondary students reside in relatively small school districts, while the remainder reside in very large districts. If, for purposes of gathering support for new revenues for public education, it pays to be small, then nearly half the state's students are at a distinct disadvantage.

School-district consolidation was a major thrust to the 1950s and 1960s, and for a number of very small elementary and high-school districts, consolidation has undoubtedly offered some important advantages. But most research on the topic suggests that insofar as there are economies of scale in education, they typically disappear when a district exceeds 20,000 students, and even then scale economies are more important in terms of school size rather than size of the district.[38]

However, school-district size is, in many respects, an historical artifact: the result of development trends that no one could have predicted easily and an outcome that is exceedingly difficult to reverse once it has been achieved. Moreover, the dependence on local property taxes for revenues for schools, in combination with the huge tax-base disparities that evolved over time, made it almost impossible to attempt large-scale reorganization of school-district boundaries.

Quite coincidentally, Proposition 13 has changed the politics of redistricting. For the first time in over thirty years, disparities in property-tax bases mean nothing to the definition of school-district boundaries and spending disparities are narrowing quickly. Consequently, for state's largest school districts, there is suddenly the opportunity to create a number of smaller independent jurisdictions free of the fiscal squabbling that would have accompanied such proposals in the past. Ironically, Proposition 13, by having centralized financing at the state level, has created the opportunity to break up large districts into smaller, more manageable and responsive units and to place opportunities for local finance of schools on a more equitable basis.

Such redistricting is wholly within the plenary power of the legislature. Never before has the state enjoyed an opportunity for redistricting less subject to local opposition. There are numerous possibilities for returning an important degree of local control over schooling while simultaneously relieving the state of full fiscal responsibility for K-12 education.

Expanding Public Choices

A third approach to returning control over schooling to the local area involves removing many of the existing restrictions on attendance patterns. Most parents have very little choice over what public schools their children may attend. In some cases, the choice is restricted because of the district's efforts to meet desegration guidelines, but more often, the choice is limited simply because of the way the district has defined attendance areas. Consequently, it is not uncommon to find children traveling relatively long distances to school because they are barred from a nearby school in a neighboring district or in a different attendance area.

Given the changes that have occurred in school finance since Proposition 13, there seems little reason to allow these restrictions to persist. With the state now picking up the full cost of K-12 education, there is no longer any economic rationale for excluding children in a neighboring district. There are some political difficulties; school policy is set by a local board elected by residents of the district, and parents in neighboring districts are therefore excluded from educational policymaking. However, the widespread use of school-site parent advisory councils would give most parents access to most of the daily aspects of their children's education.

Removing the restrictions on where parents must send their children to school would open up possibilities for parents to pursue another option: selecting a school close to their place of work rather than their home. In the vast majority of the families with school-age children both parents now work, and for them, having their children attend a school close to home has much less significance than formerly, when the mother often stayed home during the day. Not only would attending school near the work place reduce many parents' anxieties about being nearby in the event of emergencies, but also it would greatly simplify day-care arrangements because parents could organize with fellow workers to provide after-school supervision, either at the work place or at a nearby facility.

Organizing school attendance around the work place might help alleviate another problem: desegration. In most areas, the work place is far less segregated than residential neighborhoods. Moreover, because parents have the opportunity to get to know one another at work, some of the racial and ethnic tensions that accompany desegregation when the children and parents of a child's schoolmates are unknown may be greatly reduced. Finally, the problem of a child being bussed off to a school in a direction opposite from that traveled by the parent to work, further aggravating parental worries, would be eliminated. Children might still travel substantial distances to school, but they would ride with their parents.

In sum, in the wake of Proposition 13, district boundaries are archaic, needlessly inhibiting parents' choice of schools within the public system. If there are advantages to maintaining the district structure for administrative reasons—and a strong case can be made for doing so—then a relatively simple system of tuition transfers among districts would greatly expand parents' opportunities. This, combined with an explicit guarantee that parents would have access to schools near where they work, might open some interesting possibilities for making public schools more desirable.

Conclusion

Deserved or not, California has long had the reputation of being the harbinger of things to come. The state was the first to embark on radical tax and spending limitations, and since 1978, a number of other states have followed suit. To many in other states, the early euphoria that followed Proposition 13, when it appeared that taxpayers had secured a huge tax saving at no cost to services, must have seemed impossible to resist. But the costs of Proposition 13 are just now beginning to be understood. As indicated in the first section, the financial underpinnings of public education in California have deteriorated to an alarming degree, and the same is true of other public services. The current state of affairs provides a good indicator of what is in store for other states, most notably Massachusetts where Proposition 2½ has already cut deeply into school budgets.

However, out of crisis also comes opportunity, and once again California may lead the way. The state is presently entertaining a number of interesting possibilities. Whether the citizens of California will opt to abandon public education completely, adopting a broad-based system of tax credits or vouchers, or whether they will choose to unlock some of the constraints on local financing and parental choice remains to be seen. But in either event, it seems likely that in finding a way out of the difficulties that confront California's schools, public education may be completely transformed.

Notes

1. National Center for Education Statistics, *The Condition of Education: 1979 Edition* (Washington, D.C.: U.S. Government Printing Office, 1979), Stock No. 017-080-02008-4, Table 4.3, p. 146.

2. California State Department of Education, *California Public Schools Selected Statistics 1977-78* (Sacramento, Calif.: Office of State Printing, 1979), Table III-2B, p. 18.

3. For an excellent synopsis of school-finance reform in California, as well as a detailed explanation of current finance requirements, see Paul M. Goldfinger, *Revenue and Revenue Limits* (Belmont, Calif.: Star Publishing, 1981).

4. *Serrano v. Priest*, 18C.3d728 (1976).

5. Goldfinger, *Revenue and Revenue Limits*, pp. 1-3.

6. California State Department of Education, *California Public Schools Selected Statistics 1977-78*, Table IV-14, pp. 87 and 103.

7. Ibid., Table IV-14, p. 103.

8. *Serrano v. Priest*, Judgment, August 30, 1974 at paragraph 3(c).

9. For a full description of district power equalizing, see Coons, John E.; Clune, William H.; and Sugarman, Stephan D., *Private Wealth and Public Education* (Cambridge, Mass.: Harvard University Press, 1970).

10. Goldfinger, *Revenue and Revenue Limits*, pp. 3-4.

11. California Assembly Bill No. 8 (Chapter 282, Statutes of 1979).

12. National Center for Education Statistics, *The Condition of Education*, Chart 4.5, p. 151.

13. Enrollment trends and projections for Los Angeles Unified School District, the state's largest district, show that enrollments in elementary grades bottomed out in 1980-1981; enrollments in grades 7-12 are expected to stabilize in 1984-1985 and then begin growing slowly. Figures obtained from the Education and Management System Assessment Office, Los Angeles Unified School District, 450 North Grand Avenue, Los Angeles, Calif.

14. California State Department of Education, Division of Financial Services, January 1982.

15. Smith, Adam, *The Wealth of Nations* (New York: Random House, The Modern Library Edition, 1937); Thomas Paine, *The Rights of Man*.

16. Friedman, Milton, "The Role of Government in Education," in *Capitalism and Freedom* (Chicago: University of Chicago Press, 1962), Chapter VI; Coons, John E., and Sugarman, Stephan D., *Education by Choice* (Berkeley: University of California Press, 1980).

17. "Tax Credit Launched in Senate," *Education USA* 23, no. 28 (March 9, 1981):223.

18. Ibid.

19. Ibid.

20. Ibid.

21. "Prep Schools Favor Tax Credits, But. . . ," in *Education USA* 23, no. 28 (March 9, 1981):221.

22. "D.C. Voters Reject Tax Credit," *The Washington Post*, Electronic Edition: Compuserve Network, 4 November 1981.

23. Ibid.

24. See Coons, John E., and Sugarman, Stephan D., *Education by Choice*.

25. Weiler, Daniel et al., *A Public School Voucher Demonstration: The First Year at Alum Rock* (Santa Monica, Calif.: The Rand Corporation, June 1974).

26. Authors of the initiative are John E. Coons and Stephan D. Sugarman. Backers recently decided not to pursue obtaining the necessary signatures for placing the measure on the California ballot in 1982; they have indicated that they will resume their drive in 1984.

27. This idea was developed by Charles S. Benson, *The Economics of Public Education*, 3rd ed. (New York: Houghton Mifflin, 1979).

28. See, for example, Coons, John E., and Sugarman, Stephan D., *Education by Choice*.

29. See note 26.

30. "Reform of Handicapped Education Law May Elude Administration," *Education USA* 24, no. 10 (November 2, 1981):73.

31. The city of Berkeley, in 1980, approved a local square-footage tax for supporting local libraries and will vote on a similar tax for other municipal services in March 1982.

32. Proposition 13 rolled back property assessments to their 1976-1977 levels, and as long as the property does not change ownership, the assessment may increase by no more than 2 percent per year. Consequently, the tax bill of a homeowner who has lived in the same house since 1977 has risen by only 8 percent, while the consumer price index (CPI) has risen 54 percent and, in many areas of the state, home prices have more than doubled.

33. Commission on California State Government Organization and Economy, "The Los Angeles Unified School District," Sacramento, Calif.: 11th and L Building, Suite 550, 95814, June 1981.

34. Goldfinger, *Revenue and Revenue Limits.*

35. Benson, Charles S., et al, *Final Report for the Senate Select Committee on School District Finance* (Sacramento, Calif.: 1972).

36. Hoachlander, E. Gareth, "The Search for Equity in State-Local Finance: The Serrano Legacy," in *Papers of the Conference on Local Government Decisions and the Local Tax Base* (University of Southern California Law Center: The Lincoln Institute, February 1979).

37. California State Department of Education, *California Public Schools Selected Statistics, 1977-78*, Table II-2, p. 4.

38. For a review of the literature on scale economies in education, see Fox, William F., "Reviewing Economies of Size in Education," *Journal of Education Finance* 6, no. 3 (Winter 1981):273-296.

8 Financing Alternatives Available to Local Governments

Patrick C. Coughlan

Since the passage of Proposition 13 in June 1978, both the state and local governments in California have been looking for alternatives for financing essential public services. The full impact of Proposition 13 started being felt in the fiscal year beginning July 1981. Earlier many local governments had surplus funds available to them; those that did not were able to rely upon bail-out funds furnished by the state of California. It has become patently obvious, however, that the state government is no longer in a position to extend substantial aid to local governments. In addition, many state and local entities have experienced severe cutbacks in federal funds.

This chapter will present the various creative financing alternatives that cities are exploring.

Traditional Sources of Funding for Various Governmental Activities

Depending upon the activity involved, some governmental services have been financed by user fees, some by the property tax, and others by assessments based upon benefits received. In order to understand the current attempts to increase their financial bases, it is important to know how governmental services were originally financed. The following discussion is general. A government's need for new revenue sources after Proposition 13 depends considerably on how much it had been relying on property-tax revenues before 1978.

Public Infrastructure

Public works, such as sewer, water, drainage and roads, and physical improvements with low ongoing maintenance costs, were once financed by either assessment districts with one-time assessments levied against individual properties or by general obligation bonds. In recent years, even prior to Proposition 13, these methods of financing which required voter approval were not popular and had been displaced to a considerable extent by grants from higher levels of government supplemented by local general-

147

tax funds. Although the legal capacity to levy special assessments has not been eliminated by Propositions 13 and 4 (see *County of Fresno* v *Malmstrom*, 94 Cal. App. 3d 974 [1979]), the ability of cities to repay general obligation bonds out of property-tax revenues has been greatly affected.

As developments were built, cities usually demanded that the developer pay for streets, curbs, gutters, sidewalks, and in many cases improve the adjoining arterial street to cities' standards. Street maintenance was then undertaken by local government so long as the street was public. Drainage, water, and sewer facilities were similarly funded.

Local governments are now looking to developers not only to pay for constructing public works, but also to devise funding mechanisms for maintaining such facilities. Maintenance costs may be assumed by home-owners-association fees or landscape and lighting district assessments; there are drawbacks to both approaches. Unlike local property taxes, the fees paid to a home-owners association are not tax deductible to the home owner. The use of the Street Lighting and Landscape Maintenance District Act for maintenance of roads in general is of questionable legality.

Police and Sheriff Services

Police and sheriff services are extremely expensive and have traditionally been financed by general tax funds, usually property and sales taxes. Those cities that have been property-tax dependent have suffered greatly in their ability to provide efficient and effective services. A number of jurisdictions have attempted to place a tax measure on the ballot that would specifically raise funds for police or fire services. Since a direct ad valorum tax based upon the value of property is no longer permissible under Proposition 13, various flat-fee formulas have been used by cities. A few cities, Palos Verdes Estates among them, have been successful in imposing a Public Safety Special Tax.

Fire Services

Fire services also have relied heavily on general funds for their support. Many parts of the state are serviced by fire districts that rely exclusively upon property-tax revenues. Fire, like police, services are viewed as important by most electors and a number of cities have attempted to pass special taxes to support their fire services. Of course, proceeds from these special tax measures may enable the city to divert to other purposes general-tax funds previously spent for fire and police services.

Planning

Planning services have traditionally been supported by a combination of general-tax funds and user fees. Prior to the passage of Proposition 13 user fees generally did not fully reimburse communities for the planning services they provided. Many cities have conducted studies to determine the costs of planning services and are attempting to recover these costs fully from developers. Fees charged for planning services may include such items as overhead, administrative time, and even legal counsel. The more sophisticated cities, rather than adopt a flat fee, establish a fee based upon actual costs. Planning staff are required to keep records specific enough to allow the city to assess the developers the actual costs of processing each case. Payment must be made prior to the issuance of any of the necessary permits.

**Financing Alternatives Available to
Local Governmental Entities**

Cities are looking primarily to four potential sources of income to cover what might otherwise become substantial deficits in their budgets: (1) user fees and charges; (2) benefit assessments; (3) higher levels of taxation on business property; and (4) increases in special taxes generally.

    1. *Service Fees or Charges.* Service fees or charges are not new to local government and many cities have been charging for the use of parks, public transportation, and the like. But many communities are now charging for services that were previously provided free such as instructional classes, baseball clinics, and so forth.

    Since user charges and fees can be enacted by local governments without the consent of the citizens, they are the easiest to impose and therefore the most attractive to local government. Although the Gann initiative (Article XIIIB of the California Constitution, known as Proposition 4) specifically limited regulatory permit fees to the cost of regulation, the city is given discretion in accounting for such fees and may include overhead and administrative costs. In the case of *United* v. *San Diego*, 91 Cal. App. 3d 156, the court determined that the cost of regulation is a legislative matter.

    Consequently, specific findings are not necessary in setting fees, and courts will uphold any fee that is not patently arbitrary. The court upheld variable, classified, or graduated permit fees, and acknowledged that locally enacted exceptions, if reasonable, would be valid. San Diego had imposed a 100-percent penalty for failure to pay fees, and the court also upheld the penalty.

Cities may also charge more for nonresidents to use recreational facilities than they charge residents. See *Hawaii* v. *Water*, 651 F. 2d 661 (1981).

2. *Benefit Assessments.* Benefit assessments were a traditional method of financing capital improvements such as streets, lighting, sidewalks, and landscaping, authorized by a variety of California statutes such as the Municipal Improvement Acts of 1911 and 1913, the Open Space Maintenance Act, and the Lighting and Landscaping Act of 1972. Assessments may be placed on an individual's tax bill and therefore are fairly easy to collect.

The use of benefit assessments, however, is limited. The property being assessed must be enhanced in value by the improvements and the assessment levied in reasonable proportion to the benefits received. This form of levy is restricted to local capital improvements likely to increase the value of the abutting assessed property. Some public facilities and services are thought inappropriate for special assessment because the benefits are difficult to localize, such as fire and police protection.

Many governments are attempting to levy special assessments to cover maintenance charges. However, the assessment acts do not specifically authorize this use. The California legislature is considering a bill that would provide that authorization.

3. *Capital Contributions by Developers.* Although some local governments looked to developers before Proposition 13 to provide project-related public facilities, since Proposition 13 all local governments require developers to construct the public improvements necessitated by their developments. These requirements have expanded in recent years to include contributions from developers for fire stations, parks, and other public facilities.

A number of city attorneys feel that developers may appropriately be charged fees to offset the impacts of their projects on public facilities if the fee is demonstrably related to an impact of the proposed development and the money raised will be used directly to mitigate the impact. The coastal commission has been charging fees for low-income housing for a number of years on the theory that when new projects occasion the demolition of low-and moderate-income housing, developers may appropriately be required to fund replacement housing.

The attorney general of the state of California, 62 Att'y Gen. Op 673 (1979), has opined that fees for housing, fire, and police services are special taxes and therefore impermissible without the two-thirds electorate approval required by Proposition 13 and possibly illegal on other grounds even with the two-thirds voter approval.

4. *Home-Owner-Association Charges.* Many cities are requiring developers to provide for home-owner associations to maintain within their

subdivisions streets, parks, sidewalks, gutters, and sewers. Since these charges are created by contract, they are not ostensibly subject to Proposition 13's limitations.

5. *Special Taxes*. Proposition 13 allows cities and other governmental entities to adopt special taxes if approved by two-thirds of the electorate. Tables 8-1 and 8-2 list the special taxes enacted by various local governments in southern California. The difficulty in obtaining a two-thirds vote should not be underestimated. However, communities seem to be resorting to it more and more.

6. *Joint-Powers Agreements*. Cities and counties are finding it more economical to join forces in providing services to their constituents. A number of cities have entered joint-powers agreements for fire, police, and maintenance services. These creative responses by governments can save a great deal of money in the long term.

7. *Donations*. Some cities have solicited donations from their citizens to help cover the costs of essential government services. San Marino has been fairly successful in its efforts along these lines.

8 . *Donations from Developers*. Some cities have made it fairly clear to developers that projects probably will not be approved unless the developer can find some way to mitigate the impacts on police, fire, or other general services. A number of developers have responded by donating park sites, fire cars, police cars, fire engines, and, on occasion, public buildings.

9. *Financial Trade-Offs*. Cities with redevelopment agencies are using them to obtain general funds. Often a developer seeking approval of a subdivision tract map will contribute generously to various city projects in exchange for a redevelopment agency's financing and constructing some of the public facilities located within the tract. This approach can only work when the tract is actually within a designated redevelopment area. This exchange can be useful to a city even when the developer's contributed dollars are exactly equal to the project costs incurred by the redevelopment agency on the developer's behalf because profits accumulated by a redevelopment agency cannot ordinarily be spent by the city for general purposes.

10. *Service Charges*. Service charges by municipal water, electrical- and sewer-service providers, like user fees, must bear a direct relationship to actual costs; but also like user fees, a city has great latitude in calculating the overhead to be incorporated into these charges. These fees are being increased to provide reserves for future capital improvements.

11. *Fire Fee*. At least one city has imposed a fee on its residents for fire-protection services. Article 13 would raise legal barriers to such a fee except that the city involved was taking over a service previously provided by a volunteer fire department. A community can probably finance any service never previously provided by service fees as long as the fee is directly related to the cost of the service.

Table 8-1
Types of Taxes That California Cities Have Adopted

Type of Tax	Rate	Method of Collection
1. Transient Occupancy Tax	Percentage of room charge	Collected quarterly from operator who adds tax to each room-rental charge
2. Real Property Transfer Tax	27.5 per $500 paid for transferred property interest	Collected from seller or buyer
3. Business License Tax	a. Flat rate based upon gross receipts	Collected from business upon issuance of annual license which is required to lawfully operate within city
	b. Flat rate based upon number of employees	
	c. Flat rate per business regardless of gross receipts or number of employees	
4. Oil Production Tax	a. Flat rate per barrel of oil produced	Collected quarterly from operator
	b. Annual permit fee for each pumping well	Collected from operator when annual permit issued
5. Commercial Tenant Tax	$1.25 per $1,000 of rent paid by tenant per quarter	Collected quarterly from lessor who adds tax to rental charge
6. Employee's License Fee (gross receipts occupation tax)	Percentage of city-derived earnings	Collected quarterly from employer who withholds tax from employee's paycheck. Applied to both resident and nonresident employees
7. Payroll Expense Tax	Percentage of payroll paid to employee by employer	Collected from employer
8. Admissions Tax (usually imposed upon athletic events, concerts, theatrical events)	a. Flat rate per admission	Collected from operator who adds tax to admission price
	b. Graduated flat rate which increases as admission price increases	
	c. Percentage of gross receipts received from sale of tickets	Collected from operator

9. Special Events Tax (athletic events, concerts, lectures)	Flat rate per event	Collected from operator
10. Gaming Tax	a. Gross revenue license fee: graduated percentage of gross receipts which increases as receipts increase b. License fee: flat rate for specified number of tables c. Annual permit fee per club	Collected monthly from operator Collected annually upon issuance of license
11. Property Development Tax (Environmental Excise Tax)	a. Flat rate per square foot of gross floor area of new construction b. Percentage of value of new structures constructed	Collected when building permit issued
12. Park and Recreation Facilities Construction Tax (all revenues placed into special park fund)	Flat rate per square foot of gross floor area constructed	Collected when building permit issued
13. Sewer Use Tax	a. Flat rate based upon cubic feet of water consumed not to exceed maximum amount b. Flat rate per unit	Collected from consumer by adding tax to billing for city-provided utilities
14. Utility Users Tax (electricity, gas, water, telephone, cable television, refuse collection)	Percentage of charge for particular utility	Collected monthly from provider of utility service who adds tax to billing to consumer (senior citizen exemption commonly applied)
15. Parking Tax	Percentage of charge for use of parking space not to exceed maximum amount	Collected monthly from operator who adds tax to charge paid by user for parking space

Note: Some cities provide that a particular tax rate will be automaticaly adjusted annually based upon the increase in the Consumer Price Index. (CPI).

Table 8-2
Specific Tax Rates of California Cities

Type of Tax	Cities That Have Adopted This Type of Tax	Specific Tax Rate Imposed
1. Transient Occupancy Tax	Arcadia	4 percent of room-rental charge.
	Avalon	7 percent of room-rental charge.
	Azusa	5 percent of room-rental charge.
	Beverly Hills	7 percent of room-rental charge.
	Burbank	6 percent of room-rental charge.
	Carson	6 percent of room-rental charge.
	Fresno	6 percent of room-rental charge.
	Gardena	5 percent of room-rental charge.
	Inglewood	7 percent of room-rental charge.
	Livermore	6 percent of room-rental charge.
	Los Angeles	7.5 percent of room-rental charge.
	Palm Springs	7 percent of room-rental charge.
	Pasadena	6 percent of room-rental charge.
	Newport Beach	6 percent of room-rental charge.
	Rancho Palos Verdes	6 percent of room-rental charge.
	San Bernardino	6 percent of room-rental charge.
	San Diego	6 percent of room-rental charge.
	Santa Ana	5 percent of room-rental charge.
	Seal Beach	6 percent of room-rental charge.
	South El Monte	5 percent of room-rental charge.
2. Real Property Transfer Tax	Avalon	27.5¢ per $500 paid for transferred property interest.
	Beverly Hills	
	Carson	
	Cerritos	
	Fresno	
	Gardena	
	Los Angeles	
	Newport Beach	
	Pasadena	
	Rancho Palos Verdes	

Tax	City	Rate
3. Business License Tax	San Fernando, Seal Beach, South El Monte	Rates vary substantially. See text of ordinances set forth in Section 4, pp. 17-67.
	Adopted by most California cities	
4. Oil Production Tax	Long Beach (oil-well permit)	$800. per each new well for first year, $35. to $100. per well each year thereafter.
	Los Angeles	$5. per quarter for each oil well producing four hundred barrels or less, plus 12.5¢ for each barrel of oil produced by each such well in excess of four hundred barrels.
	Seal Beach	12¢ for each barrel of oil produced.
5. Commercial Tenant Occupancy Tax	Los Angeles	$1.25 per 1,000 of rent paid by tenant per quarter.
6. Employee's License Fee	Oakland	1 percent of city-derived gross earnings that exceed $1,625 per quarter.
7. Payroll Expense Tax	San Francisco	1 percent of payroll expense for persons employed within city.
8. Admissions Tax	Arcadia	20¢ per admission less than $2; 25¢ per $2-$3 admission; 30¢ per $3-$4 admission; 35¢ per $4-$7 admission; 40¢ per admission exceeding $7.
	Avalon	4 percent of gross receipts from sale of tickets for any type of amusement or entertainment.
	Fresno	5¢ per admission.
	Inglewood	35¢ per admission.
	Irwindale	10¢ per admission of $1 or less; 15¢ per $1-$2 admission; 20¢ per $2-$3 admission; 25¢ per admission exceeding $3.
	Pasadena (Rose Bowl Admission Tax)	5¢ per admission of $1 or less, plus 5¢ for each additional dollar thereafter not to exceed a maximum tax of 50¢ per admission.
9. Special Events Tax	Newport Beach	$25 per event.

Table 8-2 *(continued)*

Type of Tax	*Cities That Have Adopted This Type of Tax*	*Specific Tax Rate Imposed*
10. Gaming Tax	Bell Gardena	See text of ordinance set forth in Section 4, p. 93-121.
11. Property Development Tax (Environmental Excise Tax)	Newport Beach	15¢ per square foot of gross floor area constructed.
	Pasadena	5¢ of value of structure constructed.
	Rancho Palos Verdes	30¢ per square foot of gross floor area constructed.
	Seal Beach	1¢ per square foot of gross floor area constructed.
12. Park and Recreation Facilities Construction Tax	Beverly Hills	$2 per square foot of gross floor area constructed.
13. Sewer Use Tax	Pasadena	4.5¢ per 100 cubic feet of water consumed.
	Santa Ana	50¢ per month per unit for properties with one-four residential, commercial, or industrial units; $4 per month for five or more such units.
14. Utility Users Tax	Cerritos	10 percent of utility charge.
	Fresno	4.6 percent of utility charge.
	Inglewood	10 percent of utility charge.
	Los Angeles	5 percent of utility charge.
	pasadena	7 percent of utility charge.
	Riverside	5 percent of utility charge.
	Santa Ana	3 percent of utility charge.
	Santa Barbara	3 percent of utility charge.
	Seal Beach	5 percent of utility charge.
15. Parking Tax	Inglewood	15 percent of parking charge not to exceed 15¢ per vehicle per day.

12. *Franchise Fees.* A number of communities are looking to franchise fees as a method of raising revenue, particularly to cable television fees. A franchise fee is generally viewed as a contractual arrangement in which the franchisee is paying the franchisor for the use of the franchisor's streets and rights of way. Cable television franchise fees are limited by the federal government to a maximum of 5 percent of gross revenues. Some companies are offering to prepay franchise fees in sums of $750,000 to $1,000,000. Such fees can be a tremendous help to a city short of cash.

13. *Contracting of Governmental Services.* Although not a financing alternative specifically, many governmental entities have discovered that they can contract with private companies for services previously provided by the city at a substantially reduced cost. The dollar savings involve salaries, overhead, and, particularly, retirement costs.

Impact of Alternatives

Whether a community decides to levy special assessments, user charges, or general taxes, each has a different impact.

User charges have the advantage that the users pay their own way. Carefully monitored user charges can perform some of the functions of a pricing system by giving public-service providers information about the quality and quantity of service the public really desires. However, for services heavily used by the poor, the move to user charges can be viewed as regressive and especially harsh when the service has traditionally been supported by general tax funds. The harshness of the shift is felt just as keenly when the city elects to have the service provided by a private contractor who charges users for it.

The same advantages and drawbacks apply to assessment district financing when property owners pay for benefits received. Benefits provided to poorer areas may affect those owners and occupants least able to pay.

The imposition of special taxes and fees have varied impacts. Taxes aimed at the business community may impair those businesses' abilities to compete with firms outside the city or, if the taxes and fees are passed to the ultimate consumer, will result in higher prices.

Conclusion

Governments must balance the equities in any funding method. User charges, special assessments, and special taxes all have a place in meeting the financial needs of local governments. There is no doubt, however, that before local governments undertake efforts to increase their income, they should first ensure that required services are being offered in the most economical and beneficial way possible.

Discussion

Maxine Harris Brookner: What do you see as the legal impediments to cities acting as entrepreneurs?

Patrick Coughlan: For the charter city, I do not think there is any impediment. General-law cities, about three-quarters of the cities in California, derive their powers from legislative authorization. If there is no specific authority, can a general-law city just go ahead? Who is going to challenge their authority if the developer, the property owners, and the city are satisfied with the city's entrepreneurial efforts?

Edward Rabin: If local governments become joint venturers, cannot competitors complain? If I were a private builder competing with a government project that was whipped through lickety-split while I hung in the wind, I might have good reason to complain.

Patrick Coughlan: Your point is well taken, but I have noticed that for those government entities that have learned to process a project for themselves, the education flows for the benefit of private industry as well. They have more sympathy with the developer because they got frustrated with their own bureaucracy. In many cases processing generally has speeded up.

David Gelfand: What about antitrust liability as a result of these joint ventures, after the recent cable television case? Also, how will your plans be affected by the proposed cutbacks, under Section 103, on the tax exemption for some municipal revenue bonds?

Patrick Coughlan: You raise valid issues. It is possible the federal government will remove the use of tax-exempt mortgage-revenue bonds, especially if cities do not use good judgment. However, our current plans should not be affected.

Jack Spahn: Professor Hoachlander, how would you plan for school attendance in work areas? At present we use residential-density projections.

Gary Hoachlander: Most school districts have underutilized facilities. There are exceptions: Los Angeles, for example, has serious problems with both overcrowding and underutilization. It is an empirical question to what extent we might alleviate underutilization or overcrowding by allowing parents to opt for a school that is close to their work place. At the outset we could simply make options available to parents to the point where the school filled up.

159

**Part VI
Directions for
National Housing Policy**

9 The Trouble with Money: Is It Time To Socialize Residential Finance?

Wallace F. Smith

This chapter argues the following issues:

1. In the 1930s and 1940s Americans determined that a high-ratio, long-term, fixed rate, amortized home-owner mortgage loan was what the social objectives of the country required.
2. With continued public guidance and extensive public support, private thrift institutions evolved to serve this public purpose, attracting a significant share of private savings and creating a management-owner cadre.
3. Thrift institutions began using their leverage with the public sector to enlarge upon their role.
4. The larger role involved them in direct competition with other elements of the private financial market.
5. That competition produced or aggravated a spiral of interest costs.
6. Spiraling interest costs made it impossible for thrift institutions to provide the principal form of service for which they had been called into being.
7. Consequently, some other instrumentality, presumably a public agency, should be created to perform the role that has been abandoned.
8. To the extent that private thrift institutions are redundant and harmful to management of the economy, they should be disbanded.

We Lost It

In 1972 a young family in the United States could buy a home with 5 to 10 percent down and payments that took no more than one-fourth of the breadwinner's pay. Thanks to a concept of mortgage lending created by the federal government during the 1930s and 1940s, the long-term fixed-rate mortgage allowed the family to build equity in the home and to enjoy increasing financial freedom as the breadwinner's paycheck grew. Young families did buy homes and set about raising children. It was the American dream.

Ten years later the dream is a nightmare. Home prices have doubled or tripled. Financing charges compound the higher price, taking 40 to 50 percent of the household's income. Loan terms have reverted to those of the 1920s: short term with hazardous prospects for refinancing and greatly diminished opportunity for building equity. The family home which had been the bedrock of personal security is a financial albatross. Far worse, the house today can only be acquired by sacrificing the opportunity to raise children; it takes two incomes and the tax advantage of a fully employed, childless couple to qualify for a home loan.

The average price of homes sold in the United States in August 1981 was $88,400, and the average institutional-mortgage interest rate was in excess of 18.25 percent.[1] For a loan equal to 80 percent of the price, interest payments alone would be $12,906 per year, and if the lender permitted a 35-percent ratio of interest payments to income, the purchaser's income would have to be $36,874, roughly double the average U.S. wage-earner's yearly income. Thus the housing market has come to be based on the household with two full-time earners. It is significant that the after tax cost of mortgage interest (assuming a marginal tax bracket of 40 percent) would be only 21 percent of gross household income in this representative case. So in 1981 the one-income, child-raising family is essentially denied the opportunity for home ownership while the thrift institutions accommodate the childless and take from government almost half of the institutions' interest revenue. Like feudal peasants in Japan who had to dash their children's heads on rocks so the rest of the family could survive, most young Americans today have to choose between parenthood and a home.

In this transformation it might seem that lending institutions will prosper mightily. Inflation of house prices has magnified the security behind existing loans. Interest charges have become increasingly tax deductible to borrowers, making loan demand less interest-elastic than it would otherwise be. Loan terms are being twisted strongly to favor lenders. Government has fostered comprehensive secondary-market liquidity.

Instead the lending institutions most closely involved with home ownership are facing mass insolvency, dependent for even a faint hope of survival upon quick and massive injections of taxpayers' money. The secondary market institutions, instead of being a prop to mortgage lending, are themselves monstrous basket cases, not able to help but only join the chorus of cries for assistance. Regulatory agencies, overwhelmed by the pestilence among their charges, swing from one specious remedy to another, as though their job was to save grocery stores from bankruptcy during a famine.

How did this happen? What can we learn from it? How can we recover it? It is after all a stark and enormous economic-cum-social event, large enough to make its lesson obvious and so perilous that the nation must act.

The lesson is that whatever its other virtues the marketplace cannot manage money and credit. In two centuries of laissez-faire we have had occasion to see the limits as well as its advantages of a market economy.

Money management is one of those limits. What must be done is to complete the nationalization of monetary affairs, to go the final mile on a tortured and not-very-scenic road of defining institutions appropriate to a market-based economy.

What Happened?

In 1973 oil-exporting countries succeeded in forming a cartel and sharply increasing the price of fuel. In the United State food prices also began to rise because of an export program. Thus there were two inflationary shocks—that for oil being the more ominous perhaps. World diplomacy went limp in the face of the cartel. Economics has never been the long suit of the Department of State, and the implications of a vast change in energy prices and world terms of trade were not carefully explored.

The implications should have been clear to financial managers in the United States and in particular to those in thrift institutions (the residential-mortgage lenders). The not-so-abstruse chain of causation would go like this: Oil-price rises would induce increases in prices of substitute fuels, the supply and/or use of which could not readily expand, so the price of energy generally would rise. Since energy is a significant input in most forms of manufacturing and many activities of trade and service, there would be a tendency to shift the higher costs to consumers. Willy-nilly, financial institutions would accommodate this effort and prices would rise. The rising cost of living would, by virtue of a relationship described much earlier by economist Irving Fisher, cause nominal interest rates to rise or at least tend to do so.[2] Because of a major shift in relative prices of business inputs much capital equipment and many production techniques were made obsolete, suggesting that much of the economy of the nation be reengineered when the new set of input prices can be discerned. This implied a vast demand for savings. Expectations of inflation, however, normally discourage savings because a penny saved keeps losing its value and consumption on credit can be paid for later in cheaper dollars. Government deficits could also be expected to grow because spending power drained from the country by oil-price increases did not all come back or get replaced, thus soft spots in the employment picture were to be expected. With greater demand for borrowed funds and less supply of savings, in addition to the Fisher effect of inflation in itself, it would have been reasonable in 1973 to anticipate a prolonged period of high interest rates.

Now the essence of a residential-mortgage-lending institution (such as a savings and loan association) is that it needs a positive spread between the interest paid to depositors and interest charged borrowers. However, up to 1972 at least, most of the mortgages held by thrift institutions carried long terms and interest rates below the levels implied by the events of 1973, and there were regulatory ceilings on rates paid to depositors. As interest rates rose in other parts of the financial system, depositors in savings and loans might grow restive; the volume of new or even of existing deposits might shrink. One course of action available to savings and loans at that juncture was to begin liquidating mortgage portfolios: making fewer new loans and selling old loans in the secondary market. A case can be made that regulatory agencies should have firmly nudged savings and loans in this direction, primarily because the nation was heading into a period of credit scarcity, and the housing sector normally plays a useful counter-cyclical role by retrenching when credit is scarce. This is hindsight, of course, but the record of regulators is less than inspiring. Instead of retrenching, the lending institutions began maneuvering to keep their slice of the nation's savings pie. They got around limits on interest paid to depositors by inventing new types of deposits paying higher interest and, where necessary, securing government approval for these. These tended to keep money coming in, but it was expensive money; to pay for it, lenders let it be known they would be happy to refinance now rapidly appreciating homes (at relatively high interest rates, to be sure). Much money was lent in this way, but it was not enough to raise overall portfolio yields. New mortgages could not generally be written at rates higher than 13 percent because, even for the two-income household, incomes often could not cover the payments. Yet to keep savings on deposit lenders found themselves paying 16 to 17 percent: a large negative spread. By mid-1981 the great majority of savings and loans in the United States were operating in the red.[3]

This is not the whole story. From an economist's or an accountant's point of view, the old fixed-interest loans making up most of the savings and loan portfolios had shrunk severely in value as market interest rates went up because of the inverse mathematical relationship between the discount rate and the present value of a fixed future stream of income. If a savings and loan liquidated its portfolio of mortgages, it would typically realize far less than the amount owed to depositors; effectively, the savings and loan is insolvent.

It would be convenient if the government-sponsored secondary-market agencies could buy up these depreciated old loans at something like face value, as the Home Owners Loan Corporation (HOLC) did in the 1930s. But these secondary-market agencies are far from being independently wealthy, as HOLC was. They are independently poor, having behaved just like their client savings and loans, borrowing money at high rates and purchasing low-yielding mortgages. Though cloaked in the privileges of government, which makes talk of insolvency seem rude, they are also floating beyond the precipice.[4]

Most savings-and-loan deposits are insured by a federal agency. Is that what would save the day should depositors decide to pull the plug? No. The resources and acumen of the agency in question have always rested on confidence that this day would never come.

The Federal Savings and Loan Insurance Corporation (FSLIC) spent $1.1 billion in assisting just three troubled savings and loans in 1980.[5] There are over two hundred-fifty savings and loans on FSLIC's problem list, according to the Consumer Federation of America.[6]

Twisting in the Wind

Recall that we started this blundering epoch from a benign situation mainly constructed by government. Before the Federal Home Loan Bank system was created and the FSLIC began its work, the savings-and-loan industry was a congeries of do-it-yourself credit co-ops, often indifferently managed and locked into the most grievous illiquidity. The federal government transformed that. The most important part of the transformation was indirect: when the New Deal demonstrated the long-term, high-ratio, amortized homeowner mortgages and then stood behind that innovation until it took root. The social, let alone the economic, impact of that complex innovation would be hard to overestimate though it is, unfortunately, not much remembered by today's youthful intelligentia. It invigorated a life-style that possesses almost primitive potency, financial security, and economic citizenship for new, child-raising families by means of easily attainable homeownership.

But the mortgage reforms of the thirties left lending as a private business; a business that clearly owes its life to government normally comes to assume the government owes it a living. It was inevitable that the fraternity of residential lenders learn politics, particularly as mutual or cooperative structure gave way to profit making and a corporate ethic. The savings-and-loan industry is one of the most vigorous legislative lobbyists at both state and federal levels and has more control over the regulatory agencies than any concerned party feels comfortable admitting. The industry has used this power during the past decade, thinking it was building a bulwark against competition, but it acted so ineptly that it dug its own grave.

Mention has already been made of circumventing limits on interest rates for deposits. This culminated in authorization to match rates on Treasury bills (T-bills), subject only to restrictions that would tend to deprive small accounts of the privilege. The object was to outbid the federal government for funds, despite the fact that profitable investments were not available for much of the money thus attracted to the associations.

Belatedly noticing that T-bill accounts were unprofitable, the industry decided to have the government make them profitable. That could be done by tying mortgage-interest rates to the same T-bills or similar index of the general price of money. Eventually, this theory claimed, whenever depositors needed a bit more to stay with the savings and loan, the borrowers would provide (not just new borrowers, but also people who had taken out a loan years earlier). This system was given a variety of names: rollover, adjustable, variable interest rate, and so on. It was not referred to as the kind of mortgage arrangement common in the 1920s that led to catastrophe for legions of home owners, but that is what it is.

The ultimate weapon in the new arsenal was to be the negative amortization loan. This allows the borrower who can just barely keep up the payments on a 12-percent mortgage to start paying 15 percent, say, whenever the lender desires this to occur, by simply charging the additional payments against the home-owner's equity. At some point, of course, that equity might vanish, but there was little talk of that or of what it would lead to. From the industry's point of view, this device had two advantages: (1) It gave a savings and loan unlimited power to outbid the government, or anyone else, for savings necessary to keep the savings and loan rolling along; and (2) a large part of the additional revenue levied by the lender came right out of federal and state treasuries without any messy lobbying or embarrassing talk of subsidy because of the tax deductibility of mortgage interest. By 1980 most borrower households were probably at or above the 40-percent federal marginal tax bracket.

Would not that be enough? Would not that fulfill any normal usurer's fondest dreams? It did not work for the residental lenders, who now encountered an unexpected fact: Many people who wanted to buy houses could not afford to compete with the U.S. Treasury for the use of saver's money. Some way would have to be found to make spiraling interest rates consistent with the borrower's paycheck. Of course, government would have to lend a hand, as government always does. Ironically, the new device was named shared appreciation mortgage (SAM) (as in uncle). The concept is that for a slight break in the interest rate, the hapless borrower must turn over 40 percent or so of the property's total inflationary increase in value at a definite future time, say after ten years. As in the old story about Solomon—or was it the *Merchant of Venice?*—40 percent may be very difficult to sever painlessly. The property must in reality be turned over to the lender and the borrower, with no more than 60 percent of the equity necessary to buy another home is on the street—for good. So much for the social goal of home ownership.

How could any private industry ask for more? Their customers are locked into cost-plus contracts for a necessity of life. What the customer struggles to pay for will eventually pass into the lender's ownership. Yet there is more. By the spring of 1981 the thrift industry perceived that the new mortgage devices that they had convinced government were urgently needed were in fact only long-range solutions to their problems at best.

With persistent high cost of deposits and very little action on the borrowing side, the industries' deficits were escalating.[7] So they went to Congress to be bailed out. In June the nation's representatives were asked to underwrite a direct subsidy disguised as tax-exempt interest certificates with an estimated public cost of $10 billion or more.[8]

A literate visitor to the United States could have been excused for thinking such a proposal was doomed. The new administration was extolling the virtues of getting government off business's back. The administration was enthusiastically dismantling programs of government to save money and putting through a major tax reduction to ensure much less money would be spent in the future. The word for dairy farmers, air-traffic controllers, and hungry schoolchildren was grim and consistent: The government does not owe you a living. The federal budget was cut again and again. Eventually, even the most sacred of sacred cows, military appropriations, got the axe. How unlikely in this context is an unprecedented multibillion-dollar handout for the financial community!

The All Savers Bill became law within eight weeks of being presented and took effect six weeks after that. One would look long and hard through the history of public affairs in this country to discover clearer proof of effective self-interest by a private industry.[10]

What did the public, or even the administration or Congress get for this largesse? In return for the subsidy the thrift industry promised to stay in business. They were not asked to make long-term, fixed-rate low-interest loans to families excluded from today's housing market. Nor could the industry assure us that there would be any significant amount of new money available for the housing industry or any net increase in the nation's savings.[11] Through their economists, they whispered "trust me," and Congress bought that. Congress turned a deaf ear to state and local governments who feared the deposit subsidy would raise their own costs of borrowing. Smaller businesses, typically dependent upon the commercial paper market for their financing needs, were expected to be hurt be the All Savers Programs.

It would be incorrect to assume that the several major categories of thrift institutions stand united on deregulation, bail-outs, and the like. Savings and loans directed much of their ire in 1981 at the brash money-market funds, and the All Savers Program was evidently designed largely to puncture the growth of those funds. As it became increasingly necessary to merge failing savings and loans with stronger partners, commercial banks and their supporters in Congress and on Wall Street maneuvered to let banks do the job, getting a start on interstate banking in the process. Naturally, savings and loans take a dim view of competitive behavior by the other segments of the thrift industry. Savings and loans also wage legal and lobbying war on loan assumptions and seller-assisted financing.[12]

Why Savings Should Not Be Indexed

Nothing riles a businessman quicker than being ridiculed for acting like a businessman. Given the presumption that the thrift industry is a business, all the strategems mentioned earlier are not only understandable but they are right. Customers should, after all, have to pay a price that covers the cost of production; insisting that borrowers pay what savers require is an application of the same principle. It is a corollary of the theorem about supply and demand: If supply is limited, price will rise, and a rising price will simultaneously encourage an increase in supply and discourage some demand, resulting in equilibrium at a higher level of cost and price. Businessmen use up their acumen implementing this scheme and cannot be expected to spend a lot of time reflecting on cases in which the theorem is wrong.

The thrift industry happens to be such a case. One way to show this is to make a very simple model of indexed savings: a situation in which the price of money includes a real component and a correction factor for price level changes, as Irving Fisher believed it should.[13]

If the nominal rate of interest is partly determined by the inflation rate, it is also true that part of the inflation rate is due to changes in the nominal interest rate, as many current critics of the CPI point out. To apprehend the nature of their interaction we can start with these definitions:

Let A = aggregate spending on resources other than savings

I = aggregate spending on savings

$B = A + I$

D = aggregate debt

i = the nominal rate of interest

w = the real return on capital

$\alpha = \Delta A / A$;

$\beta = \Delta B / B$ (that is, the economy's price index)

$i = w + \beta$;

$I = Di$;

$\Delta I = D(w + \beta) - Dw.$[14]

Now suppose there occurs a one-shot increase ΔA in money spent on an unchanged amount of real goods. If saving is indexed, the nominal interest rate i will rise, inducing a further increase in total spending, B, and, in turn, a further increase in i, and so on. The result will be an increase α in real-resource prices by the following relationship:[15]

$$\beta = \Delta A/(B - D) \tag{9.1}$$

Since $\alpha = \Delta A/A$, the multiplier relationship between the initial shock, α, and the ultimate change in the price level , β, is:

$$\beta/\alpha = A/(B - D) \tag{9.2}$$

The fact worth noting is that B is a flow, such as gross national product, (GNP), while D is a stock, as a limit the value of the nation's entire real capital; thus it is likely that D is large relative to B and might exceed it. As D approaches B the multiplier approaches infinity; only draconian monetary restrictions can then check inflation, an inflation not caused by money managers in the first place nor by a public deficit no matter how financed and not attributable to formation of a major cartel, but simply to the indexing of savings. The philosophy that savers are entitled to a small cost-of-living raise, or the erection of a market system for thrift that facilitates an escalation of opportunity cost, will destroy the economy.[16]

A numercial example might be useful. If we let $A = 1,000$, $D = 200$, and $w = .03$, then a 10-percent real price increase ($\Delta A = 100$) produces a 12.4-percent increase in the overall price level and raises the interest rate from 3 percent to 15.4 percent. But this assumes the aggregate of indexed saving capital amounts to only one-fifth of real output. If $D = 500$ the price level increase from a 10-percent increase in goods prices would be 19.4 percent; if $D = 900$, the price index would rise by 78.7 percent.

All of these cases assume a passive monetary authority, which is really another story. There is also another significant assumption: namely, that only savers enjoy indexed incomes. Put another way, our model in effect designates as savers the indexed segment of the economy. It would be possible to generalize the model to allow for any degree of indexing, but the important result of that exercise is obvious: If everyone is sheltered from inflation by cost-of-living contracts, any inflationary shock (for example, a crop failure) implies an infinite rate of inflation. Inflation demands the redistribution of real goods, and until the incidence of that redistribution is settled the inflationary spiral will continue.

Indexing, not savings, is the root of the problem. What gives the thrift industry its special significance is the fact that debt, the base for saving's claim to income, is large in proportion to national product. A financial economist might object to the model presented on the ground that the evidence of debt (say, a bond) loses value as the interest rate rises, thus offsetting the tendency for interest payments to aggravate inflation. But that argument would be tantamount to assuming away indexing, forcing savings-and-loan depositors, for example, to accept and realize capital losses if they try to move their accounts. That is not the contractual structure of the thrift industry. Savers can demand cash, not depreciated mortgage paper.

Another distinguishing characteristic of the thrift industry is the fact that interest income is a transfer. One can argue that morally the saver is entitled to something like the real marginal product of capital, but this argument wears thin when the interest return generates its own increases by the process described earlier and real income is siphoned continuously from wage earners to renters long after the act of saving.

Allocative Inefficiency

Another compelling reason for not allowing savings to be indexed against inflation is that we do not index borrowers. An increase in the nominal interest rate has an adverse real effect on particular segments of the economy or of the public.[17] In particular, families in the housing market and their surrogates (the builders, building-supply manufacturers, and so on) lose command of resources not just to other producing sectors of the economy but to savers when saving is indexed. A borrower offered a long-term, fixed-rate contract may have the better of a risk bargain if lenders lack foresight and rates eventually climb, but the borrower facing a contractually indexed saver is at an unequivocal disadvantage, forced to bear risks that savers supposedly get paid to bear and that lending institutions are chartered to assume. That historic allocation of risk was designed to achieve a social purpose: to encourage homeownership and the financial security of the American family. Backing away from it, on whatever argument, is a repudiation of that explicit national value; any knowledgeable person who can not concede this is a charlatan.

In real terms the indexed-savings (IS) function beloved of Keynesian textbook producers has a negative slope; rising interest rates mean declining employment. The logic is that the real interest rate is the sieve of capital formation; the higher the cost of money, the fewer new investments that will pay their way. The downward-sloping IS curve seems to contradict the positively sloped supply curve of savings that common sense suggests: That is, we will save less if interest rates are low and more if rates are high. Of course, we have GNP on the horizontal axis in the one case and the microeconomic quantity of savings in the other. But still, if interest rates rise, is there more saving or less?

It is more fruitful to specify the source of the rise in interest. Assume it is due to the phenomenon that Irving Fisher had in mind: a rise in the price level. Then in nominal terms the microeconomic supply curve of savings—if those savings are not indexed—shifts downward. Borrowing is encouraged beyond the funds available and nonprice rationing of funds must occur. Institutional arbitrage becomes a source of sterile profit: That is, bankers get rich.

If that profit leaks out to savers, virtually indexing those who control savings, secondary inflation and interest-rate increases will occur as our model suggests. The nominal rate of interest will rise beyond the increase in the value of real resources so producers will have to curtail investment plans. Thus marrying the naive interest-savings supply curve with the interest-GNP IS function it seems that the supply curve of savings has both a positive and negative slope in different ranges of the interest rate. That is, it is backward bending.[18]

Indexing savings is thus bad for employment and GNP. It produces high nominal rates that disturb international economic relations as well, tending to spread unemployment and the skewing of purchasing power toward the owners of thrift accounts. We are reminded almost daily that the Federal Reserve System sticks to a tight-money, high-interest-rate regime in order to reduce inflation. We are less well informed about the theory behind this, but on the supposition that the Fed is Keynesian the reasoning may be that high interest will discourage investment and thus reduce employment and consumption spending. If the Fed is Monetarist, on the other hand, the idea might be that there is too much money chasing too few goods so the policy is to restrain growth of the money supply; high interest rates would be just an inadvertent by-product of the scarcity of money. This chapter suggests that inflation continues as long as the several sectors of the economy manage to keep up with rising prices by raising prices and wages anew; it stops when they are defeated in this effort by an insufficiency of money or credit, imposing a substantially random incidence of the real transfer that inflation represents.

Interest rates may be an attractively simple way to allocate savings, but they seem to have no unambiguous role in governing the quantity of savings. One can argue that control over nominal interest rates has become the exclusive object of national economic policymakers. If tight credit succeeds in reducing inflation, it will do so by lowering real income, which is inflation by another name: less goods for the same money. No, the benefit of reducing inflation is lowering nominal interest rates, and that benefit accrues to a particular class of financial intermediaries.

A Thrift Regimen

This is a good catalog of complaints about the private thrift business. It does not manage its own affairs well; it gets unwholesomely close to government even while begging to be free; it can and probably does grievously compound inflationary situations that may arise; it countermands an explicit social declaration and rewards the idle and roils the trade of nations. It should not be a private business.

The thrift institution has been a much-regulated private business in the past; we could revert to that, but even if the politics of that could be finessed we would have to hope savers forget about the joys of disintermediation and that thrift-institution managers put down their *Wall Street Journals* once in a while and go fishing.

It would not be sensible to buy out the savings and loans and other savings institutions. As they are largely insolvent, the price would not be great but there would be an odd problem about the liquidation rights of depositors.

This seems to leave a system in which government makes home loans on terms that will permit the home-ownership option to survive. Funds could come from any combination of sources but old-fashioned values suggest principal reliance on a wartime-style, compulsory-savings program crossed with social security. Similar programs appropriate to other long-term credit needs (local government, utilities, and so on) could be devised. This would be credit allocation. Most countries do plan capital formation by broad sectors at least; Japan is an outstanding example and proof, if any is needed. that public management of credit does not take the zing out of capitalism.

Present actions are futile.[19] We are helping an industry that was created and nurtured for a public purpose to transform itself into an unnecessary and evidently dangerous turkey shoot. The game must be called off; but where is the referee?

There is some irony in the prospect that the most conservative national administration in memory may be forced to nationalize a large slice of the nation's financial work. But the thrift industry is in a state of collapse and the child-raising family has become endangered species. The range of public options is rapidly narrowing. It is the culmination of ten generations' experience: time now to acknowledge that whatever one's economic philosophy, the business of money is the public's business.

Our money troubles in this decade results from assuming that money is a commodity, suitably produced and alloted by an unfettered market. Money—in all its forms—is a public institution and a social responsibility.[20]

Notes

1. *Wall Street Journal*, 1 October 1981 and 7 October 1981.

2. An interesting review and discussion of the relationship between interest rates and price-level changes was presented in the *Wall Street Journal*, 2 October 1981.

3. Total losses by savings and loans in 1981 were projected at $5 billion by the head of the Home Loan Bank Board. *San Francisco Chronicle*, 11 September 1981.

4. For the third quarter 1981, the Federal National Mortgage Association posted a record loss $79.5 million. Losses for the first nine months of 1981 were $119.6 million versus a profit of $13.5 million for the year earlier period. *Wall Street Journal,* 13 October 1981.

5. *Wall Street Journal,* 20 February 1981.

6. "MacNeil-Lehrer Report," July 8, 1981. Total reserves of FSLIC approximate $6.7 billion. *Wall Street Journal,* 29 October 1981.

7. In the first half of 1981, for the first time in forty years of record keeping, the aggregate net income of insured savings and loans was negative: a $1.5 billion loss. *Wall Street Journal,* 29 September 1981.

8. One estimate of the tax cost of All Savers was $14 billion. *Business Week,* 31 August 1981.

9. In the beginning of June 1981, the secretary of the treasury proclaimed, "We have to free the thrift institutions." *San Francisco Chronicle,* 1 June 1981. The All Savers subsidy bill was introduced three weeks later.

10. It is naive to suppose that the savings and loan industry is out to do any favors for savers. In September 1981 the industry objected strenuously to a federal agency ruling that allowed higher interest on passbook accounts: the locked-in savers. *Wall Street Journal,* 24 September 1981. While industry economists preach against savers sudsidizing borrowers, the industry does not mind at all if savers subsidize savings-and-loan operators. The secretary of the treasury, responding to pressure from the savings-and-loan associations, took immediate steps to rescind the DIDC ruling on passbook interest.

In August 1981 the Home Loan Bank Board proposed a scheme of acquiring low-rate mortgages from savings and loans and announced a drastic revamping of accounting rules to let savings and loans avoid recording losses when an old mortgage is sold; the loss can be spread over several years. *San Francisco Chronicle,* 18 August 1981.

11. The head of the largest savings and loan in Miami opined just before All Savers certificates went on sale that the program would not have a perceptible effect on mortgage interest rates; savings & loans would find it advantageous to use any new deposits to buy old mortgages at bargain prices from FNMA, FNMA realizing losses in the process. *San Francisco Examiner,* 20 September 1981.

A financial analyst for Merrill Lynch remarked that "prudent management won't rely heavily on All Savers for new mortgage lending because it's one-year money." A spokesman for a major home-building organization said, "We've spent a lot of time studying the All Savers bill. Our basic reaction is that it isn't going to help housing in a material way." *Wall Street Journal,* 21 September 1981.

12. On September 24, 1981, again responding to pressure from the savings-and-loan industry, the secretary of the treasury issued proposed regula-

tions preempting state laws and court rulings that allow home buyers to assume existing, low-rate mortgages. Kenneth Harney, "The Nation's Housing," *San Francisco Chronicle,* 4 October 1981.

13. The argument being made here is not to be equated with the comment now frequently heard that housing costs distort the CPI. For a typical expression of that view, see the editorial "CPI: Confusing Price Index," *Wall Street Journal,* 30 September 1981. That position is simply that interest enters into the price index in an unreasonable way. Plans have been made to purge the CPI of mortgage-market effects. *Wall Street Journal,* 28 October 1981. This is reminiscent of the dullard who, encountering a difficult part of his textbook, simply ripped that chapter out of the book and threw it away. A fact that nicely exposed the uselessness of modern U.S. economics just had to be swept under the rug. Our concern is that price inflation can generate a continuing upward spiral in interest rates.

The term *indexing* as used here is to be distinguished from the indexing of tax rates, which has almost the opposite implication. In this chapter, indexing means tying a payment to the general price index. Escalator clauses in wage contracts are illustrative, but indexing is a more inclusive concept. Indexing tax rates, on the other hand, means expanding income-tax brackets as general price inflation proceeds so that a particular taxpayer whose income rises only as much as prices do will not lose real income to the government through bracket creep.

14. Some readers might feel better if a third term, $w\beta$, were present in this expression. A miniscule amount in any case, it has been omitted here to minimize clutter.

15.
$$
\begin{aligned}
\beta &= \Delta B/B \\
&= (\Delta A + \Delta I)/B \\
&= (\Delta A + D[w + \beta] - Dw)/B \\
&= (\Delta A + D\beta)/B \\
\beta B - \beta D &= \Delta A \\
\beta &= \Delta A/(B - D)
\end{aligned}
$$

16. It is hard to understand why prominent economists have not been much heard recently on the hazards of financial-institution deregulation; the profession has long considered the disadvantages of income indexing to be self-evident. For example,

> . . . if every contract is covered by a full escalator clause, then there may be *no limit* on the amount of inflation which will result." [Emphasis in original.] Paul Wonnacott, *Macroeconomics* (Irwin, 1974) p. 307.

In 1969 the Federal Home Loan Bank Board published a four-volume set of papers by prominent economists, *Study of the Savings and Loan Industry;*

several of the papers anticipated the current problem. MIT Professor Paul Cootner's contribution, "The Liquidity of the Savings and Loan Industry," cautioned against cumulative-inflation/interest-rate effects if residential lenders undertake a regime of monetary stringency, saying: "Any stabilization of housing activity . . . counters the effectiveness of monetary policy." The result, he warned, could be "further tightening of the monetary screws" (pp. 335-336). It is surprising, too, that members of the economics profession would tolerate the suggestion that families must finance their principal asset—the home—which directly or indirectly they will use for forty to fifty years, on credit terms fast approaching those of a thirty-day note.

17. Interest on the federal debt is the fastest-growing component of federal expenditures, rising from about 7 percent of the total in the 1970s to 13 percent in 1981. *Business Week,* 21 September 1981.

Interest income is the fastest-growing component of personal income in the United States. *Business Week,* 5 October 1918.

The surge in interest rates is forcing major redirection of the life-insurance industry. *Business Week,* 14 September 1981.

18. Any resemblance to other backward-bending curves is purely coincidental. The correlation coefficient between aggregate personal savings as a percent of aggregate disposable income on the one hand, and the average conventional first-mortgage interest rate for loans on existing houses on the other, over the period 1970 to 1980, was -0.57. Thus on the practical assumption that the mortgage interest rate reflects interest available to depositors, it appears that saving is stimulated by *lower* interest rates, not by higher rates (see figure 9-1A). The same date source (national-income statistics appearing in the *Survey of Current Business*) shows a *positive* correlation between the savings rate and a CPI-adjusted or real mortgage rate, a coefficient of 0.71, suggesting figure 9-1B. Figure 9-1B resembles the supply schedule of microeconomics: The higher the price (interest), the more will producers (savers) put on the market. But there are problems with figure 9-1B. One is that savers may know what the real interest rate was *last* year, but they will not know what it will be during the time their money is on deposit; their decision to save must be based on something else. The data show a strong negative relationship between the savings rate and the price index (correlation coefficient -0.80), suggesting that the real mechanism is that as *inflation* proceeds some would-be savers fall behind and cannot afford to save. This is consistent with the by-now-standard Keynesian concept that relates the aggregate levels of GNP, savings, and investment with the *real* interest rate: an inverse relationship as in figure 9-1A. The logic is that as borrowing becomes more costly, businesses find fewer opportunities for profitable investment so that investment activity falls and unemployment is created.

Nominal
interest
rate

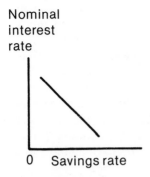

0   Savings rate

Real
interest
rate

0   Savings rate

Figure 9-1A.   **Figure 9-1B**.
One Theory of the Savings Rate   Another Theory of the Savings Rate

Interest
rate

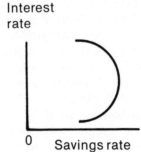

0   Savings rate

Figure 9-1C.
Long-Term View of the Savings Rate

Whether we are talking of *nominal* interest rates or *real* rates, the picture that emerges is figure 9-1C. Starting at a low level of reward for saving, saving increases as that reward—interest—rises. Beyond some point, however, if inflation plus money-market competition pushes the rate very high, businesses cut back, GNP falls, aggregate savings is reduced, and would-be savers fall behind in real income so they save less.

From the individual thrift institution's point of view, of course, figure 9-1B is the whole story. Paying a higher interest rate than the bank across the street pays will bring in more deposits. In the aggregate, however, this competition can lower total savings. Concern for externalities of this sort is the rational person's justification for government involvement.

19. Banker-economist Albert M. Wojnilower has provided an illuminating perspective on credit crunches since World War II in "The Cen-

tral Role of Credit Crunches in Recent Financial History," in W.C. Brainard and G.L. Perry, eds., *Brookings Papers on Economic Activity*, 2 (Washington, D.C.: The Brookings Institution, 1980). Reminding us of Bagehot's observation that money will not manage itself, Wojnilower contends that steps to shelter first one segment of the market and then another from cyclical contractions give increasingly free rein to the casino instincts of financial markets and contribute to secular increases in prices and interest rates.

20. Harvard Professor Nathan Keyfitz, writing in the winter 1980 issue of *The Public Interest*, provides excellent perspective on the social-security system and what should be done about the problem it faces. In "Why Social Security is in Trouble," Keyfitz argues that the system should be constructed on an actuarial cohort-funded basis, at least to the extent of supplementary coverage, replacing the present pay-as-you-go basis. Payments into the present system, which aggregated $95 billion in 1977, draw no interest and are, in fact, forced savings which impact the population regressively. Mandatory funded pensions are being introduced in the Netherlands, Switzerland, Great Britain, and Sweden, Keyfitz points out.

If our system were funded, the reserves would have to be invested in something, of course; we are suggesting that housing is an obvious candidate. Coincidentally, the aggregate reserve that Keyfitz estimates would be required now to put social security on a funded basis is approximately equal to the aggregate residential mortgage debt outstanding: something over $2 trillion. If people's money were thus available to finance people's housing, the interest rate on deposits and on mortgages would be essentially arbitrary—a wash—and this part of the credit market would be insulated from the remainder, to the benefit of all. That was the original concept behind building societies.

Linking savings accounts to housing credit is not a new idea and it has many variants. In West Germany, for example, *Bausparkassen* enter into contracts with prospective home buyers; depositors agree to a low-interest regular savings program in return for a future mortgage commitment at a guaranteed rate of interest, recently 4.5 to 5.0 percent. In West Germany the ratio of a personal savings to personal disposable income was 14.5 percent in 1979 versus 5.6 percent in the United States. Evidently it is not a high interest rate that motivates people to save. The savings ratio in Japan, in 1979, was 20.1 percent. The prime rate in Japan, in mid-1981, was 6.75 percent. See Bruce Stokes, *Global Housing Prospects: The Resource Constraints,* Worldwatch Paper 46, September 1981.

Several countries—Japan, West Germany, France, and Canada among them—provide expensive tax subsidies to steer savings into particular kinds of thrift institutions, the same principle as our tentative All Savers scheme. A vital factor is what the taxpayer gets in return: more hous-

ing, easier business credit, less inflation, and so on. In most countries the
link is quite clear and effective; in Japan, for example, the mid-1981 inflation rate was 4.7 percent. The U.S. approach, on the other hand, is essentially a no-questions-asked donation to a set of troubled financial institutions that are angling to get out of the housing business. See *Business Week,*
1 September 1980 and 24 August 1981.

10 Rental Housing: Shortage or Surplus?

Ira S. Lowry

One year ago, I became increasingly puzzled by newspaper stories about a national crisis in rental-housing markets; the assertions they made seemed inconsistent. I investigated the matter and soon became fascinated by the gaps in logic between evidence and conclusions. Eventually I came to the judgment that we were all confused about what was going on in the nation's housing markets and that the main reason for that confusion was inflation. Incomes and prices were changing so rapidly and unevenly that we lost track of real changes in the production and consumption of housing services.

According to the press, the rental-housing market was in a state of crisis in 1980. Rents were escalating and vacancy rates were at an all-time low. Millions of Americans could not afford to own homes and could not find affordable rental housing. Yet landlords were going broke and investors were shying away from an obviously unprofitable market. A report by the General Accounting Office made it official and urged immediate federal action.

I searched for statistical evidence of this crisis—especially in trying to distinguish nominal changes in prices from real changes in purchasing power and real changes in the production and consumption of housing services.

This chapter briefly summarizes my research. The discussion will begin with the demand side of the market and then turn to the supply side.

First, throughout the 1970s, the price of rental-housing services rose, but by less than the CPI. Thus any renter whose income kept up with the CPI was able to afford more housing consumption at the end of the decade than at the beginning, as figure 10-1 illustrates.

Second, the median real income of renter households dropped during the decade by 19 percent, as shown in figure 10-2, and the median rent-income ratio rose from 0.21 to 0.25.

Third, real consumption of rental housing increased by 8 percent per household and 22 percent per capita, as shown by figure 10-3.

The drop in renters' real income reflected two events: a radical change in household composition, and a shift by the more prosperous renters to home ownership. Although the number of renter households increased by 14 percent over the decade, the number of persons in those households hardly changed. Average household size decreased by 14 percent, and the number of rented dwellings occupied by only one person increased by 45 percent. The new single-person households were mostly young people and

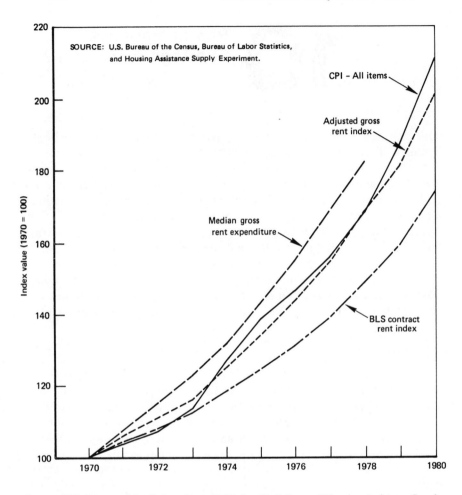

SOURCE: U.S. Bureau of the Census, Bureau of Labor Statistics, and Housing Assistance Supply Experiment.

Figure 10-1. Price Indexes for Urban Rental Housing and All Consumption

divorcees. The consequence was that nearly the same aggregate amount of real income was divided among more households, so the average household income dropped.

Also, the more prosperous renters lined up to buy homes, leaving behind the less prosperous. Contrary to much folklore, rising home prices in the 1970s broadened rather than narrowed the market. Although home ownership expenses rose faster than rent (see figure 10-4), the proportion of households that were homeowners increased at every level of real income

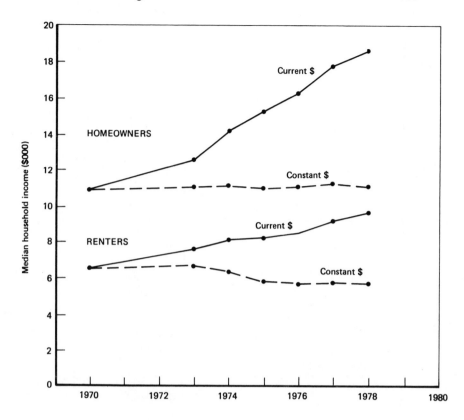

Source: U.S. Bureau of the Census.
Figure 10-2. Median Household Incomes of Urban Homeowners and Renters

over $12,500 (see figure 10-5). The reasons for this shift of households that traditionally had been renters into home ownership are fairly clear. Because of bracket creep, the tax advantages of home ownership were increasing, but more importantly, the prospects of capital gains from property appreciation were alluring. I estimate that the typical home buyer of 1970 with a fixed-interest mortgage and average property appreciation was getting his housing free by 1976, as shown in figure 10-6.

So the drop in renters' average real incomes did not mean that individual renters were getting poorer. Rather it meant that they were becoming prosperous enough to set up separate households instead of living with relatives or unsatisfactory spouses. Those who bought homes were no longer counted in the renter-income statistics. The 22-percent increase in rental-housing consumption per capita reflected in roughly equal parts more space per person and better-quality dwellings.

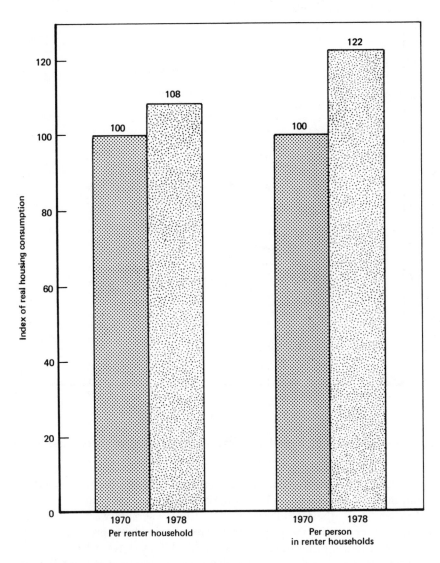

Source: U.S. Bureau of the Census.
Figure 10-3. Indexes of Real Housing Consumption by Urban Renters

Let us turn now to the supply side of the market. We do not have good
national statistics on the cost of supplying rental housing, but there was
enough data to construct satisfactory indexes of rental revenues and costs.

First, landlords' revenue per unit of rental-housing service rose by 87
percent during the 1970s, as figure 10-7 indicates, whereas the CPI rose by

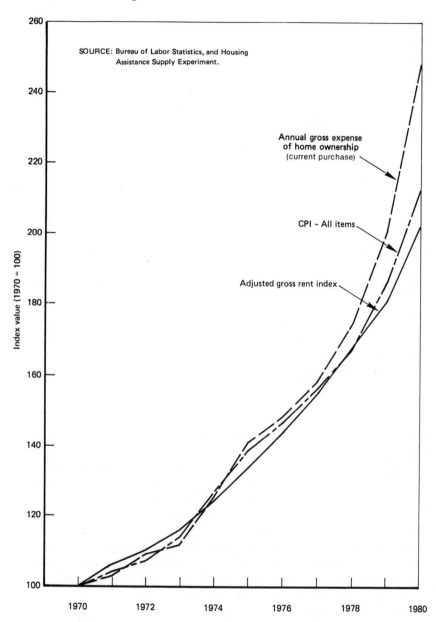

Source: Bureau of Labor Statistics, and Housing Assistance Supply Experiment.

Figure 10-4. Price Indexes for Urban Rental Housing, Home Ownership, and All Consumption

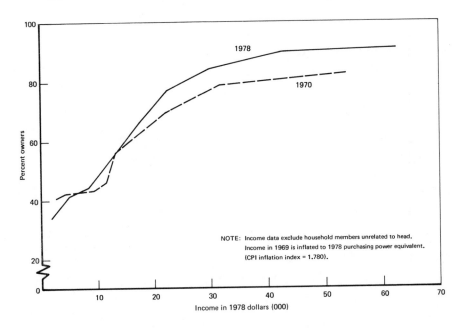

Source: U.S. Bureau of the Census and Bureau of Labor Statistics.

Figure 10-5. Owners as Percent of All Urban Households Within Each Income Interval

113 percent. So the statistical evidence does not support the widespread belief that landlords have taken advantage of a tight market to raise rents outrageously.

Second, operating costs rose by 141 percent, or 1.6 times faster than revenue, as shown in figure 10-7. It thus appears that landlords have not even been able to pass through their cost increases.

In fact, net operating return (the amount available to service mortgage debt and provide a return on equity) increased by 34 percent in current dollars during the decade. But the purchasing power of that return *decreased* by 37 percent, as figure 10-8 reveals. Mortgage lenders took some of the loss because their interest rates were fixed when the mortgage was made. Landlords, the equity owners, took the rest.

When net return from rental property is capitalized at current interest rates, we find that the implied current dollar-asset value of rental property did not change much during the decade. The average real value of rental-property assets declined by nearly 50 percent. Unfortunately, there is no way to confirm these calculations by direct observation. We do not have a national statistical system covering the market values of all rental properties.

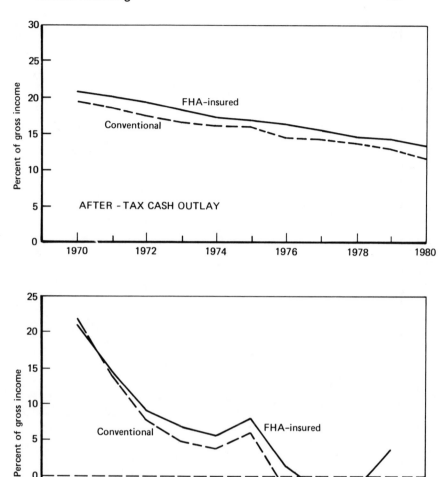

Sources: U.S. Department of Housing and Urban Development, Federal Home Loan Bank Board, and Housing Assistance Supply Experiment.

Figure 10-6. Illustrative Financial Outcome of a 1970 Home Purchase

However, my estimates, if they are correct, do explain events in the rental market that might otherwise seem puzzling. Despite what the press describes as a critical shortage of rental housing and prohibitive rents, landlords are doing their best to get out of the rental business. In inner-city

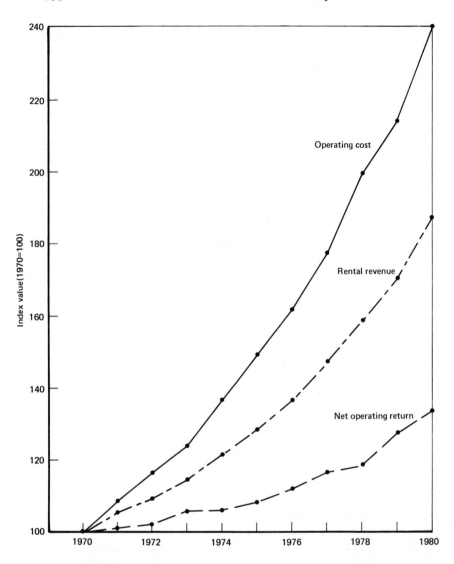

Source: U.S. Bureau of Labor Statistics, U.S. Bureau of the Census, and Housing Assistance Supply Experiment.

Figure 10-7. Indexes for Urban Rental Revenue, Operating Cost, and Net Return

neighborhoods, that best is often abandonment; in more prosperous neighborhoods, it is condominium conversion. Today, the market value of rental property appears to depend less on its expected operating return than on its value as a nonrental property.

The central mystery seems to be: Why didn't rents rise faster? If there were really a rental-housing shortage, landlords should have reaped extraordinary profits; instead, they were selling rental-housing services below long-run average cost.

The only satisfying answer is to reject the proposition that there is a rental-housing shortage. Instead it seems that there is a surplus of rental housing in the sense that more is available than people are willing to buy at a price that covers the cost of providing it. A common retort to this assertion concerns the rental-vacancy rate, alleged to be at an all-time low. The vacancy rate is low likely because rents are bargains. Landlords prefer to lose money on a full house than on a half-empty one.

This is a complicated idea that bears illustration. Imagine a one hundred-unit apartment building with a 10-percent vacancy rate. The landlord could fill the building by cutting his rents by 10 percent. In either case, his total revenue would be the same. Which operating policy should he prefer? For several reasons, most landlords would prefer the full house. But whichever policy he chooses, unless revenues provide a competitive return on capital, the landlord will soon be withdrawing his capital from the rental market. That characterizes the rental market of the 1970s.

Let us now turn to the policy implications of this analysis. The remedies for the rental-housing crisis that have been generally proposed include the following:

1. measures to restrict rent increases in privately owned rental dwellings
2. measures to restrict the removal of such dwellings from the rental inventory
3. measures to encourage the construction of new rental dwellings
4. measures to subsidize the operation of existing rental dwellings

Except for 4., all these remedies seem counterproductive.

There are certainly a few energy boom towns in Colorado and Wyoming where housing of any kind is extremely scarce because of rapid population growth. But persuasive evidence of a *general* shortage of rental housing, even in cities such as Los Angeles where public concern is intense, is not readily apparent. More accurately, in many places renters are unable to find dwellings of the size and quality they have come to prefer at rents they are accustomed to paying.

For those whose incomes are not indexed, the rent increases of the past decade have imposed a measurable hardship. For those whose incomes are indexed, the underlying source of dissatisfaction is that real incomes grew less rapidly during the 1970s than during the preceding decade. Aspirations for higher levels of consumption have become harder to satisfy.

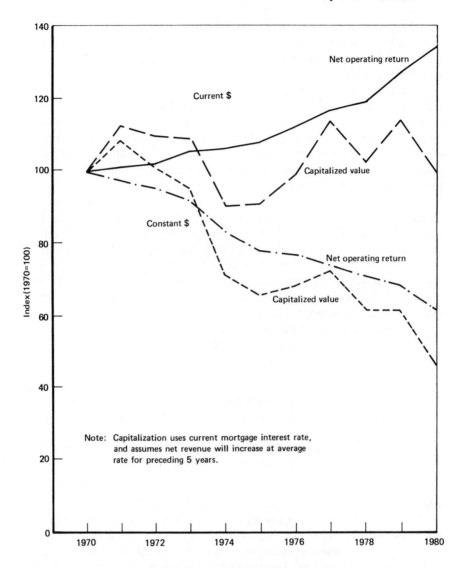

Source: U.S. Bureau of Labor Statistics, Federal Home Loan Bank Board.
Note: Capitalization uses current mortgage interest rate and assumes net revenue will increase at average rate for preceding five years.

Figure 10-8. Return to Capital Invested in Existing Urban Rental Properties

Rents *have* risen rapidly but not fast enough to keep pace with general price inflation or to offset the rising cost of supplying rental housing. The prospective crisis is not rising rents but a general loss of interest in building or owning rental property. If the rent lag continues, we should also expect increased withdrawal of capital from rental property and of dwellings from the rental inventory by undermaintenance, abandonment, and conversion to nonrental uses.

If perchance the pace of rent increase were to pick up, the demand for rent control, already widespread, would be politically overwhelming. But successful rent controls, those that truly restrict rent increases, will both expedite the withdrawal of existing capital and discourage new construction. Both rent controls and restrictions on condominium conversions may benefit sitting tenants, but only at the expense of (1) landlords and (2) other would-be renters and owners. Such restrictions do not improve the property owner's prospects or encourage the production of rental housing.

By deep subsidies (roughly 25 to 30 percent of annualized cost), the federal government can stimulate new construction. But new rental accommodations compete with the existing inventory. By increasing the supply of rental dwelling, such a policy might restrain rent increases throughout the inventory, although empirical evidence does not clearly warrant that inference. It would certainly increase vacancy losses and thereby add to the financial problems of existing rental properties.

Subsidizing the rents of existing dwellings while encouraging landlords to raise rents would perhaps be more helpful. This seems to be the outcome of Housing and Urban Development's (HUD) Section 8 program for existing housing; when a dwelling enters that program, its average rent increase has been about 26 percent, with no change in physical facilities. The assisted tenant does not mind because HUD picks up the check; the landlord is presumably grateful. The drawback of this policy is that is is done at the taxpayer's expense, transferring income from higher-income home owners to poor renters and their landlords.

To summarize, I believe that both renters and home owners benefitted substantially from price inflation during the 1970s. Relative to incomes and prices generally, rental housing was a bargain, so renters spread out, consuming both more space per capita and better quality housing. Those who could raise a down payment on a house did even better at least on paper: home-owner properties appreciated so rapidly that capital gains more than offset out-of-pocket expenses.

Landlords have not done so well. The real rate of return on rental property dropped throughout the decade as operating expenses outpaced revenue. For properties in good locations, condominium conversion often yielded large profits; elsewhere, landlords have withdrawn capital by undermaintenance, and in some places, abandonment. It is not surprising that the demand for new rental construction has dwindled.

The question for the future is: how would controlling inflation affect housing markets? A lot of home owners would probably find themselves in financial trouble, rental demand would pick up, and rents would rise relative to home prices. It appears that landlords have the greatest stake in general price stability.

Discussion

Allen Baldwin: The title of your chapter is Searching for a Crisis. I am not sure whether you found a crisis.

Ira Lowry: I am not sure either. Rental housing is vanishing. If that is a crisis, we have one. But I could not find a crisis in the consumption of housing. In 1980 both renters and home owners were better off than they were a decade previously.

Alfred Bell: You examined the period from 1970 to 1980 rather carefully. Do you believe that period marked a distinctly different pattern of relationships between rental housing and the total housing market from previous experience? Can the same relationships be assumed to extend into the future? Or was there a watershed in the late 1970s in which basic relationships changed? In either case, what are the prospects for those who simply do not have the capital to purchase housing of their own?

Ira Lowry: The events I described are reasonably continuous with the 1960s; I ran all my indexes back to 1960. Two things were different in the 1970s. One was the much more rapid rate of increase in all price indexes but especially in indexes of home prices. The second, toward the end of the decade, was the jump in mortgage interest rates, which had held steady until 1977. The movements of these indexes with respect to each other are quite important. It does not take a lot of calculation to figure that, for example, if the rate of property-value appreciation is 15 percent and the effective after-tax interest rate is 10 percent it is better to buy now than to save. But when that relationship reverses, so does the incentive to invest in home properties.

As to the future, the demanders of rental housing are increasingly lower-income people. Until the existing superabundance of rental housing is worked off by one means or another, they are going to have lots of choices. I do not think that landlords will be keeping places up with much vigor, but there is going to be plenty of rental housing around.

Cary Lowe: You may have overgeneralized. There have been spurts in the rental-housing market and whatever the differences were between 1970 and 1980, there were times during that ten-year period when dramatically different things happened. There may well have been a general increase in access to home ownership, for example, but that was abruptly cut off in the last three years due to the rise of mortgage interest rates. So people at the affluent end of the renter scale who were moving to ownership dramatically slowed down in doing that by 1977-1978.

When you talk about the availability of rental units, it may well be that competition gets stiffer depending on family characteristics, such as low-income families with five or six children.

Ira Lowry: You suggested that I needed disaggregation in two dimensions, one in time and the other in segments of the market.

Cary Lowe: Could I add just one more disaggregation? There have been political developments that also led to a public perception of things perhaps being worse than they are, but the public perception is frequently what generates political responses. The easiest example is Proposition 13: the perception of renters that they were left out, the response of at least an observable number of landlords of raising rents when people expected them to drop, and the dramatically accelerated demands for rent control that succeeded in many places in a period of just a few months. It did not matter what had happened in the preceding five years. The point was, in a very narrow six-month period something dramatic changed in the rental market and led to a public demand for official response.

Ira Lowry: I certainly agree with that. But in fact, the national data I collected is thoroughly disaggregated in time. I have annual time series on everything that I was using. Of course I see lots of bumps. But I saw no reversals in pattern during those those two decades, the 1960s and the 1970s. So I do not feel especially sensitive on that score. On the question of sectoral disaggregation, I do feel uncomfortable because what is true in one community may not be true in another, what is true for rich people may not be true for poor people and so on. I am acutely aware of that. There is a certain protection in looking at averages, though. If an average goes up, for example, then either a few extreme cases carried it, which is most improbable when the data includes many millions of households, or a big section of the distribution of cases moved to push up the average.

Cary Lowe: But that segment could all be in the upper third.

Ira Lowry: It could, possibly, but, in fact, preliminary data suggest the contrary. We have just run numbers for the Los Angleles/Long Beach SMSA covering 1970 to 1977, using an annual housing survey as our base. We disaggregated by income level, by race, by family composition, to see what was happening to renters here. To our immense surprise, the people who came out best during that period, in the sense that their relative circumstances in 1977 as compared to 1970 were most favorable, were the lowest-income group. Their real incomes went up, whereas the real incomes of higher-income groups went down. Their rent-to-income ratios dropped slightly and their housing consumption stayed about the same. There are some exceptions to that: One is Hispanics. The data suggests that new immigrants start out with very little income in crowded quarters and in the course of five or so years integrate into the system and come out looking much better at the end of that time.

David Shulman: Would you agree that instead of having a shortage of physical housing units, we have a shortage of acceptable neighborhoods? Much of our housing stock is in the wrong locations.

Ira Lowry: I would certainly agreee that we have enough housing in the United States and within most metropolitan areas to house all the people there at least as well as they were housed a decade ago and usually better, as far as the structure, the space, and the number of rooms is concerned. It is clearly the case that much of that housing is not where people would prefer it to be located. For example, inner-city neighborhoods are no longer acceptable for many people.

Otto Hetzel: Your statements seem misleading. The President's Commission on Housing reports that of 16.8 million persons of low or moderately low income at least 73 percent are paying over 30 percent of their income and 24 percent are paying over 50 percent of their income. These are renter households only. When you say there is no shortage of rental housing, you are misleading us about the plight of these people.

Ira Lowry: If I mislead about the plight of that group, it is certainly without intention. Poor people have a problem; they do not have enough money. Characteristically they spend 30 to 50 percent of their income for housing. My only point is that, so far as I can decipher from national statistics, their circumstances did not get worse during the decade.

Otto Hetzel: Are you sanguine about that?

Ira Lowry: I am glad that their circumstances did not worsen, if that is what you mean. I have a certain amount of sympathy for people without money and I am glad they are not in more trouble in 1980 than they were in 1970. The question of whether they are entitled to help is, it seems to me, a very different question from the question of what is going on in rental-housing markets.

Otto Hetzel: You indicate that the typical home buyer of 1970 has been getting his housing free since 1976. Your conclusion suggests that the only hope for renters is subsidy, a strong call for redistribution of some kind to equate the differential that is starting to grow between those two segments of society.

George Lefcoe: I have heard Jack Lowry's speech a number of times and I can report that Jack's argument has been in favor of income-redistribution systems like vouchers and against subsidizing housing units. The people with the low incomes may not be the ones to whom subsidized units are targeted since they require deeper subsidies than moderate- or middle-income families. If the poor are the beneficiaries, large subsidies are required for each unit built. If not many units are produced, a lottery is created with most poor people left in the cold. Over time, subsidized housing tends to drive out market-rate housing, diminishing total supply and injuring those who did not win the lottery instead of just leaving them where they were. Housing subsidies can only make sense when there is a shortage of housing and not when the problem is the inability of people to afford it. That is the point that Jack has been trying to make. You misdirect public effort if you analyze this as a housing problem instead of an income problem.

Ira Lowry: This reminds me of a few weeks ago when I was addressing the National Association of Housing and Redevelopment officials on this subject: A panel of distinguished housers reluctantly agreed that the poor people's problem was money, not the availability of housing. Then each person in turn stood up and proposed construction subsidies.

Tony DeVito: In my data there has been no growth in any of the Northeast, Midwest population centers in the past ten years except for state capitals. But it does not do me any good out here where I am paying double what I was paying in Detroit for my rental housing. There is no shortage of rental housing in Detroit and New York.

Ira Lowry: Certainly you have a point. There is no national housing market, only a congeries of local housing markets. The numbers I have got so far tell very much the same story for Los Angeles as the aggregate national statistics show. For example, the price of rental housing in Los Angeles during the 1970s went up at almost exactly the same rate as other prices. I do not have good specific operating data for Los Angeles but, if the production function is anything like it is elsewhere, the cost of supplying rental housing went up faster than the prices that people were paying for them.

Tony DeVito: When you aggregate data from older neighborhoods under lower fixed-rate mortgages with rental housing in the desirable, newer areas where people want to be, you can get an average that looks pretty good. But it is not telling the whole story.

Ira Lowry: That may be true, but as President Carter said, "Life is unfair." When consumers speak of housing shortage, they usually mean that if the price of housing were lower they would consume more. When developers speak of a housing shortage, they usually mean that the market is so saturated they cannot find any good opportunities for development. When I speak of a housing shortage I would expect to find landlords making out like bandits. What I find instead is landlords trying to get out of the rental business even in places such as Los Angeles. That does not square with the shortage you are describing.

Debra Alpert: Wallace Smith, would you please comment on the regulation Q elimination through 1986 and its effect on the housing market?

Wallace Smith: I think our financial institutions are going to be restructured. Many people do not think we will continue to have a savings-and-loan industry that does nothing but finance housing.

David Shulman: With no-growth land-use controls, putting new mortgage capital into the market translates into nothing but higher prices, not more houses.

Wallace Smith: Yes, and isn't that an argument for federalizing the function? Bankers should never finance speculation; they should finance the creation of real resources. But in fact the thrift industry did finance inflationary turnover during the 1970s. One of the arguments for making home finance a public function is to better control the use of financial resources.

Cary Lowe: A report from the U.S. General Accounting Office about a year and a half ago calculated that two-thirds to three-fourths of all new rental housing in this country was being produced at least in part and sometimes entirely through public finance agencies. Is an extension of this trend what you are urging?

Wallace Smith: My forecast is that the United States is headed toward a situation that exists in most of the rest of the world, where rental housing is a public function.

Fred Kahane: Many people during the 1970s switched their investment capital into home ownership because they thought that the social-security system was not adequate as a form of long-term investment. Now the pension funds are investing in housing.

Wallace Smith: I think pension-fund investment in housing has great potential. In terms of housing, though, there is a problem. A pension fund is forced savings. If it is lent at 6 percent, say, then fund beneficiaries, who are not also borrowing, grumble if T-bills are yielding 16 percent. Pension-fund management is not insulated from the money market. It is the insulation we need.

11 Conclusion

Arlo Woolery

I would like to share a few observations about certain chapters in this book. When I read Wallace Smith's chapter for the first time, I was shocked. I read the chapter a second time and started to write in the margin, "I agree." By the time I had been through the chapter a third time, I began to feel empathy with Smith. Then I realized that he does what I do. Tenured people have an obligation to offer outrageous ideas since young people fighting for tenure can not.

Many local savings and loans are in trouble. We are embarking upon a new era in this country that is going to give us a national mortgage market with firms like Sears and Roebuck and Merrill, Lynch providing mortgage funds on a nationwide basis. Smith's chapter argues implicitly that not only have the industry and the markets failed, but the regulators have failed as well. Smith then concludes by urging that the business be turned over to the regulators. He restates the Keynesian concept that increasing interest rates breed increased unemployment. In 1933 interest rates were hovering around 1 percent. The city of New York was borrowing at one tenth of 1 percent. In the Weimar Republic, October 1923, interest rates went to 10,000 percent. High interest rates did not breed savings. Instead, people got paid in the morning and rushed to the stores to spend their earnings by lunchtime.

I was interested in Donald Hicks's chapter and Katharine Lyall's response to it, and especially their shared concern for unemployed people who may elect to remain in depressed areas. Most Americans are descendants of immigrants: I happen to be Norwegian. Between 1825 and 1875, half of the population of Norway immigrated to the United States: They had to learn a new language and endure other discomforts related to their resettling. I can not understand how those people in the face of all those difficulties were able to make this kind of a transition. Now we are talking about people being locked into the Eastern communities that are suffering decay and we are worried about whether to subsidize them to stay or to move. Has our system lost something, or have we?

Richard Lamm's thesis urges us to measure government's performance as a land manager. We need to know more about how government functions as a land manager, either to criticize or commend the government control and ownership of vast tracts of land, especially in the West.

The California tax administrators a few years ago were interested in why state or local governments were paying about twice as much for small water companies as private investors. Was it because they have no cost of capital or because their revenues are tax exempt? Even with all those differences, why should government pay more than one dollar more than the private sector to acquire any property? At one dollar more, government would be the high bidder. So if we are trying to evaluate government performance we had better look at why government pays more than one dollar more than the private sector for anything.

Barnaby A. Allison
Stradling, Yocca, Carlson & Rauth

Debra E. Alpert
Assistant Controller
International Mortgage Company

Allen P. Baldwin
City of Lake Elsinore

Commissioner Norma Bard
Los Angeles County Regional
    Planning Department

Alfred C. Bell
Associate
The Planning Center

Diana Bradford
Acting Director
Community Redevelopment
    Agency

Dr. Maxine Harris Brookner
Consultant
Senate Local Government
    Committee

Sidford Lewis Brown

Professor W. Elliot Brownlee
Department of History
University of California

Daniel Cartagena
Planning Director
City of Carson

Professor Fred Case
Department of Real Estate &
    Urban Land Economics
Graduate School of Business
    & Management
University of California

Gloria Casvin
Valencia Corporation

Professor Jeffrey Chapman
Public Administration & Urban
    Planning
University of Southern California

Geoffrey D. Commons
Executive Director
Pasadena Development Corporation

Kathleen Connell
Director of Housing Division
Community Development
    Department

Marlee T. Coughlan
Citizens Planning Council of
    Los Angeles County

Patrick C. Coughlan
Richard, Watson, Dreyfuss
    & Gershon

Ellis Crow
Manager
Long Range Planning
City of Long Beach

Bill Crowe
Deputy to Supervisor Schabarum
Los Angeles County Board of
    Supervisors

Paul Curtis
Associate Director
Community Development

Mary C. Davey
Housing Advisor, Santa Clara
    County

Dennis A. Davis
Deputy Director
Rio Salado Development District

Phillip DeLao
Executive Planner
Summa Corporation

Professor Donald R. Denman

Anthony DeVito
Chief Deputy
Los Angeles County Department
    of Regional Planning

David J. Dmohowski
Government Relations Manager
The Irvine Company

David R. Doerr
Chief Consultant
Revenue and Taxation Committee
State Capitol

Commissioner Roy W. Donley
Los Angeles County Department
    of Regional Planning

Lee Eckel
Vice President
M.J. Brock & Sons, Inc.

Joseph P. Edmiston
Executive Director
Santa Monica Mountains
    Conservatory

Bruce A. Eisner
Santa Monica Mountains
    Conservancy

Professor Virgil L. Elliott
Golden Gate University
Graduate School of Public
    Administration

Frank Fargo
Senior Vice President
Wainwright & Ramsey

David Fine
Legal Counsel
Southern California Association
    of Governments

Maureen E. FitzGerald
Consultant, Local Government
    Chronical, England

Professor M. David Gelfand
Pace University
School of Law

Peter B. Giles
President
Santa Clara County Manufacturing
    Group

Linda Gilster
E.L. Pearson & Associates

LeRoy Graymer, Head
Public Policy Program
UCLA Extension

Deni Greene
Director
Office of Planning & Research

Robert H. Gustafson
Chief of Operations
Statistical Research & Consulting
 Division
State Board of Equalization

Professor Donald G. Hagman
University of California Law
 School

Max Halfon, Esq.

Professor Peter Hall
University of Reading
England

Gary W. Hambly
Government Affairs Director
Building Industry Association
 of Northern California

James E. Hartl
Division Chief
Los Angeles County Regional
 Planning Commission

Martin Helmke
Consultant
California Senate Office of
 Research

Professor Otto J. Hetzel
Wayne State University Law School

Ann Marie Hickambottom
Land Use Coordinator
California Association of Realtors

Donald A. Hicks
Associate Professor of Sociology
 and Political Economy
The University of Texas at Dallas

Professor E. Gareth Hoachlander
School of Education
University of California

Stanley R. Hoffman
Regional Economist

Ronald R. Horn
Vice President
Sikand Engineering Associates

Frank Hotchkiss
Director of Planning
Southern California Association
 of Governments

Bruce P. Howard
Professor of Law
University of Southern California
 Law Center

Theodore B. Howard
President
Economic Development
 Corporation of Los Angeles
 County

Elbert T. Hudson
President
Broadway Federal Savings & Loan

Fred L. Johnson
Fred Johnson Investments Inc.

Trixie Johnson
Chairperson
Santa Clara County Industry
   and Housing Management
   Task Force

Professor Francis E. Jones, Jr.
University of Southern California
   Law Center

Stephen L. Jones, Esq.
Latham & Watkins

Fred Kahane
Housing Director
Southern California Association
   of Governments

David Kamm
Policy Analyst
Summa Corporation

Professor Gideon Kanner
Loyola Law School

Raymond Kappe, FAIA
Director
Southern California Institute of
   Architecture

Michael F. Keeley, Esq.
Riordan, Caps, Carbone &
   McKinzie

Dale L. Keyes
Director
Environmental and Energy
   Programs
Battelle, Columbus Laboratories

Larry J. Kimbell
Director
UCLA Business Forecasting Project
Graduate School of Management

Clark King
Santa Monica Mountains
   Conservancy

Kaya Koral
Highland Engineers

Diane M. Kozub
Senior Consultant
Assembly Revenue & Taxation
   Committee

Professor James A. Kushner
Southwestern University School
   of Law

James C. Lamb
Economic Development Officer
City of Long Beach

Richard D. Lamm
Governor of Colorado

Professor George Lefcoe
University of Southern California
   Law Center

Dr. Cary D. Lowe
Instructor
University of Southern California
   Law Center

Ira S. Lowry
Senior Economist
Management Sciences Department
The Rand Corporation

Dr. Katharine C. Lyall
Vice President for Academic
   Affairs
Univeristy of Wisconsin

Steve Mabs
Senior Planner
Environmental Management
    Agency
Information & Housing
    Development Office

Dennis Macheski
Program Manager
Southern California Association
    of Governments

Carole A. Maher
Director, Playa Vista Program
Summa Corporation

Lindell L. Marsh, Esq.
Nossaman, Krueger & Marsh

Norma K. Mencacci
Santa Clara County Executive
    Office

Ellen Michiel
Director of Governmental
    Affairs
Goldrich & Kest

Professor Frank G. Mittelbach
Graduate School of Business
    Management
University of California

Jim Monaghan
Assistant to Governor Lamm
Denver, Colorado

Marie J. Moretti
Executive Director
Brown Institute of Government
    Affairs

Norman Murdoch
Planning Director
Los Angeles County Department
    of Regional Planning

Commissioner Delta Murphy
Los Angeles County Department
    of Regional Planning

Donald H. Nollar
City of Pasadena

George Nony
Assistant City Manager
City of Burbank

H. Pike Oliver
Manager, Planning Policy
The Irvine Company

Norman T. Oliver, Esq.
Oliver, Stoever & Laskin

F. William Olson
Environmental Management
    Agency
    Information & Housing
    Development Office

Jerry Y. Oren
Oren Realty & Development
    Co. Inc.

Alexander Pope
Los Angeles County Assessor

Professor Edward H. Rabin
University of California School
    of Law, Davis

Neal Roberts, Esq.
Wyman, Bautzer, Rothman, &
    Silbert

Paul Robinson
Administrative Assistant
California Democratic Party

Rosemary Schroeder
City of Pasadena

Professor Alan Schwartz
University of Southern California
    Law Center

Professor Donald Shoup
School of Architecture & Urban
    Planning
University of California
Los Angeles

Professor David Shulman
Graduate School of Administration
University of California
Riverside

Mark S. Siegel
Deputy to Councilman Wachs
Los Angeles

Edwin M. Smith
Associate Professor of Law
University of Southern California
    Law Center
Research Associate
Institute for Marine & Coast
    Studies

Professor Wallace F. Smith
University of California
Schools of Business Administration

Jack R. Spahn
E.L. Pearson & Associates

Edward J. Sullivan, Esq.
O'Donnell, Rhoades, Gerber,
    Sullivan & Ramis

Radoslav L. Sutnar
President
Sutnar & Sutnar, Inc.

Linda L. Unruh
Assistant to the Speaker
California State Assembly

Roger Van Wert
Supervising Regional Planner II
Los Angeles County Department
    of Regional Planning

Raymond Watt
Chairman of the Board
Watt Industries

Gary A. Wayne
Project Manager
Ramsgate

Richard E. Webb
Vice President
Summa Corporation

Kathleen A. West
Social Services Commission
City of Whittier

Peter Wiersma

Thomas F. Winfield III, Esq.
Brown, Winfield & Canzoneri, Inc.

Professor Lowdon Wingo
University of Southern California
    School of Urban & Regional
    Planning

Bill Wojtkowski
Director
Community Development
Claremont, California

Jennifer Wolch
Assistant Professor
University of Southern California
  School of Urban & Regional
  Planning

T.C. Wolff, Jr.
Executive Vice President
Summa Corporation

Arlo Woolery
Executive Director
Lincoln Institute of Land Policy

Sharon Woolery
Lincoln Institute of Land Policy

About the Contributors

Patrick C. Coughlan is a partner in Richards, Watson, Dreyfuss & Gershon, a Los Angeles law firm specializing in public law and land use law. He has extensive experience in representing various governmental entities and corporations in planning, zoning, construction, land development, and environmental matters.

Donald R. Denman was responsible for setting up the Department of Land Economy and the Honour School in the subject at Cambridge University, England. He is now professor emeritus and emeritus fellow of Pembroke College, Cambridge, and of sundry national and international institutions. He practices as consultant and adviser to governments and universities on a world-wide scale in the field of land economics, land policy and marine resource development. He is author of 17 books and numerous articles in the national and international press.

David R. Doerr has been chief consultant to the California Assembly Revenue and Taxation Committee from 1963 to the present and was an elected member of the Board of Trustees of the San Juan Unified School District from 1976 and 1981.

Peter Hall is professor of geography at University of Reading, England. He taught at Birkbeck College and at the London School of Economics. His books include *London 2000* (1963, 1969), *The World Cities* (1966, 1977, 1983), *Europe 2000* (1977), and *The Inner City in Context* (1981). He has advised the British government on a number of official councils and committees. In a 1977 address to The Royal Town Planning Institute he first suggested the idea of the enterprise zone for the revival of depressed inner cities.

Donald A. Hicks is associate professor of sociology and political economy at the University of Texas at Dallas and was the senior urban-policy staff member for the Panel on Policies and Prospects for Metropolitan and Nonmetropolitan America in the Eighties for the President's Commission for a National Agenda for the Eighties. He authored the final urban-policy report for the commission, *Urban America in the Eighties: Perspectives and Prospects* (1982). Dr. Hicks has published numerous articles in a variety of policy-science and urban-issue areas, including problems of metropolitan service delivery, suburban exploitation of central cities, patterns of residential relocation, and public-private sector alliances in municipal service delivery.

E. Gareth Hoachlander is director of the Project on National Vocational Education Resources, School of Education, University of California, Berkeley. Dr. Hoachlander is a general partner in Planning Management Research Associates, Inc., a consulting firm specializing in public sector management, planning and research.

Bruce P. Howard is associate professor of law at the University of Southern California Law Center. He received his law degree from the Harvard Law School, where he was a noted editor on the Harvard Law Review. His current teaching subjects include real estate and property.

Dale L. Keyes has been involved in energy and environmental affairs for over ten years. His professional interests have focused on technical strategies and economic effects of achieving air-quality standards, market-based approaches to pollution control, and energy-environmental linkages. Dr. Keyes holds degrees in chemistry, biochemistry, urban planning, and geography.

Larry J. Kimbell is director of the University of California, Los Angeles, Business Forecasting Project and associate professor of business economics at the Graduate School of Management. His research involves large-scale econometric models and general equilibrium models.

Richard D. Lamm was inaugurated January 14, 1975, as the Governor of Colorado and has served in that position to the present. Before that he was a professor of law at the University of Denver. A 1961 graduate of the University of California Law School, Berkeley, he not only practiced law but served as a certified public accountant.

Ira S. Lowry is a member of The Rand Corporation, a nonprofit institution devoted to research on public policy. He has specialized in research on housing, urban spatial organization, and urban demography. He recently completed the Housing Assistance Supply Experiment, a ten-year research project sponsored by the U.S. Department of Housing and Urban Development.

Katharine C. Lyall is vice president for Academic Affairs of the University of Wisconsin. She has served on the research staff of the Chase Manhattan Bank, been a member of the faculties of the Maxwell School at Syracuse University and The Johns Hopkins University, and served as executive director of the Committee on Evaluation Research for the Russell Sage Foundation. During the Carter administration, she was deputy assistant secretary for Economic Affairs at the U.S. Department of Housing and Urban Development. Prior to coming to Wisconsin, she was professor of political economy and director of the graduate program in Public Policy at The Johns Hopkins University. Dr. Lyall has authored numerous books and articles in the fields of public finance, economic development, policy analysis and evaluation research.

George E. Peterson has been director of the Public Finance Program of the Urban Institute since 1976. He previously taught economics at Harvard University. While at the Urban Institute Dr. Peterson has directed studies and published writings on federal tax policy, state and local pension funding, capital financing, grant-in-aid impacts, and public-employee compensation.

David Shulman is associate professor of administration and economics at the graduate school of Administration, University of California, Riverside, and consulting economist at the University of California, Los Angeles, Business Forecasting Project. He does research in finance and urban economics.

Edwin M. Smith is associate professor of law at the University of Southern California Law Center, and research associate at the Institute for Marine and Coastal Studies. He has also been staff attorney for the National Oceanic and Atmospheric Administration Office of General Counsel, Northwest Region.

Wallace F. Smith is professor of business administration at the University of California, Berkeley, and has been a member of the Berkeley Business School faculty since 1958. He is author of a number of books and monographs on real estate and urban land economics, including *Housing: The Social and Economic Elements* (1970) and *Urban Development: The Process and the Problems* (1975).

About the Editor

George Lefcoe is Henry W. Bruce Professor of Equity at the University of Southern California Law Center where he has taught since 1962. A graduate of Dartmouth College and the Yale Law School, Professor Lefcoe has taught at the law schools at Boston University, the University of Utah, and Yale University. His publications include *Land Development in Crowded Places: Lessons From Abroad* (1979) and *Land Development Law* (1974). Currently, he serves as chairman of the Regional Planning Commission, Los Angeles County, and has served as consultant or advisor to state and federal agencies including the U.S. Department of Housing and Urban Development and the California Assembly Committee on Revenue and Taxation. For the past five years he has been on the faculty of the Lincoln Institute of Land Policy.